P9-DTK-708

Restraint

A volume in the series

CORNELL STUDIES IN SECURITY AFFAIRS

edited by Robert J. Art, Robert Jervis, and Stephen M. Walt

A list of titles in this series is available at www.cornellpress.cornell.edu.

Restraint

A New Foundation for U.S. Grand Strategy

Barry R. Posen

Cornell University Press

Ithaca and London

First published 2014 by Cornell University Press

Printed in the United States of America

Library of Congress Cataloging-in-Publication Data

Posen, Barry, author.
    Restraint : a new foundation for U.S. grand strategy / Barry R. Posen.
        pages cm — (Cornell studies in security affairs)
    Includes bibliographical references and index.
    ISBN 978-0-8014-5258-1 (cloth : alk. paper)
    1. Hegemony—United States. 2. United States—Foreign relations—
2001–2009. 3. United States—Foreign relations—2009– 4. United States—
Military policy—21st century. I. Title. II. Series: Cornell studies in
security affairs.
    JZ1312.P67   2014
    327.73—dc23   2013049498

Cornell University Press strives to use environmentally responsible suppliers and materials to the fullest extent possible in the publishing of its books. Such materials include vegetable-based, low-VOC inks and acid-free papers that are recycled, totally chlorine-free, or partly composed of nonwood fibers. For further information, visit our website at www.cornellpress.cornell.edu.

Cloth printing   10 9 8 7 6 5 4 3 2 1

For Cindy

Contents

List of Tables and Maps	ix
Preface	xi
Acknowledgments	xv
Introduction: The Evolution of Post–Cold War U.S. Grand Strategy	1
The Path to Liberal Hegemony	5
The Strategic Position of the United States	16
Causes and Consequences	20
1. The Perils of Liberal Hegemony	24
Direct Costs	24
The Balance of Power	28
The Allies	33
Identity Politics and Intervention	50
Military Power and Intervention	54
Overstated Benefits	60
Persistent Problems	65
2. The Case for Restraint	69
The Geopolitical Interests of the United States	69
Nuclear Weapons: Dilemmas, Dangers, and Opportunities	71
The Struggle with Al-Qaeda and the Enduring Risk of International Terrorism	83
Implementing Restraint in Key Regions	87
The Problems of Transition to Restraint	129
Integrated Reforms	131

3. Command of the Commons: The Military Strategy,
   Force Structure, and Force Posture of Restraint   135
       "Command of the Commons"   136
       The Insights of Maritime Strategy   136
       Force Structure   144
       Global Force Posture   158
       Affordable and Effective   162
   Conclusion: A Sustained Debate   164
       Critiques of Restraint   168

   Notes   177
   Index   225

Tables and Maps

Tables

1. U.S. nonnuclear force structure: proposed and actual,
   1997–2013   12
2. Distribution of global capabilities, 2011   17
3. Defense burden sharing, 2011   36
4. Capabilities of the principal European states   88
5. Capabilities of the principal Asian states   92
6. A future multipolar world?   94
7. Persian Gulf oil production and proven reserves   107
8. U.S. nuclear attack submarines: proposed force structure   152

Maps

1. Political Asia   42
2. Major chokepoints   137

Preface

The United States has grown incapable of moderating its ambitions in international politics. Since the collapse of Soviet power, it has pursued a grand strategy that can be called "Liberal Hegemony," which is unnecessary, counterproductive, costly, and wasteful. The purpose of this book is to explain why this grand strategy works poorly and to offer an alternative grand strategy and associated military strategy and force structure. Three major events affected my thinking—the enlargement of NATO to include the former vassal states of the Soviet Union, the war in Kosovo, and the war in Iraq. The first expanded U.S. obligations in ways that did little for U.S. security and needlessly antagonized Russia. Kosovo was an elective war, rationalized on the basis of information that was at best poor, and at worst deliberately mischaracterized by motivated policy entrepreneurs, and nearly bungled militarily due to the war's founding illusions. The 2003 Iraq war echoed the mistakes of the Kosovo war, but on a larger scale and with much greater costs. Military spending has been excessive throughout this period, because the political ambitions that it serves have been more ambitious than national security required. This is a track record. The United States needs a change of grand strategy.

The United States, like all other countries, must live in the world as it is—a world without a single authority to provide protection. Any state can resort to arms to enforce its claims, so the United States wisely remains prepared to enforce its claims, if it must. The most important claim is to sovereignty, territorial integrity, and safety. That said, the development of military force is expensive, and the use of military force is terrible. Great American generals from William Tecumseh Sherman to Dwight Eisenhower remind us that war is hell and that war is waste. The United States needs military power and needs to be prepared to use it. But this is no casual matter. Military power must be subjected to the discipline of political analysis. That is the purpose of grand strategy.

In this book I offer a critique of the present grand strategy, "Liberal Hegemony," and offer the outline of an alternative, and the military strategy and force structure to support it, "Restraint." Restraint advises us to look first at the elemental strengths of the United States, which make it an easy country to defend. The United States thus has the luxury to be very discriminate in the commitments it makes and the wars it fights. Although the United States has been much at war since the end of the Cold War, only one fight was forced on us—the Afghan War. And even there, the United States was not forced to fight that war in the naïve and profligate fashion that it chose.

The United States is a wealthy and capable state. It can afford more security than most states. But the United States has extended the boundaries of its political and military defense perimeter very far. Taken separately, each individual project has seemed reasonable and affordable, at least to its advocates. Taken together, however, they add up to an embedded system of ambitious and costly excess. For these reasons, I have signed up with the advocates of Restraint. The United States should focus on a small number of threats, and approach those threats with subtlety and moderation. It should do that because the world is resistant to heavy-handed solutions. It can do that because the United States is economically and militarily strong, well-endowed and well-defended by nature, and possessed of an enormous ability to regenerate itself. It is not smart to spend energies transforming a recalcitrant world that we could spend renewing a United States that still needs some work.

In the Introduction, I trace the evolution of the post–Cold War U.S. grand strategy debate. Though it may seem inevitable that the United States took the path it did, there was much discussion in the 1990s about how to proceed. One can identify four different strands of opinion. Sadly, these have been reduced to two—the establishment consensus on Liberal Hegemony and Restraint. Four factors helped make Liberal Hegemony the victor. First, with the collapse of Soviet power the United States became the most capable global power in history. Nothing stood in the way. Second, the Western liberal model was triumphant. History vindicated the rightness of our system and made it in our eyes the appropriate model for others. Third, the Cold War ended with U.S. forces "manning the ramparts" around the world. Insecurity and disorder beyond the ramparts quickly created demands from within and without to move them outward. Fourth, the United States had built giant organizations to wage the Cold War and squadrons of national security experts to manage them. Most organization theorists will tell you that organizations never want to go out of business; if they succeed at their first task, they will try to find another. For these reasons, a more rather than a less ambitious strategy emerged after the Cold War, even before the September 11, 2001, terrorist attack on the United States, which supercharged the whole effort.

In chapter 1, I lay out why these policies are not working. At bottom, they run up against three problems, which will get worse. First, other countries want security as much as we do. When we define our security expansively, we encourage some of them to compete more intensely. Others welcome our help, and because they can count on the United States, are stingy with their own defense spending. They "cheap ride." Second, global trends will make U.S. expansiveness ever more costly because other states are growing in power, as are peoples and groups, as the U.S. government's National Intelligence Council has been reporting for several years. More capable states are more able to push back and hence more inclined to do so, as are individuals and nonstate actors. Third, perhaps since the middle of the nineteenth century, ethno-nationalist, religious, and class identities have become heavily politicized. Globalization and modernity have the paradoxical effect of intensifying these identities rather than weakening them. These identities ease the way for the political mobilization of power—for street action, for voting, for civil and international war, for terror. They provide both purpose and motive force. Strong politicized ethno-national and religious identities dislike rule by other groups, or foreigners, above all else. Liberal Hegemony puts the United States in that role, or close to it, too often. Finally, although modern high-technology weaponry has created the impression that military power is a scalpel that can be used to excise diseased politics, in my view it remains a club, which in the end mainly allows us to beat problems into grudging submission at best, remission at worse. Liberal Hegemony is not only unnecessary, it will prove increasingly costly.

In chapter 2, I offer the outline of an alternative grand strategy that is responsive to the deep problems encountered by our present policies. I identify three important security challenges for the United States—the maintenance of a balance of power in Eurasia, the management of nuclear proliferation, and the suppression of international terrorist organizations that choose the United States as a target. I offer moderate policies to address these three challenges and review in detail how the United States should comport itself in four areas of the world: Europe, the greater Middle East, East Asia, and South Asia.

In chapter 3, I develop a military strategy and force structure to implement the Grand Strategy of Restraint. This is essentially a maritime strategy, which I have called "command of the commons." The United States should invest its scarce military power in the maintenance of an ability to access the rest of the world. It should reduce, however, its regular military presence in the rest of the world. The United States should avoid certain missions altogether, especially coercive state and nation building. Thus the United States can radically cut the ground forces that seem most apt for garrison duties and counterinsurgency. Major force structure cuts should allow the United States to save significant amounts of money, cutting the defense budget to perhaps 2.5 percent of GDP.

A single book cannot do justice to the problem of a new grand strategy. I offer a framework and address what I consider to be the most important problems. I do not, however, explore every problem or explore all plausible solutions. Readers may ask, "But what about . . .?" I invite them to imagine how a Restraint advocate would answer after having seen my treatment of the larger issues.

Acknowledgments

Since the beginning of this project, I have given dozens of talks about it. I wish to thank all those who attended these talks, listened patiently to views that may have seemed heretical, and offered constructive criticism.

I owe a huge debt to Harvey Sapolsky. He, Daryl Press, and Eugene Gholz (the latter two graduate students at the time) had the courage and imagination to argue for a very different grand strategy for the United States in the immediate aftermath of the Cold War, from that contemplated by most in the national security field, including me. The very best thing about having good colleagues and good students is that they challenge one's own thinking.

Keren Fraiman, Brendan Green, Kelly Grieco, Miranda Priebe, and Noel Anderson served ably as research assistants. They labored without much direction from me. But when in the course of writing, I had occasion to open the files they had assembled for me, my morale would get a boost from the head start provided by their work. Josh Shifrinson served ably both as an RA, and a sounding board for the manuscript. In this latter role he enjoyed some payback for all the criticisms I have offered on his papers and thesis materials. I thank Shai Feldman, Robert Jervis, Richard Samuels, Harvey Sapolsky, Stephen Walt, and an anonymous reviewer for comments on the final draft manuscript.

Four institutions provided the research support to complete this book, and I am grateful to all of them. My home institution, the Security Studies Program, Center for International Studies, Massachusetts Institute of Technology, which I have had the privilege to direct, provided summer funding. The Carnegie Corporation of New York provided a generous grant to the Security Studies Program. The Woodrow Wilson Center in Washington, DC, provided funding, and for one semester, a superb base.

[xv]

The Dickey Center at Dartmouth College provided funding and a wonderful environment in which to write.

Finally, I wish to thank my wife, and colleague, Cindy Williams. Her iron self-discipline when finishing her own books set a great example. Her support and encouragement helped me through the low periods that at least some authors experience when trying to produce a book. And, she agreeably accepted my adversaries as her adversaries.

Restraint

Introduction

THE EVOLUTION OF POST–COLD WAR U.S. GRAND STRATEGY

A grand strategy is a nation-state's theory about how to produce security for itself. Grand strategy focuses on military threats, because these are the most dangerous, and military remedies because these are the most costly. Security has traditionally encompassed the preservation of sovereignty, safety, territorial integrity, and power position—the last being the necessary means to the first three. States have traditionally been quite willing to risk the safety of their people to protect sovereignty, territorial integrity, and power position.

A grand strategy enumerates and prioritizes threats, and potential political and military remedies to threats. Remedies include alliances, intelligence capabilities, military power, and the underlying economic and technological potential on which it is based. The threats of greatest importance arise from other nation-states, especially states of comparable capability, which can pursue their own interests with any means they choose because they are unconstrained by world law or world government or world police. Though we have seen that private organizations can do great harm though terrorism, their capacity pales against the potential of other nation-states. Grand strategy is ultimately about fighting, a costly and bloody business. The worst threats are military. A large well-handled military in the hands of another state can produce rapid damage to one's interests, if those interests are undefended. A grand strategy contains explanations for why threats enjoy a certain priority, and why and how the remedies proposed could work. A grand strategy is not a rule book; it is a set of concepts and arguments that need to be revisited regularly. Sometimes nation-states write their grand strategies down in one place, sometimes they do not.

[1]

A grand strategy is a key component of a state's overall foreign policy, but foreign policy may have many goals beyond security, including the improvement of the prosperity of Americans at home, or the economic welfare or liberty of people abroad. These are appropriate goals for a foreign policy, but great care should be taken not to conflate them with security goals as they have historically been understood, lest one fall into the trap of prescribing expensive and dangerous security means for their solution. Environmental change, the risk of global pandemics, human rights, and free trade may be important and worthy concerns for US foreign policy problems. There may be an argument that such problems strongly affect the sovereignty, territorial integrity, power position, and safety of the United States—the basic security of the country. But this needs to be demonstrated, not assumed. It may be that the massive U.S. defense budget, the peacetime deployment of large U.S. forces around the world, the U.S. alliance structure, and the employment of U.S. military power in war significantly affect our ability to address these issues, but this too needs to be demonstrated. Finally, even if these connections can be drawn, we must consider the cost-benefit relationship of military solutions to these problems. National security is a term of enormous emotive power in some nation-states, especially the United States, and every analyst or group with an overseas agenda has a powerful interest in implying a connection between their specific interest and national security.

Similarly, grand strategy is not about every major national policy decision, though it may influence those decisions. Given that national power is based on a healthy economy and a vital population, it is tempting to turn national debates about all such decisions into grand strategy debates. This would be overreach. First, it is simply a fact of life that the domestic politics of any country will affect choices between guns and butter. Grand strategy makes its argument for the military share, but a complex domestic political process ultimately influences how much "security" a state will buy. Rarely will the security situation be so dire that domestic politics ceases to play a meaningful role. Second, some might say that grand strategy must be about both guns and butter, indeed that it should be about everything, otherwise, it is not "grand" enough. This would, however, dilute the most important purpose of grand strategy, which is to address the fact that the state exists in a world where war is possible. The state needs some focused thinking about this problem, given its importance, even if the conclusion to that thinking were that the state is too weak to defend itself, and surrender is the wisest course. Third, although grand strategy depends on the sinews of national power, these sinews reflect a wide range of factors about which the specialists in threat assessment, alliance management, and combat—strategists, diplomats, and soldiers—know little. They should confine their advice to what is germane to the generation of military power; otherwise their amateurism may prove counterproductive.

In this book I employ a narrow definition of national security—sovereignty, territorial integrity, power position, and safety. Sovereignty is a nation-state's ability to make its own national decisions in its own way. Territorial integrity is largely self-explanatory, though neighboring states often dispute where precisely a boundary is to be drawn. Power position is the sum total of a state's capabilities relative to other states, which permits the state to defend sovereignty, territorial integrity, and safety against threats by other states. Capabilities include population size, health, and skill; economic capacity of all kinds, including industrial power, agricultural land, and raw materials; and military power. The relationship among these power factors is complex and varies across history. Some of these factors are amenable to state policy, but others are not. Even small states pay attention to these capabilities in order to deal with whatever threats they can, even from stronger states. Finally safety of the society is important, but this is a murkier concept. States wish to protect their people from harm to the extent possible. Deterrence of attack is one way to do this. Nevertheless, modern nation-states have typically been willing to accept dangers to their population if war proves necessary to protect sovereignty, territorial integrity, and power position. States do what they can to avoid being forced into this situation, and the desire to keep one's population from harm, even in wartime, affects military strategy. And it should be emphasized that in a world full of the kinds of destructive capabilities that modern technology has generated, as well as the vulnerabilities inherent in modern economies, that perfect safety is a chimera. Chasing perfect safety is itself a recipe for disaster. I conceive threats narrowly to these values. I focus on direct, imminent, and plausible military threats, mainly by other nation-states, but include of necessity threats by well organized, violent, nonstate actors. Throughout, I remain skeptical of "domino theories" that string together a chain of individually imaginable, but collectively implausible, major events, to generate an ultimate threat to the United States and then argue backward to the extreme importance of using military power to stop the fall of the first domino. Some may argue that my approach ignores the complexity of international politics, and the many plausible interconnections among issues of different types—economic, political, military, social, and technological. We know that everything is related to everything else, but this insight is not useful in the real world of strategy, which is a world of scarcity and high cost. My purpose here is to concentrate narrowly on the main problems, to generate an appropriate grand strategy, and then ask how comfortable we feel with the product.

[3]

States have often gone without clearly stated grand strategies but they do so at their peril. Grand strategies serve four functions. First, resources are invariably scarce. If a grand strategy includes clearly stated priorities, it provides a guide for the allocation of these scarce resources. Strategists have long agreed that it is best to be very strong where it matters. Efforts to defend everything leave one defending not much of anything. The standard example is U.S. strategy for the Second World War. Although the United States extracted as much as 40 percent of its gross domestic product (GDP) for military purposes, this did not permit equal efforts everywhere. Prewar contingency planning called for a focus on Germany because it was the most capable potential enemy. Despite the fact that Japan attacked the United States, and despite the emotions mobilized by that attack, on the whole the United States pursued the war effort according to these prewar priorities.

Second, in modern great powers, several large and complex organizations must cooperate to achieve a state's security goals. Micromanagement of this cooperation is difficult. A clearly stated grand strategy should help these organizations to coordinate their activities in peace and war. The U.S. grand strategy for the competition with the Soviet Union aimed to contain the Soviet Union, prevent it from conquering weaker states, and patiently wait for it to reform its policies or collapse. Presuming the USSR to be a militarily capable and expansive state the United States and its allies decided to deter Soviet adventurism through the credible threat of very costly resistance, including possible escalation to nuclear war. Large "conventional" forces were maintained, but they were not expected to carry the burden of deterrence and were not structured for an open-ended conventional war, lest deterrence be eroded. Similarly, the United States and its allies did not settle on a campaign to liberate Eastern Europe and did not maintain forces adequate to that task. On the whole, it was understood that the goal of Western military power was to preserve the status quo and wait, and in a very rough sense, Western diplomatic, intelligence, and military activities oriented themselves in that direction.

Third, deterrence and persuasion of potential adversaries and reassurance of allies and friends is preferable to the actual use of force. Grand strategies communicate interests. The strategy of containment conveyed to the Soviet Union the U.S. interest in defending Western Europe. So did past U.S. behavior. Soviet strategists would not have had to do much research to discern that the United States had geostrategic reasons for defending Europe, or more specifically, ensuring that no single empire consolidated itself on the Eurasian land mass. The United States is a great continental power; the only real challenge to its security would be another great continental power, of comparable or superior economic capacity. The United States, like the British before them, waged war in Europe to prevent such an outcome in the Second World War. The Soviets had good reason to believe the United States would do it again, especially after the United States backed its commitment with very large forces.

Finally, clearly stated grand strategies assist internal accountability. They permit criticism and correction when they are proposed; they organize public discourse when new projects are suggested; and they allow for evaluation of such policies after the fact. Grand strategies are good for democracy. Grand strategy has sometimes constrained unfortunate behavior. During the Cold War, strategies of roll-back or preventive war were occasionally suggested.[1] The logic of containment helped to turn these bad ideas aside.

THE PATH TO LIBERAL HEGEMONY

Over the twenty-plus years since the collapse of the Soviet Union, the foreign policy establishment has gradually converged on an activist grand strategy for the United States. There is little disagreement among Republican and Democratic foreign policy experts about the threats that the United States faces and the remedies it should pursue. Early in the 2009 presidential race the three most viable candidates—Hillary Clinton, Barack Obama, and John McCain—all published articles on national security in the establishment journal *Foreign Affairs*. All three saw terrorism, nonstate actors, and weak or failed states as threats to the United States. All were concerned about rising powers. All insisted on the need for U.S. leadership. All believed in the use of force to prevent atrocities abroad. All three candidates strongly supported NATO, although they all wanted it to do more. Obama and Clinton subscribed to the unilateral use of force; McCain was silent on the matter in the articles. All rated nuclear proliferation as a very serious problem; all agreed Iran must be prevented from getting nuclear weapons and were open to a military solution to Iran's nuclear programs.[2]

G. John Ikenberry observes that since World War II, the United States has built a "liberal hegemonic order," which it continues to manage, and thus I dub the consensus grand strategy Liberal Hegemony.[3] The strategy is hegemonic because it builds on the great power advantage of the United States relative to all other major powers and intends to preserve as much of that advantage as possible through a range of actions, including a sustained investment in military power whose aim is to so overwhelm potential challengers that they will not even try to compete, much less fight. Despite some important disagreements among its proponents, it is liberal because it aims to defend and promote a range of values associated with Western society in general and U.S. society in particular—including democratic governance within nation-states, individual rights, free markets, a free press, and the rule of law. The spread of these values is not only seen to be good in its own terms, it is seen to be positive, if not essential, for U.S. security. The view is that the United States can only be truly safe in a world full of states like us, and so long as the United States has the power to pursue this outcome, it should. The notion that U.S. foreign policy should try to spread these values has a complex history.[4] It originates instrumentally with Woodrow Wilson but intellectually goes back to the earliest ideas about the United States relative to the rest of the world, and the progressive example that it provided. These ideas were given new energy by the victory over Soviet totalitarianism, and the sudden realization that the United States might actually have sufficient power to spread its ideas about domestic governance and international order.

Proponents of Liberal Hegemony see threats emanating from three major sources: failed states, rogue states, and illiberal peer competitors. Failed states are a serious threat, because they may produce or nurture terrorists, but also because they are often plagued by religious, ethnic, or nationalist politics that produce civil war, human rights violations, refugees, and crime. Refugees and crime were believed to have knock-on consequences for Western security, as they overflow borders, carrying instability with them. "Rogue" states, with interests and forms of government different from our own, a willingness to use force, and in the worst case, an inclination to acquire nuclear weapons, remain a closely related threat because they may assist terrorists, and because they restrict U.S. freedom of action wherever they emerge. Because of their undemocratic governments, "rogue" states can become "failed states." The rise of one or more peer competitors is a threat to the U.S. power position, which is directly central to U.S. security and would complicate the spread of liberal institutions and the construction of liberal states. Until recently this was seen as a distant possibility. China's sustained rapid growth, coupled with the Great Recession in the United States, and the specter of huge near-term budget deficits, have generated a perception that China is coming on faster than had been expected. This concern explains the Obama administration's trumpeted "pivot to Asia."

This grand strategy consensus did not emerge immediately at the end of the Cold War. At that time four sets of ideas competed for the affections of the U.S. foreign policy establishment—Cooperative Security, Primacy, Selective Engagement, and Isolationism.[5] The present consensus is a fusion of two of these sets of ideas—Cooperative Security and Primacy. This fusion did not fully emerge until the aftermath of the September 11,

[6]

2001, Al-Qaeda attack on the United States. My alternative, discussed later, draws on Selective Engagement and Isolationism.

Cooperative Security was developed by several prominent defense intellectuals and former and aspiring Pentagon public officials associated with the Democratic Party during the last years of the George H. W. Bush administration, as it became clear that the Soviet Union had well and truly passed away.[6] Advocates of this strategy sought to create a stable peace. Threats to stable peace included unreformed "rogue" states, failed or failing states, and the proliferation of nuclear weaponry. These issues were seen to be tightly interrelated. Rogue states, a catchall term for heavily armed authoritarian survivors of the Cold War, might want nuclear weapons; if they had them they would develop aspirations that could lead to war, including the use of nuclear weapons. Neighbors would also want nuclear weapons; regional arms races would further raise the risks of nuclear weapons use. Even a regional nuclear war would be bad for the United States.[7]

Then UN ambassador, and later secretary of state, Madeleine K. Albright was a key advocate of the view that there was "a gray area of regional conflicts and potential conflicts that does not fit neatly into any national security framework but which, if left unattended, could erode the foundation of freedom and threaten world peace."[8] Weakened regimes or failed states would succumb to civil war, which would in turn produce war crimes and refugee flows and havens for criminals. Rogue states might turn into failed states as authoritarian leaders wielded violence to preserve their power. Ensuing refugee flows might themselves spread instability and conflict. Unpunished war crimes would set a bad example for others. Just as cold war seemed to have given way to great power peace, a new set of threats was poised to prevent the emergence of a better world.

Cooperative Security advocates had three interrelated answers: arms control, cooperative security institutions, and Western technological superiority. The first would prevent proliferation and limit other kinds of military competition; the second would marshal the energies of like-minded powers, mainly liberal democracies, to oppose rogue states and stabilize failed states; and the third would permit military interventions that would be cheap, quick, and relatively free of collateral damage. These solutions would also work together and be mutually reinforcing. Arms control would make it hard for any state to have enough military power to threaten others. The presence of even small nuclear powers might deter stabilizing military interventions by the United States and its allies, so nuclear proliferation would need to be prevented to protect the freedom of action of the peace-loving states.[9]

[7]

Cooperative security institutions would ensure that any state that disturbed the peace would always be outnumbered, and that the defenders of order would not fall into pointless disputes among themselves. Western military technology would deter miscreants and stiffen the backbone of the liberal coalition. Cooperative security institutions and arms control would delicately adjust the military forces of the great powers such that none of them could threaten anyone else, or each other. The United States would be a special case, controlling the high-technology enablers of military superiority—command, control, communications, and intelligence, and air power and precision-guided munitions—to better serve as the leader of any necessary military operation. Other states would tolerate U.S. superiority because the United States would bind itself to security institutions. There was some discussion that the United States would retain conventional ground forces too small to invade and occupy others, and thus render its control of the most advanced technology unthreatening. And these others could depend on the United States to help defend them. An extra source of cohesion would arise from the fact that many of the great powers were liberal democracies, and the supposition that these were naturally peaceful toward one another, and particularly capable of cooperation.[10]

Primacy emerged quickly after the collapse of the Soviet Union as the strategic orientation of the Republican Party. Some analysts observed that the United States suddenly enjoyed a level of preeminence seldom seen in world affairs, and it did not take long for them to conclude that the United States needed to preserve that position. Foremost among the fears at the time was a resurgent Russia. Some already foresaw the rise of China. A few were concerned about Japan, the economy of which had grown ferociously in previous years but had not yet plunged into the doldrums where it has languished ever since.[11] The preservation of primacy quickly became a vital interest, as the leaked draft of the final Defense Policy Guidance of the first Bush administration famously argued.[12]

> Our first objective is to prevent the reemergence of a new rival, either on the territory of the former Soviet Union or elsewhere, that poses a threat on the order of that posed formerly by the Soviet Union. This is a dominant consideration . . . and requires that we endeavor to prevent any hostile power from dominating a region whose resources would, under consolidated control, be sufficient to generate global power. . . .
>
> Our strategy must now refocus on precluding the emergence of any potential future global competitor.[13]

Primacists were also very concerned about nuclear proliferation, because nuclear weapons in the hands of rogue states could interfere with the exercise of U.S. power, a concern they shared with Cooperative Security advocates.[14] Columnist Charles Krauthammer, one of the original primacists, argued that "the post-Cold War era is thus perhaps better called the era of weapons of mass destruction. The proliferation of weapons of mass destruction and their means of delivery will constitute the greatest single threat to world security for the rest of our lives. That is what makes a new international order not an imperial dream or a Wilsonian fantasy but a matter of the sheerest prudence."

Primacists were a coalition of two types of thinkers. Old-fashioned realists such as then secretary of defense Richard Cheney, Henry Kissinger, and even Democrat Zbigniew Brzezinski simply wanted the United States to remain comfortably at the top of the international pecking order, because what could be better in an anarchic world? This did, however, imply picking up the pieces of the Soviet Empire and integrating them into the North Atlantic Treaty Organization. The most assertive proponents of Primacy, however, were the "neoconservatives." Their ideological agenda then was less clear than it became when they rose to policy prominence in the first term of the George W. Bush administration.[15] They assuredly did want the United States to maintain its preeminent position and proposed energetic military and political action to achieve this. They had plans, however, for what they wanted to do with all this power—the spread of democracy and market economies.[16] Though they shared that objective with Cooperative Security advocates, by contrast they remained deeply skeptical of international security institutions.[17]

The convergence of Cooperative Security" and Primacy began in the Clinton administration and was for all intents and purposes completed during the subsequent administration of George W. Bush. Two facts drove the Clinton foreign policy team toward the Primacy camp.[18] First, they discovered in the Balkan wars that liberal democracies could not cooperate in security matters without a powerful leader. Coalitions are always subject to collective action problems, and given the diffuse nature of new threats and the normal functioning of liberal democracies, a large democratic coalition proved unwieldy and slow. The democracies need a leader willing and able to shoulder a disproportionate share of the costs and risks; it helped that it could promise inexpensive victories. The U.S. military had regular employment. Secretary of State Madeleine Albright gave eloquent voice to this discovery when she coined the term *indispensable nation* for the U.S. role in international security projects. It is also noteworthy that the Clinton administration became comfortable with the use of military force, albeit on a modest scale. It elected to escalate U.S. military involvement in Somalia, coerce the abdication of the government of Haiti and then occupy the country, employ air strikes coercively in Bosnia and follow with another occupation, wage an intensive air war

[9]

to eject Serbian forces from Kosovo and follow that with still another occupation, launch several small and medium air attacks against Iraq, and
launch a major raid on an Al-Qaeda camp in Afghanistan and a smaller
raid on a presumed chemical weapons plant in Sudan.[19] Second, the
Clinton administration came to understand that a presumed claim to national security expertise, and greater understanding of and sympathy for
the military, was a principal message of the Republican Party, so they lost
interest in careful management of the inner workings of the Department
of Defense, including controlling the future growth of procurement, operations, and personnel costs. The Clinton administration did reduce the
overall force structure—personnel and combat units—from its Cold War
level by 35–45 percent and by many estimates did not fully fund the large
force that remained. More deliberate management and greater force
structure cuts were required. Instead, legislators and Pentagon execu-
tives alike retained the large force structure, pushed plausible costs into
future years, and provided ever increasing remuneration and benefits to
thank both busy military personnel and their less busy retired pre-
decessors.[20]

The Democratic Party's embrace of Liberal Hegemony is evident in the
last, little read strategy statement of the Clinton administration. "More
than ever, prosperity and security in America depend on prosperity and
security around the globe. In this age, America can advance its interests
and ideals only by leading efforts to meet common challenges. We must
deploy America's financial, diplomatic and military resources to stand
up for peace and security, promote global prosperity, and advance democracy and human rights around the world."[21] The document em-
braces a central role for military power, declaring that "strategic mobility
is critical to our ability to augment forces already present in the region
with the projection of additional forces for both domestic and international crisis response. This agility in response is key to successful American leadership and engagement."[22]

A group of like-minded policymakers and academics participated in a
forward-looking strategy study in 2004–6, the *Princeton Project on National Security*, which echoed the earlier Clinton administration document and declared that the protection of the American people and way
of life required three specific aims: "1) a secure homeland, including protection against attacks on our people and infrastructure and against fatal
epidemics; 2) a healthy global economy, which is essential for our own
prosperity and security; and 3) a benign international environment,
grounded in security cooperation among nations and the spread of liberal democracy."[23] The authors, several of whom later served in the
Obama administration, called for large U.S. military forces to secure a
liberal order.

[10]

The United States should work to sustain the military predominance of liberal democracies . . . an effort that must include providing for a large part of the defense of other states, assuring friends that they will remain free, generally dissuading aggression and revisionism, and keeping sea lanes of communication open. Maintaining a balance of power in favor of liberal democracies is likely to require a continued high level of U.S. defense spending, together with substantial contributions from our allies.[24]

Of equal interest is the victory within the Primacy camp of the neoconservatives over the realists. Early in the George W. Bush administration, the strategic rhetoric was distinctly realist. The Bush team was concerned with relations among the great powers.[25] Evidence for any interest in the spread of democracy and other liberal institutions through the application of U.S. military power was sparse. Humanitarian military intervention was famously dismissed by future national security advisor Condoleezza Rice just prior to Bush's election.[26] The 2002 National Security Strategy focused on potential great powers and declared as an explicit goal that the United States should remain so powerful militarily that it would "dissuade potential adversaries from pursuing a military build-up in hopes of surpassing, or equaling, the power of the United States."[27] The attacks of September 11, 2001, catalyzed a conversion.

The neoconservatives argued that the sources of Al-Qaeda terrorism were rooted in Muslim, especially Arab, society. These societies needed to be turned toward liberal democracy. In any case, a world of liberal democracies would increase the "number of nations likely to be friendly to the United States."[28] References to "democracy" almost quadrupled from the 2002 Bush national security strategy to the 2006 version.[29] The invasion of Iraq, and the overthrow of Saddam Hussein, represented an opportunity to begin the process, though this was only one of several arguments advanced for the war. Rice was a noteworthy convert to these ideas, declaring when she became secretary of state that "the greatest threats now emerge more within states than between them. The fundamental character of regimes matters more than the international distribution of power. In this world it is impossible to draw neat, clear lines between our security interests, our development efforts and our democratic ideals. American diplomacy must integrate and advance all of these goals together."[30] More broadly, Republicans came to agree with the Cooperative Security advocates that failed states did indeed constitute a threat to the United States. A new reason was added based on a popular reading of the experience of Afghanistan: failed states could turn into hatcheries or base areas for international terrorists.

[11]

The Military Power Consensus

So foreign policy specialists on both sides of the aisle now agree that the United States must remain the strongest military power in the world by a very wide margin. There have been disagreements about just what this meant specifically, but the principle is now enshrined in the political discourse of the security establishment. Colin Powell had the most expansive view, as illustrated by the "Base Force" structure that he recommended for

TABLE 1. U.S. nonnuclear force structure: proposed and actual, 1997–2013

	Base Force Powell	Clinton BUR[1]	DOD 1999[2] (CBO Real)	DOD March 2005[3] (real)	QDR 2010[4] The plan 2011–15	Obama Plan FY2014 "objec- tive force"[5]
Army						
Active divisions	12	10	10	10	10[6]	10
Reserve divisions	6	8	8	8	8	8[7]
Total	18	18	18	19	18	18
Marines						
Active divisions	2⅓	3	3	3	3	3
Reserve divisions	1	1	1	1	1	1
Air Force[8]						
Active wings	15	13	13	13		11
Reserve wings	11	7	8	8		5
Total	26	20	21	21[9]	17[10]	16[11]
Navy						
"Total battle force" ships[12]	450	346	317	324	289	291
Carriers	13	12	11	11	10–11	11
Attack Subs	80	45–55			57–59	55
Amphibs.	50	44			29–31	31
Personnel						
Active (thousand)	1,626	1,450,	1,386	1,383	1,406	1,361
Reserve (thousand)	920	905	869			834
Budget Authority (then year billion dollars)	281 (FY97$)	243 (FY97$)	276 DOD (FY2000 Appropriation)	400.0	548.9 (FY2011 request)	526.6
Constant 2005 dollars[13]	367	318.5	349.2	400	471.7	435.2

[1]BUR is the Bottom-Up Review conducted by Les Aspin as secretary of defense. For Base and BUR Force structures, see Barry R. Posen and Andrew L. Ross, "Competing Visions of U.S. Grand Strategy," *International Security* 21, no. 3 (winter 1996/97): 10, table 2.
[2]Dan Crippen, director of the Congressional Budget Office, "Budgeting for Defense: Maintaining Today's Forces," Statement to U.S. Senate, Committee on the Budget, 106th Cong., 2nd sess, September 14, 2000, 9–11, http://www.cbo.gov/doc.cfm?index=2399&type=1.

[3]Base Realignment and Closure Commission, *2005 Defense Base Closure and Realignment Commission Report,* "Appendix D: Force Structure Plan," September 8, 2005, D-5.

[4]*QDR,* 2010, xvi–xvii. Office of the Under Secretary of Defense (Comptroller)/CFO, *United States Department of Defense Fiscal Year 2011 Budget Request: Overview,* U.S. Department of Defense, February 2010, 3–1, 8–1.

[5]Under Secretary of Defense (Comptroller), *Overview, US DOD FY 2014 Budget Request,* http://comptroller.defense.gov/Budget2014.html, A1, is the source of the Obama administration's projected force structure figures below.

[6]The QDR 2010 and FY2014 budget documents report the number of brigade combat teams (BCTs) instead of the number of divisions. Three or four BCTs are usually commanded by one division. In FY2010 forty-five active and twenty-eight reserve BCTs were in the force. The FY 2014 plan projected thirty-seven active BCTs and twenty-eight reserve BCTs. The number of divisional headquarters in the FY 2014 plan remained at ten active and eight reserve.

[7]The army seems to be conflicted on how many divisions it has, and what kind. Presently it lists ten active divisions, two "integrated" (combined active and Guard), and three Army National Guard divisions, in its force structure, http://www.army.mil/info/organization/unitsandcommands/divisions/. Elsewhere at the same web site, it lists three additional guard divisions, http://www.army.mil/info/organization/unitsandcommands/national guardunits/. Three of the guard divisions presumably serve mainly in homeland security missions. For the last several years the army has treated divisions mainly as command elements and counts its combat power in terms of brigade combat teams of which there are typically three or four assigned to each division.

[8]The DOD sometimes has reported wings, and sometimes squadrons. Typically, three or four squadrons are assigned per wing. The Air Force consists mainly of active duty units, but has a small number of reserve combat units. The Air National Guard, legally under the command of state governors, provides the bulk of the reserve units.

[9]For an opaque accounting, See IISS, *The Military Balance 2005–2006* (London, 2005), 28–30, which suggests fifty-four active and thirty-three Air National Guard squadrons, which could constitute roughly thirteen active and eight reserve wings, identical to the original Clinton plan.

[10]Ten to eleven "theater strike," and six "air superiority" wings; the QDR provided no breakout between active and Air National Guard and no squadron totals; F16CJ air defense suppression aircraft seem to be omitted, which understates the total relative to previous years.

[11]Forty active fighter squadrons, three air force reserve, and twenty-one Air National Guard.

[12]"Battle force ships . . . include both active duty and Naval Reserve Force combat ships as well Navy- and Military Sealift Command-operated auxiliaries—such as oilers, ammunition ships, dry cargo ships, and multiproduct resupply ships—that transport supplies from shore to navy combat ships operating at sea." Ronald O'Rourke, *Navy-Marine Corps Amphibious and Maritime Prepositioning Ship Programs: Background and Oversight Issues for Congress,* RL32513, Updated July 10, 2007, 4, fn.4.

[13]Office of Management and Budget, "Table 10.1 – Gross Domestic Product And Deflators Used in the Historical Tables: 1940–2018," in *Budget of the United States Government Fiscal Year 2013 Historical Tables,* online at http://www.whitehouse.gov/sites/default/files/omb/budget/fy2014/assets/hist.pdf; Office of Management and Budget, "Gross Domestic Product And Deflators Used In The Historical Tables: 1940–2015," in *Budget of the United States Government Fiscal Year 2011* (Washington, DC: Government Printing Office, 2010), 210 (Historical Tables), table 10.1.

[13]

the post–Cold War world. But the Clinton administration was not far behind. Table 1 illustrates the relative accord across the parties on U.S. force structure. Despite their complaints about the Clinton defense effort, the George W. Bush administration kept the Clinton force structure intact, even into the fourth year of the War on Terror (this remains the basic U.S. conventional force structure today). In real terms Bush initially spent more than Clinton, but not so much more as to suggest a significant difference of opinion. The projected force structure of the Obama administration remains very large, even as it faces serious budget constraints. Maintaining a wide margin of military superiority will be more demanding, however, as China and others grow economically, and if they behave as other rising powers have and allocate some of their new wealth to military capability.

There is consensus that the United States should stand ready to use force on a variety of issues. The Obama administration has made its views clear:

> America's interests and role in the world require Armed Forces with unmatched capabilities and a willingness on the part of the nation to employ them in defense of our national interests and the common good. The United States remains the only nation able to project and sustain large-scale operations over extended distances. This unique position generates an obligation to be responsible stewards of the power and influence that history, determination, and circumstance have provided.[31]

Preventive war is typically associated with the primacists of the Bush administration in the aftermath of the September 11 attacks.[32] But Madeleine Albright made the case for preventive war while she was Clinton's secretary of state.[33] James Steinberg, deputy secretary of state in the Obama administration, gently embraced the idea before returning to government.[34]

Stopping the proliferation of nuclear weapons is now agreed to be a vital interest of the United States. President George W. Bush strongly implied that he would be willing to wage war to prevent a nuclear armed North Korea or Iran and argued for war against Iraq because Saddam Hussein purportedly had a viable nuclear weapons program. Though the Obama administration's 2010 Quadrennial Defense Review (QDR) was silent on preventive war as a general nonproliferation policy, the language about preventing nuclear proliferation remained very strong. The QDR did suggest a willingness to use force preventively in the event that a state appears to be in danger of losing control over its nuclear weapons.[35] At the March 4, 2012, America Israel Public Affairs Council annual policy conference, President Obama publically committed to the use of force to stop Iran's nuclear programs, if diplomacy failed.[36]

Both parties agree that the United States should directly manage regional security relationships in any corner of the world that seems to matter strategically, which increasingly is every corner of the world. The Clinton administration and the subsequent Bush administration agreed that large U.S. forces should remain stationed around the world. Though Clinton called some of the Cold War legions home, when he left office very large forces, more than a quarter million troops, remained abroad ashore and afloat, including 117,000 in Europe, 111,000 in Asia, and 18,000 in the greater Middle East.[37] There are still nearly 175,000 troops stationed abroad, not including those deployed on operations.[38] In his final national security strategy review, President Clinton extolled the virtues of military presence around the world.[39] The Bush administration concurred, though its 2004 Global Force Posture Review did call for a paring of U.S. bases and forces abroad, in part to reduce the stresses on the force arising from the global war on terror and the campaigns in Afghanistan and Iraq. The Bush Pentagon planned to concentrate a higher proportion of forces at home, but so arrange the remaining traditional bases and newer access agreements abroad to support rapid deployment to unpredictable emerging crises.[40] They planned to bring 70,000 troops home, along with 100,000 dependents, and close a third of U.S. bases, installations, and facilities, mainly in Europe.[41] Most of these changes did occur.

The Debate on International Institutions

The key difference between the two political parties remains attitudes toward international institutions: Democrats like them, Republicans do not.[42] Republicans accuse Democrats of a willingness to sacrifice U.S. sovereignty to these organizations. This charge misses the point. In the abstract, Democrats believe that international institutions can help create among nations the same kinds of rational, peaceful, ordered relations among nation-states that democratic societies create for themselves. Democrats also like international institutions because they think that the great power of the United States will permit it to write the rules and dominate the outcomes. The legitimacy of any given outcome achieved in an international institution will rise due to the processes that have been followed, but these processes can be controlled to produce the outcomes that the U.S. desires. Legitimacy will lower the costs for the United States to get its way on a range of issues. Despite the fact that these institutions will inevitably constrain the United States somewhat, and in particular will generate lengthy decision-making processes, Democrats expect that they will produce a net gain in U.S. influence. On the whole international institutions find a good deal of support in the American public, though the depth of this support is unclear.[43]

[15]

Many Republicans remain deeply skeptical of international institutions, especially security institutions. They seem certain that international institutions will restrain the United States at critical moments; even a whiff of constraint arouses their suspicion. Walter Russell Meade locates these beliefs most strongly in the Tea Party movement, which he ties to the Jacksonian tradition in U.S. foreign policy: "Although they value allies and believe that the United States must honor its word, they do not believe in institutional constraints on the United States' freedom to act, unilaterally if necessary, in self-defense."[44] Even if in the end the United States gets its way, Republican primacists fear that lengthy decision-making processes in a crisis will also prove a major problem. Instead, in the words of Danielle Pletka, head of the American Enterprise Institute, "Republicans are more willing to upset the global status quo." Her article on the contours of a Republican foreign policy is devoid of references to international institutions or multilateralism, with one exception, a disparaging allusion to the U.N Security Council, but otherwise conforms to the tenets of Liberal Hegemony.[45] Republicans have a different model of international institutions. Institutions should formally or informally recognize U.S. leadership. NATO and the U.S.-Japan Security Treaty are the favored models. International institutions that include liberal countries are more trusted than those that have a universal membership.[46] Former secretary of defense Donald Rumsfeld caricatured this view during the run up to the 2003 war, when he lauded the loyalty of the "New NATO" members—small former vassal states of the Soviet Union dependent on the United States for their security and then willing to approve almost anything the United States wanted to do. Though decisions in NATO are nominally achieved through consensus, the alliance works because it has a recognized leader. This is even more true for the alliance with Japan. Rarely do the Japanese assert themselves in this relationship. Japanese military planners barely know how the United States intends to use the fifty thousand military personnel it bases in Japan.

THE STRATEGIC POSITION OF THE UNITED STATES

Any critique of U.S. grand strategy should begin with a review of key facts.

The United States is an enormously powerful country. Some believe that the United States is living in a "unipolar" moment, in which U.S. power so dwarfs that of others that it lives in a league of its own. I agree with this characterization, though I also believe that change is coming. At present the United States produces roughly 21.5 percent of gross world product measured in dollars at prevailing exchange rates. There is no other country in the world that generates this much output. China is the next most productive single country, but remains perhaps half as capable economically.[47] Economic power is the source of U.S. power in the wider world, including military power. These figures do not mean that the United States has no security problems. They do mean that the U.S is very well placed to address them.

China is the most likely challenger to U.S. primacy and may catch the United States in terms of economic output at market exchange rates by 2030; even then it will still need to spread that GDP across a much larger population, reducing somewhat its ability to translate its rapidly developing economic potential into military power and global leverage.[48] A composite index of power indicators devised by the U.S. National Intelligence Council based on GDP, population size, military spending, technology, health, education, and governance projects that China could roughly equal the United States by 2045.[49] If China can maintain its recent economic momentum, and even if the United States performs reasonably well, some analysts nevertheless expect that its GDP at market exchange rates could be twice that of the United States by 2050.[50] If and when China does become the world's largest economy, the United States will likely remain in second place and India third, though the European Union collectively would be slightly ahead of the United States. Once-mighty Japan could fall to a distant fifth place, outproduced by China by a factor of six.[51]

TABLE 2. The distribution of global capabilities, 2011[1]

Country name	GDP (trillion USD)	Share of world GDP	GDP at purchasing power parity (trillion international dollars)	Population (million)	Military expenditure share of GDP (2010)
United States	15.09	21.57%	15.09	311.59	4.83
European Union[2]	17.55	25.08%	16.53	503.68	1.79
China	7.30	10.43%	11.35	1,344.13	2.01
Japan	5.87	8.39%	4.38	127.82	0.99
India	1.85	2.64%	4.53	1,241.49	2.46
Russia	1.86	2.66%	3.03	141.93	3.94
World	69.97	100.00%	81.17	6,973.74	2.62

[1]*Source*: World Bank, "World Development Indicators," http://data.worldbank.org/indicator.
[2]European states are displayed as an aggregate for convenience; individual European nation-states retain control over most state functions, especially defense and foreign policy, but have created a single European market, and a sizeable body of agreed regulation that permits a high degree of economic integration.

[17]

The United States will need to plan carefully for this kind of strategic future. In particular, a strategic competition with China probably cannot be managed by Cold War methods. The Soviet Union never had an economy more than about half as productive as that of the United States.[52] China could ultimately prove a much more formidable economic and strategic competitor. If such a rivalry emerges, the United States will need real allies, contributing more to the common defense than the security dependencies it protected during the Cold War. As the distant sea power, the United States, like Great Britain historically, should be able to find allies among states proximate to China, who will have better reasons for concern about Chinese power than we do, and better reasons to fear China than to fear the United States.

The United States has important assets that will allow it to remain competitive with the other consequential powers, even as their economies grow. The United States has a large, diverse, and talented population, the third largest in the world. This population continues to grow both from natural births, and from immigration. The population is demographically better balanced than that of many of our peers. One should also note that the U.S. economy, coupled with its immediate neighbors Canada and Mexico, is insulated geographically from major disruptions abroad. The U.S. economy is diverse, producing manufactured goods, advanced technology, raw materials, energy, and foodstuffs. Connections with Canada and Mexico further broaden the base. Though free trade is beneficial, the United States can go it alone if necessary; others are not so well placed.

The U.S. dollar is an important security asset because it is the world's reserve currency. Liberal Hegemony does not make the dollar the world currency; the dollar as world currency enables Liberal Hegemony. Having the world currency is both a strategic advantage and a trap. In times of trouble the U.S can borrow vast sums; at the same time the willingness of others to hold dollars allows the United States to live beyond its means even when it is not in trouble. Governments hold massive quantities of U.S. government securities against economic and political emergencies; the price of many important commodities such as oil is typically denominated in dollars in international trade. Though massive U.S. borrowing has made those who hold large reserves of dollar securities nervous, there are still not many alternatives. Certainly there is evidence that these others are trying to diversify their portfolios, and it seemed for a time that the euro had become a kind of junior partner as a reserve currency.[53] When international politics seems unstable, or when the global economy is roiled, businesses and governments still seem to want dollars. One can imagine why. Though currencies strengthen and weaken due to the economic fortunes of the moment, holders of government securities want to be sure that they will be repaid in the long term. Foreigners know that the United States is a relatively conservative, democratic, capitalist country. The government will not fall, nor will wealth be expropriated. The United States is secure from conquest. And the U.S. economy is sufficiently large and diverse that holders of dollars can expect to find something in it that they might want to buy. Only the European Union comes close to the United States by these criteria, but it still suffers from the absence of a strong central government.

Geography still matters in national security. The United States has long enjoyed the benefits of ocean barriers and relatively weak neighbors. The oceans constitute a formidable defense against conventional invasion if the United States retains the naval and air power to fight on, above, and under them. Though the invention of nuclear weapons makes it easy to damage the United States from long range, even here the U.S. location helps. Costly and complex systems are needed to deliver nuclear weapons reliably against the United States at long range, and these systems can only be produced by a handful of wealthy and economically capable states. Though an unusually competent and lucky terrorist group could acquire or improvise a nuclear explosive device and smuggle it into the United States, the capacity to damage the United States heavily resides in states, which have return addresses for the massive U.S. nuclear retaliatory force, and lots to lose. Canada and Mexico are strategically weak neighbors and cannot threaten the United States. Though it is seldom discussed due to the delicacy of national feeling, neither state is free to align itself with an enemy of the United States. The United States would and could prevent it.

Nuclear weapons are an important strategic fact. There is no way to offer this observation without seeming silly. As noted above, they have increased the damage that other nation-states and even nonstate actors can do to the United States. At the same time, because the United States is an advanced economic power, with more experience with nuclear weapons than any other, and with a massive nuclear force capable of devastating retaliation against other nation-states under any conceivable conditions, nuclear attacks on the United States are suicidal. In the event of such an insane gambit, U.S. revenge would be cold comfort to us, but prospective attackers must count on that revenge, which would end their societies. Nightmare scenarios of insane leaders launching nuclear attacks will remain a concern, but it takes more than one individual to launch a nuclear war, even in autocratic states. This strategic situation of mutual assured catastrophe (if not complete destruction) is true of relations among all advanced economic powers who choose nuclear armaments. Nuclear weapons do more than deter nuclear attack; a nonnuclear invasion of a nuclear power would be incredibly risky; the attacker could not count on the defender to leave its most powerful weapons unused. The existence of nuclear weapons mutes great power security competition. The risk of a weapon falling into the hands of a group that has no values to hold hostage is real, however.

There is not yet a new candidate for hegemony in Eurasia, though China's economic growth means that its policies bear watching. The United States waged two hot wars and one cold one in Eurasia in the last century because this is where we find the greatest concentration of economic power.[54] The United States has ensured that no single hegemonic power arises in Eurasia, unites its disparate states by the sword, commands its economies, and develops enough capacity to challenge the United States in its hemisphere. Germany and the Soviet Union were candidates for hegemony, and the United States opposed them. Japan attempted to achieve hegemony in Asia and was thwarted. Since the Cold War ended, there has been no such candidate challenger in Eurasia.

There is a rough balance of power among the key powers in Eurasia, including Russia, India, and Japan and the cluster of capable medium and small powers that cooperate as the European Union. These all jostle one another in different ways. At the moment, not all are equally capable, and China is the most capable of them all. None of them, including China, is presently capable of mounting a bid for hegemony, and if one of them tried, the others could combine against it. These states can currently defend themselves, or can do so with much less assistance from the United States than we currently provide. This could change in the future, and a Grand Strategy of Restraint aims to husband U.S. power, and energize local capabilities, for that day.

CAUSES AND CONSEQUENCES

Four important causes serve as the foundation of this book: the anarchical condition of international politics; the propensity of modern people to identify with groups larger than themselves—nations, ethnic groups, or religions; the enormous and obvious destructive power of nuclear weapons; and the propensity of war, once underway, to create a system of action resistant to human control. These causes have been integrated into theories, which I discuss below. These theories are not merely clusters of ideas; they are causal arguments, which have been repeatedly tested, formally or informally. We do not know, perhaps cannot know, whether these theories provide complete and fully reliable explanations of what has occurred, high-confidence predictions of what will occur, or high-confidence advice on how to proceed. We can be confident, however, that

[20]

these causes are important and that they often seem to produce certain effects. The theories have stood the test of time. Social scientists, strategists, and historians return to them repeatedly because they provide important insights. Combined with extensive study of the facts of the case, and assisted by careful judgment, they can help us make sense of our situation.

My entire analysis is premised on a realist theory of international politics. Even many of the facts about economic vitality and geography enumerated above seem important only in light of this theory.[55] Realists depict the international political world as an anarchy—a realm without a sovereign. In this realm, self-help is the rule. Any state can resort to armed force, so all will want at least some armed force, and the material and human assets that contribute to armed force, to ensure themselves against the worst case. Most states wish to achieve as much autonomy as possible. States thus seek power; some pursue what they perceive to be "sufficient" power to defend, while some chase all the power that they can. Some chase power recklessly, while others are shrewd and cautious, waiting for opportunities. Ironically, superior relative power is one such opportunity; the strong typically wish to get stronger and their superior capability may allow them to do so.[56]

Most autonomous states wish to survive. They will balance against powerful states, especially those that seem greedy for even more power, wondering what they intend to do with it.[57] In the face of buildups or aggression by others, they will build up their own capabilities, or seek allies, or both.[58] States will also "buck pass." To husband their own power, they will encourage others to deal with international problems, until they are forced to deal with these problems themselves.[59] States will "free ride" and "cheap ride" if another state is willing to do the heavy lifting.

Nuclear weapons profoundly affect the relationships among the states that possess them. Nuclear weapons in the hands of an adversary raise the stakes of any great power clash. Because they are immensely destructive, and quite small relative to their destructiveness, nuclear weapons are easy to deliver and easy to hide. They are also comparatively cheap. Thus moderately advanced states ought to be capable of developing an assured ability to retaliate against a nuclear attack by their peers, a secure second-strike capability. Even a ragged retaliation puts much of an adversary state's wealth and population at risk. This is not difficult for statesmen to understand, and thus they will be very cautious in dealing with other nuclear weapons states. Deterrence should prove stable. Nuclear powers are difficult to coerce, and incredibly difficult and costly, if not impossible, to conquer and thus nuclear weapons strategically favor the defense.[60] Nuclear weapons have, however, created one peculiar risk.

[21]

Should a nuclear device fall into the hands of a nonstate group, deterrence logic might not hold, because targeted states have nothing to threaten to retaliate against.

Identity politics is a strong feature of the modern world. Though people identified with and battled for their families, tribes, and clans in antiquity, modern nationalism raises these inclinations to a larger scale.[61] Since the French Revolution we have seen the propensity for very large groups of people without family ties to connect their fates together on the basis of shared language, culture, and history.[62] These "imagined communities" seek political power to advance their collective interests and ensure their collective survival and prosperity.[63] Ambitious politicians find that appeals to nationalism are particularly effective in periods of physical and economic insecurity. Thus is born the nation-state. Nationalism has been one of the most powerful political forces of modern times—providing the political energy that sustained the two world wars, the wars of decolonization, and the numerous conflicts that followed the collapse of Soviet power, and the subsequent collapse worldwide of multiethnic states that had survived largely due to the superpower dole.

Political scientists argue vehemently about the sources of nationalism, and whether or not nationalism per se is a source of conflict.[64] That said, intensification of nationalism has traveled with conflict quite often, as cause or consequence. Nationalism is a powerful political tool for military mobilization.[65] And nationalism has been resurgent since the end of the cold war ideological competition. It must be acknowledged, however, that other identities have proven powerful. Religious identities are often part and parcel of national identities. Some states are inhabited by multiple ethnic groups struggling to determine the content of a national identity, or striving to secede to establish their own nation-states. Most important, the spread of modern nationalism makes states hard for outsiders to conquer and govern because it facilitates mobilization and sacrifice.

Though essential for the achievement of security in international politics, military power is a blunt instrument. Students of war, and practitioners, understand that war is costly and not easily controlled. Carl von Clausewitz, perhaps the greatest military practitioner/theorist, tells us that war is an extension of politics, and that every act in war should be connected to the ultimate political end.[66] Otherwise war is simply meaningless violence. He explains at length that this advice is hard to follow. War is an intense competition, subject to strong emotions and random events. Once war is under way, states will dig deeply into their potential resources to avoid defeat. Clausewitz was a student of nationalism himself and observed how the emergence of nationalism in revolutionary France permitted that country to mobilize vastly more resources for war

[22]

than any other country in Europe had been able to mobilize. He famously observes that war creates an environment of its own—of fear, fog, and friction. Fear is easy to understand; military power has the purpose of doing harm, especially to other militaries. Warfare has always been quite destructive but has proven especially destructive since the industrial revolution. Fog arises because information in warfare is particularly unreliable, in part because one's enemy does not want one to have accurate information. And warfare often consists of many tactical engagements, separated in space and time, and information on each one usually cannot be effectively integrated in one place. (The United States today leads the world in the exploitation of technology to solve this problem, but debates persist on the extent to which fog can be banished.) It is difficult for the commander to interpret the meaning of these engagements. Finally, problems of fear and information interact with the sheer magnitude of battlefield projects. Most military forces are large complex organizations that must drag with them onto the battlefield (or if at sea or in the air into the battlespace) what they need to fight and to live. Even without any enemy violence this is a major physical problem. Something is always going wrong. Friction is however magnified once combat begins, once the enemy is trying to do damage, and deny information. Indeed, in Clausewitz's view, fear, fog, and friction combine and interact. Each helps intensify the other. The discriminate control of force and the achievement of political purposes are thus quite difficult. War is a blunt instrument. It is enormously cruel and its natural tendency is toward tremendous waste. It should be taken up rarely, and only with enormous determination not only to see the war through if necessary, but of equal importance to keep it under political control.

The United States is compelled by the enduring circumstances of international politics to make preparations for defense. The U.S. strategic situation is remarkably good relative to others. It is rich, distant from other great powers, and defended by a powerful nuclear deterrent. Other great powers are at present weaker than the United States, close to one another, and face the same pressures to defend themselves as does the United States. Finally the employment of military power is always fraught. Even weak states may be able to call on an aroused nationalism to assist in their defense. The theories that inform my strategic thinking, and the particular facts of the U.S. situation, suggest to me that U.S. grand strategy can be and should be quite "restrained." It has not been. I turn now to a critique of the grand strategy that did emerge in the United States after the collapse of the Soviet Union and the end of the Cold War. This grand strategy is significantly more active, and more militarized than seems necessary.

[23]

[1]

The Perils of Liberal Hegemony

Liberal Hegemony has performed poorly in securing the United States over the last two decades, and given ongoing changes in the world it will perform less and less well. The strategy has been costly, wasteful, and counterproductive. The United States has spent hundreds of billions of dollars on unnecessary military preparations and unnecessary wars, billions that it can no longer afford. The wars have needlessly taken the lives of thousands of U.S. military personnel and hurt many thousands more. The strategy molds the U.S. military in a way that will leave it simultaneously large, expensive, and fundamentally misshapen. The strategy makes enemies almost as quickly as it dispatches them. The strategy encourages less-friendly states to compete with the United States more intensively, while encouraging friendly states to do less than they should in their own defense, or to be more adventurous than is wise. This in turn creates additional defense burdens for the American people. Below I discuss these errors in greater detail and explain why our policies are misdirected and self-defeating.

DIRECT COSTS

The United States has waged four wars since the election of William Jefferson Clinton in 1992: the 1999 war with Serbia over Kosovo, the 2001 invasion of Afghanistan and the subsequent counterinsurgency, the 2003 invasion of Iraq and subsequent counterinsurgency, and the 2011 war to oust the Gaddafi regime in Libya. Only the invasion of Afghanistan can be defended as a necessary response to a clear national security threat: those responsible for the September 11 attacks on the United States could

[24]

not be allowed to continue their relatively comfortable existence in that country. The war in Kosovo was initiated to achieve humanitarian and ideological goals. The war in Iraq was launched for a variety of reasons. Charitably, it arose from a series of intelligence failures; poor information was rendered frightening due to the September 11 attacks. Less charitably, it was a grand ideological project that aimed to transform Arab society in a way that would produce governments favorable to the United States. The Libya war was publicly motivated by the expectation of imminent massacre of civilians, but Western leaders seem also to have wanted to play a role in the "Arab Spring" for ideological reasons and may have hoped that siding with the rebels against a leader widely despised across the Arab world would recover a better opinion there of the United States. The United States also fought limited military engagements in Somalia and Bosnia for humanitarian purposes. Somalia began as a mission of humanitarian assistance and ended in a bloody fight as U.S. leaders succumbed to the temptations of nation and state building. Bosnia had a similar evolution. In Bosnia and Kosovo, the United States followed its "kinetic" operations with lengthy peace enforcement and nation- and state-building efforts involving tens of thousands of U.S. (and allied) troops for many years. The same evolution occurred in Afghanistan and Iraq, at much greater cost. United States troops are still present in Kosovo, despite the great stresses on U.S. forces arising from other military operations. In Haiti the United States threatened military force to overthrow a military junta and followed that group's exit with a deployment of tens of thousands of peacekeeping troops. The United States avoided putting troops into Libya to affect the shape of the postwar government, but immediate developments pointed to the emergence of a weak state beset by factional violence. The United States also used force many times against Iraq between the 1991 war, Operation Desert Storm, and the 2003 war, Operation Iraqi Freedom.

The United States has incurred large direct costs in money and casualties from its post–Cold War activism, because the U.S. military is an expensive tool, and even poor enemies can prove dangerous. By 2010, the United States had spent $784 billion on the Iraq war, and another $321 billion on Afghanistan and other worldwide activities associated with the "Global War on Terror."[1] Even the entire series of relatively limited operations in the 1990s cost the United States roughly $40 billion (all dollar figures in this paragraph given in 2011 dollars).[2] Relative to past wars, these costs are very high. The United States spent more on the Iraq war in real terms than it did on the Vietnam War, in which it faced an enemy backed by the Soviet Union and China. It spent almost twice as much as it spent in the Korean War. In its peak year, Iraq war spending amounted to 1 percent of U.S. GDP.

Beyond money, these wars have more tragic costs for American and Allied soldiers killed and wounded, and their families. The U.S. military is highly skilled and extraordinarily well equipped, so the human cost of these wars to the United States has thankfully been lower than one might have expected from past experience. According to the Pentagon, 4,422 Americans died during the Iraq War, and nearly 32,000 were wounded.[3] Enduring Freedom, and other associated counterterror operations accounted for 2,229 deaths, and 18,675 wounded.[4] One hundred thousand U.S. service members who deployed to the Iraq and Afghan wars have been diagnosed with post-traumatic stress disorder. Over 200,000 suffered mild to severe traumatic brain injury occasioned by proximity to explosive blasts, which at the time did not produce an obvious exterior wound.[5] Many of the wounded, and many others who fought in these wars, will require significant medical care for the remainder of their lives. Aside from the personal price they have paid, the country is honor bound to look after them for years to come, so the dollar costs of these wars have not yet been fully realized. These wars also have significant effects on the people of the countries in which they take place, including deaths, wounds, and displacement. Well over 100,000 Iraqis died violently during the U.S. operation.[6]

The direct costs of these wars tell only part of the story. The size of the annual U.S. defense effort necessary to sustain the grand strategy, now roughly 4 percent of GDP, is excessive. The sheer extent of the global military effort is one driver of costs, but there are also less obvious drivers. Though both patriotism and the challenges of military life motivate many to serve, the United States has high personnel costs because it has a largely professional military: pay, retirement, and health benefits must compete with the private sector.[7] Because military personnel are expensive, the United States cannot afford many of them, so it buys them the most sophisticated and lethal technology man can devise, in order to sustain global capabilities with a relatively small force. This creates a demand for even more skilled and more costly personnel.

For ethical reasons, cold economic reasons, and political reasons defense planners, senior military leaders, and politicians have an interest in spending vast amounts of money to prevent even a single casualty. Americans properly honor military service persons and wish to subject service members to the least risk possible. The professionals are expensive to train and hard to replace. Rising casualties are also the surest way to elicit skeptical public attention to a war, so commanders and particularly politicians have a political interest in "force protection." Thus a marginal dollar spent on force protection always seems cost effective.

Because it is the U.S. ambition not only to deter attack but to deter any peacetime military competition, an open-ended quest for clear, decisive, and somehow, enduring technological superiority is the result. The United States thus has very high military research and development costs. Once research and development efforts yield a producible design, it turns out that the quest for technological superiority has resulted in an enormously costly weapon. For the reasons outlined above, Republican and Democratic politicians agree that the U.S. military should have the best weapons money can buy, and are not competent in any case to judge when the law of diminishing returns sets in for military acquisition.

In its quest for Liberal Hegemony the United States consistently accounted for a little more than a third of all the military spending in the world during the 1990s. All potential adversaries and competitors combined spent a bit less than 20 percent. Allies of the United States accounted for a bit less than a third of all spending, and the rest of the world perhaps 15 percent.[8] The figures are even more lopsided today, with the United States accounting for 41 percent of all global military spending. This level of effort would seem to buy more insurance than the U.S. needs. At best, this amounts to a subsidy to other prosperous nations that could defend themselves if they spent a little more on defense; at worst this is pure waste; perhaps the others spend less because threats are less than we think.

The opportunity cost of overinvestment in military power is illustrated by comparisons to the effort of other nation-states. If, prior to the attacks of September 11, 2001, during the 1990s, the United States had consistently only spent as large a share of GDP on defense as its most militarily committed, globally activist, and prosperous allies, Britain and France, we could have diverted approximately 0.75 percent of GDP— roughly $75 billion annually—to nondefense activities. France then averaged 3.1 percent, the UK 3.2 percent, and the US 3.95 percent.[9] Today the disparity is roughly double. Including expenditures on the wars, the United States was spending 4.8 percent of GDP on defense in 2011, while these allies were averaging 2.25 percent[10] Others spend an even lower share of GDP. On a sustained basis these differences translate into hundreds of billions of dollars in foregone U.S. domestic investments in everything from debt reduction to infrastructure.

The U.S. military effort, both in peacetime, and in wartime, has been costly and is destined to become even more difficult and expensive if Liberal Hegemony remains the grand strategy. Although the U.S. military may easily defeat "rogue" states or occupy "failed states," the subsequent work of reconstruction and counterinsurgency will probably get even more difficult. And it is improbable that major states, growing in wealth, can be cowed into permitting the United States an open-ended military superiority.

[27]

The Balance of Power

Statesmen and strategists have long believed that states tend to join together to "balance" the power of capable states and coalitions. The United States has thus far faced only limited balancing but will likely face a lot more in coming years. As mentioned in the Introduction, international politics is an anarchy, a system without a sovereign. If actors within that system value their autonomy, they have an incentive to keep a wary eye on the most capable among them, lest the unrestrained powerful choose to attack. There is no central authority to call on for help. When one state grows too strong and threatens the sovereignty of the others, there is a tendency for the others to concert action and accumulate military power in order to defend themselves. This process is not a law, it is a tendency.

"Balancers" face many obstacles to success. Cooperation is difficult, and the more capable the target the greater the risk to those in opposition. If it takes too many independent actors to balance the power of one, the process becomes difficult indeed. Modern Europe has been the cockpit of balance of power politics, and a series of aspiring hegemons have tried and failed to establish their dominance. That said, these failures implicated others in one or more hugely destructive wars. Louis XIV, Napoleon, Kaiser Wilhelm, and Adolf Hitler all had good runs before being brought down. And it took a half-century of containment and nuclear deterrence to exhaust the energies of the Soviet Union. Balancing is difficult and dangerous work, but there are incentives to attempt it for states that value their independence.

The United States is perhaps the most capable power in history. This incentivizes others to balance but also makes balancing against the United States costly and difficult. The factors that make it possible for the United States to "go it alone" also make it possible for the United States to have great global ambitions. In the last two decades the United States has pursued these ambitions. The United States has sought very high levels of influence in most parts of the world, and often intrusive management of the internal affairs of other states large and small. The United States has been profligate in the use of military force to achieve these objectives. On the basis of U.S. capabilities, and demonstrated U.S. intentions, we should see other states balancing against the United States. Do we?

External Balancing

Most observers agree that the United States has faced little balancing.[11] Why might this have been the case? Because the United States is at a great distance from other states, true conquest of others is a costly matter, which both mutes U.S. ambitions and increases its costs, so its power may appear less threatening. Other factors, such as the nuclear weapon, also defend weaker powers against the risk that the United States could turn highly aggressive. The U.S. strategy has not aimed for formal empire or territorial conquest and annexation. Finally, the distribution of capabilities among other states has made the formation of balancing coalitions difficult. At present, the aggregate capabilities of three disparate states would be required to arithmetically exceed U.S. capabilities (see table 2). In the real world of alliance management, this is problematical. It is also the case that the rest of the consequential powers in the world are concentrated in Eurasia, which tends to make them more fearful of one another than they are of the powerful, but distant United States.[12]

Balancing efforts have occurred, however, and more are to be expected. The level of U.S. power, as well as the activist strategy that it enables, are likely to be perceived as a problem by other independent actors. At the same time, a "diffusion of power" is underway, as China and India ascend to the top ranks of world powers, and a handful of states such as Russia, Japan, and perhaps Brazil remain sufficiently capable to matter as allies. Thus some states will be more able to tilt with the United States on their own, or more able to form smaller and more manageable balancing coalitions.

Scholars following the trajectory of the "unipolar moment" have debated whether or not balancing is present. A new, somewhat useful distinction has been drawn between "soft" and "hard" balancing. "Soft balancing" captures concerted behavior by other states to increase the costs of the activist hegemon, short of the use or threat of violence, or the mobilization of material capabilities.[13] Many scholars have observed that hegemons typically attempt to legitimate their power position.[14] They would like others to believe that their might is also right. This helps the hegemon control costs. Soft balancing aims to deprive the hegemon of that legitimacy. Thus it consists mainly of diplomacy, particularly in venues that the hegemon hopes to employ to legitimate its action. The United States, as a liberal hegemon, is particularly vulnerable to this kind of action. Students of soft balancing point to action by Russia and France to deprive the United States of a U.N. security council resolution to authorize Operation Iraqi Freedom as an example. One could argue that China is engaged in soft balancing in its effort to protect traditional norms of sovereignty versus new interpretations advanced by the United States and other Western states.[15] China has used its position in the U.N. Security Council to slow U.S.-led efforts to pressure Iran into giving up its nuclear enrichment projects. Iran is a close associate of China. Given China's growing dependence on oil and gas imports from the Persian Gulf, it is plausible that Beijing is balancing U.S. power in that region.

Russia and China have collaborated to keep the Syrian civil war off the agenda of the UN Security Council. Soft balancing is consistent with its modifier, and it is difficult to argue that it has done much to slow U.S. behavior. That said, the practice is a leading indicator that U.S. hegemony does not sit well, sometimes even with its friends. "Hard balancing," the assemblage of military capability, provides the real energy in international politics. "External" balancing aims to concert hard power, or the threat of hard power, through alliances. International diplomacy is often about generating the concern in the bumptious target state that a coalition could be formed against it.[16] At some future point, that potential coalition could be a military coalition. But developments need not go that far. Balance of power diplomacy has usually stopped short of building formal alliances. During the Cold War, analysts accustomed themselves to the notion that balancing coalitions would be accompanied by formal institutions such as NATO or the Warsaw Pact with bureaucracies, command structures, and permanently stationed military forces, or the elaborate U.S. base structure that had become attached to the U.S.-Japan Security Treaty. In the past this kind of institutionalization has not occurred until well into a war, if at all.

Today balance of power diplomacy is already widely practiced. Russia and China do have a weak standing institution, the Shanghai Cooperation Organization.[17] More remarkable has been the significant sales of top-of-the-line Russian armaments to China.[18] Students of the Cold War will recall that the Soviet Union and China became bitter enemies, and the United States profited from this under President Nixon. The end of the Cold War precipitated a shift of affections, even as tensions between the United States and China quickly developed.[19] Despite the obvious fact that those parts of Russia bordering China are quite vulnerable to Chinese military action, and are the subject of long-standing irredentist claims, Russia has sold China advanced fighter aircraft, surface-to-air missile systems, warships, and naval weapons. Of course, some of this is merely a business proposition; Russia wants to keeps it arms industry viable and exports are a way to do so. But it is equally clear that Russia is happy to help China create risks for the United States and probably views the sale of arms to China as less risky to itself due to the evolving tension between China and the United States.

Russia has also done what it can to limit the extent of U.S. penetration of their former republics in Central Asia. More generally, Russia has become assertive and is trying with some success to build a sphere of influence on its periphery. And it has used force in one case, Georgia, to make the point that it believes it has a *droit de regard* in these regions. United States strategists see Russian behavior of this kind as aggressive. The possibility that prior Western activities are prompting a Russian balancing response is seldom conceded. NATO "enlargement" is conveniently forgotten; Russia should not mind that the alliance that crushed its Soviet parent has been picking up all the chips on Europe's poker table and moving its frontier inexorably in Russia's direction. Moreover, diplomatic historian Mary Sarotte finds that U.S. and German officials verbally assured Soviet leader Mikhail Gorbachev that NATO would not do this, though the assurances were never written into a treaty.[20] So to the evident creep of NATO's power in an easterly direction was added the experience of bad faith. Balance of power theorists would have expected Russia to push back as soon as it had the power; it has a little power, and it is pushing back.

The Western powers themselves have not been immune to the lure of balance of power diplomacy. Even U.S. allies in Europe have done what they can to punch up the capacity of the European Union for independent foreign policy action, including the development of a shadow military command structure outside of NATO.[21] The purpose here is limited, to have a capability in reserve against the possibility that the United States could prove capricious, and the Europeans would have to go it alone. This should not be exaggerated; progress on EU integration is slow. What is surprising is that it has happened at all in an institution whose members typically find the very question of military force to be distasteful.

The United States has, ironically, noted the power trends and reached out to India in case China grows too strong. The Bush administration cut a deal with India to permit it to import U.S. nuclear technology, despite that country's independent nuclear weapons program. This undercuts the Nuclear Non-Proliferation Treaty's (NPT) bargain to offer civilian nuclear technology only to states that forswear nuclear weapons.[22]

Internal Balancing

Internal balancing aims to strengthen a state militarily or deliberately to improve a state's economic position to mobilize military power at a later date. Efforts to dull the U.S. military advantage are widespread. Nuclear proliferation in some cases is motivated primarily by fear of the United States. North Korea seems to want nuclear weapons in part because it has no other answer to U.S. military superiority. Iran pursues "near nuclear weapons" status to improve its power in the Persian Gulf, a region the United States has strategically dominated since the end of the Cold War. China has taken Iran's part in its dispute with the United States over its efforts to master the technology that would permit it to build atomic weapons. Both Russia and China have sold advanced weaponry to Iran.

China is working very hard to improve the quality of its military forces, technologically and professionally. Aside from its imports from

[31]

Russia, its domestic arms industry strives to produce more internationally competitive weapons, and judging from appearances it is having some success. China is also developing strategic materials and energy stockpiles, presumably to allow it to ride out a U.S. blockade, enabled by U.S. command of the sea.[23] On a smaller scale, Iran too has tried to develop a capable independent arms industry. Though its products are much less advanced than those of the top producers, they seem to have made important progress, especially in their ability to produce unguided and guided rockets and missiles. There is also some evidence that they are producing night vision devices, portable surface to air missiles, and signals intelligence gear.[24] The performance of their clients, especially Hizbollah in its 2006 war with Israel, and the so-called "special groups" in Iraq, both suggest some impressive skills in Iran's military. The trade in expertise is likely two way; Iran teaches others some techniques but itself profits from the combat experience of its friends.[25]

Thus far the combination of soft and hard, external and internal balancing encountered by the United States has been inconvenient, but not deadly. The diplomatic resistance to the United States over Iraq cast a shadow over the U.S. effort, making it harder for some allies to sign up and easier for them to leave. It also helped shape the backdrop of politics across the Arab world, legitimating assistance to Iraqi insurgents opposed to the United States. We cannot measure this, however, and the actual impact may be slight, given the expected patriotic opposition of at least some Arab Iraqis to the United States, and the particular opposition of Sunni Arab Iraqis, whose hold on power the United States broke. In the world of hard balancing, China's internal improvements are the most decisive. Its overall economic progress, however, cannot be attributed to a desire to balance the United States per se, but rather to a larger desire to build China's wealth and prosperity. As many have observed, China's export-led growth strategy depends in part on the liberal international economy that U.S. hegemony aims to sustain and protect. At the same time, however, China is working steadily to improve its military power. And it is hard to see any immediate object of this buildup other than the United States. United States strategic planners have taken note. China is making it very difficult for the U.S. military to reach the Asian littorals. The debate on "anti-access area denial capabilities" in the U.S. defense community, and the emergence of the "air-sea battle" concept, with its concomitant requirement for significant expenditures on the most advanced offensive capabilities, testifies to the military progress China has already made and is expected to make.[26] As China improves its littoral warfare capabilities, U.S. projection assets may simply be pushed away. I expect this to occur, but only after the United States spends a great deal of money trying to prevent it.

[32]

Realists argue that states try to husband their power, because power is the means to security in an anarchical world. Capable states are expected to balance against other great powers, especially great powers that are trying to improve their overall position, or who demonstrate malign intent. Some capable states have balanced against the United States, though not with much energy. More states have taken a different route. Many middle and small powers "cheap ride" on the U.S. security effort and underspend on defense because the United States seems very willing to carry the burden of securing them against their regional adversaries. Some are bolder; they count on the United States to defend them even if their own ambitions get them into trouble; they drive recklessly.

The United States is a good ally. Aside from the massive capabilities it can bring to any problem, U.S. leaders have been obsessed with the credibility of their commitments and have accepted the idea that failure to stand up anywhere will lead to challenges everywhere.[27] Indeed, the obsession with credibility goes even farther; there is great concern that allies will lose faith in U.S. promises. The peculiarities of domestic politics also tend to make commitments sticky once they are in place. The American people do not naturally believe that problems in distant places matter to them, so their leaders, as well as policy partisans, oversell new commitments to them, and infuse those commitments with value—our friends are always doughty liberal democratic underdogs, beset by criminals and aspiring tyrants. The U.S. record of looking after its friends during the Cold War is exemplary. Many U.S. allies take advantage of this U.S. propensity. And many aspire to be U.S. allies, because they understand this propensity.

Because U.S. allies are wealthy, and do generate some military power, partisans of Liberal Hegemony are loathe to consider new arrangements in which they would assume greater responsibility for themselves. These allies are not, however, straightforward additions to U.S. power. Allies of the United States remain autonomous actors, and they contribute what they wish to U.S. security problems. The main contingency that causes an ally to add its capability to that of the United States is a shared perception of threat. The weaker that shared perception, the smaller the contribution. Finally, the weaker the ally, the less they are able to contribute, but also the less their contribution matters, and they know it. If the United States cares enough about them to offer an alliance, then it cares enough to defend them whatever they do themselves.

Present day U.S. alliances do not resemble the grand alliance of the Second World War, or even the Cold War. In World War II the United States, Britain, and the Soviet Union had the single objective of destroying

Nazi Germany. All had a great deal of economic potential to bring to the fight, and all contributed the maximum possible to that project because all feared Nazi Germany. During the Cold War the situation differed. Though the Western European members of NATO all feared the Soviet Union, even the largest were individually incapable of contributing enough to balance its power. The U.S. role in the alliance was central; NATO was more a grand U.S. security guarantee than it was a partnership of military equals. Though the allies did contribute to their own defense, it was generally the case that they underprovided for their own security, counting on the United States to carry the load. The United States had an interest in doing so, fearing that the Soviets could "run the table" in Europe and become a true continental hegemon, able to challenge the United States in a global competition.

Presently, the net U.S. gain from its alliance relationships is considerably less than it was in the Cold War and is not commensurate with the cost. The bargain has become unprofitable to the United States and requires renegotiation. The United States provides security around the world. This was understandable when a powerful Soviet Union potentially threatened prosperous, middle-sized countries on its periphery. This is no longer the case. The Europeans in the North Atlantic Treaty Organization, and Japan, do face some potential threats, but not enough to elicit serious military efforts, especially given the U.S. guarantee. Whatever residual threat Russia poses to Europe could easily be addressed by Europeans themselves. China does not presently pose the threat to Japan once generated by the Soviet Union, but China's power is growing and probably will grow more significantly over the next several decades. Japan could make a much more significant contribution to its own defense today and could make significant contributions in the future. Europe and Japan could also make larger contributions to security problems farther afield, in which they have an interest, but to which they contribute less than they could.

The limited efforts of its principal allies have several negative consequences for the United States. The most obvious negative consequence is that the United States overspends on its military. If these countries did more, the United States could do less. Second, these alliances play a strange role in the U.S. security policy debate. Advocates of particular U.S. programs and policies often claim that failure to follow their advice will weaken our alliances. This is related to a third problem, these alliances are institutionalized and within U.S. policy debates are portrayed as alliances, rather than what they are, U.S. guarantees. United States policy advocates can use these allies to make it appear that their projects have deeper international support than they do, and help to make it seem that any given project will garner more contributions than it will,

[34]

even though these claims are difficult to measure. Polls consistently show that Americans are more likely to support the use of force when they have allies involved.[28] Thus the U.S. share can be made to appear low up front, when in fact the United States will likely end up bearing the lion's share of the project's cost.[29]

The United States also provides security in less formal relationships. Several of these have generated a different problem. Small states, or non-state actors, which for any number of reasons have become confident in the U.S. commitment, behave recklessly.[30] They pursue their own narrow interests even when these are at variance with the interests of the United States. In each case there is a unique set of problems that make it difficult for the U.S. government to discipline these actors. Among them are, or have been, various Israeli governments, the Kosovo Liberation Army in 1998–99, the government of Georgia in 2008, the Democratic Progressive Party government of Taiwan in 2000–2008, a series of governments in post-Ba'ath Iraq including the Nouri al-Maliki government, the Kurdish parties in Iraq, and the Karzai government in Afghanistan. The Philippines and ironically, Vietnam, may also be developing a taste for reckless driving. These problems will be discussed below.

Cheap Riding

Evidence of allied deficiencies is found in three areas: their overall defense efforts, their specific nonperformance in agreed medium-term improvement plans, and their finely tuned contributions to combined operations. To be fair, the allies do quite a lot for their own security and to make the United States happy. They could, however, do more, but they do not because the United States carries the weight. They would argue that the United States does what is in its interests, and they follow with what is then in theirs. This is true in isolation. I argue, however, that this grand strategy is no longer in the U.S. interest, and the limited contribution of the allies is one of the negative factors in the present grand strategy.

The United States has rich allies who contribute a far smaller share of GDP to military purposes than does the United States and spend much less overall (see table 3). They contribute far less on a per capita basis. Even if per capita GDP is considered, and we accept that the average U.S. citizen is still wealthier than a citizen of an EU country or Japan, the allies still spend less than their "fair share" on defense. The Europeans do field more people in their armed forces, but coupled with their lower spending overall this has the unfortunate effect of diverting a great deal of money to salaries and other personnel costs, which contributes to much lower spending per soldier on equipment and training. Thus European

[35]

TABLE 3. Defense burden sharing—2011

Country or group	GDP[1] (trillion USD)	GDP per capita (USD)	Military spending (billion USD)[2]	Military spending as a share of GDP (percent)	Military spending per capita (USD)	Military personnel	Military expenditure per soldier[3]
United States	15.09	48,111	687.0	4.56	2,205.00	1,564,000	439,260
NATO (Europe)	17.45	31,140	282.5	1.6	418.00	2,027,000	139,370
Japan	5.9	45,902	59.83	1.02	469.00	248,000	241,250

[1]GDP figures from World Bank, "World Development Indicators."
[2]U.S. and Japanese military spending and personnel figures from IISS, *Military Balance 2013* (London, 2013), table 25; NATO Europe figures from NATO, "Financial and Economic Data Relating to NATO Defence," April 13, 2012, http://www.nato.int.
[3]I have calculated this myself. It is a crude indicator of relative investment in the overall quality of the force. Excluding both war spending, and the 100,000 troops added for the wars, the U.S. figure would drop to roughly 360,000 per soldier.

forces are on the whole not nearly as well equipped or technically advanced as U.S. forces. European states probably have too many people in their armed forces relative to their current defense needs; they would be better off spending these resources on more and better equipment for a smaller force.

If the United States did less, and the allies perceived that this reduced their security, they could clearly afford to spend more. The United States has jawboned its allies for years in an effort to get them to do more, but this has produced few results. In some ways, the U.S. effort to elicit more contributions from allies has waned. During the latter years of the Cold War, the Congress required the Pentagon by law to assess "Allied Contributions to the Common Defense." This report enumerated the efforts of the allies and assessed those efforts on the basis of ability to pay. DOD asked for and the Congress approved an end to the reporting requirement, and it was formally ended in 2008, though no report had been produced since 2004 in any case.[31] The document was meant to be replaced with a new report assessing the efforts of the NATO allies by different and more relevant metrics, but this has never appeared publicly.[32]

After the Cold War ended, the members of the North Atlantic Treaty Organization turned to the question of how to reform the alliance to preserve its relevance, given the disappearance of the Soviet threat, its original purpose. This occurred gradually, as it was initially unclear that

Russia would shed almost all of its offensive capability. NATO, under U.S. leadership, chose to expand rather than contract its horizons. The alliance became a key element of Liberal Hegemony. The inclusion of former Warsaw Pact states became the first project, locking in the Cold War victory, but assuming a new set of security commitments.

During the NATO operations against Serbia over Kosovo in 1999, the alliance held its fiftieth anniversary celebration and committed itself to a new and more expansive agenda. The alliance would address

> uncertainty and instability in and around the Euro-Atlantic area and the possibility of regional crises at the periphery of the Alliance. . . . Ethnic and religious rivalries, territorial disputes, inadequate or failed efforts at reform, the abuse of human rights, and the dissolution of states can lead to local and even regional instability. The resulting tensions could lead to crises affecting Euro-Atlantic stability, to human suffering, and to armed conflicts. Such conflicts could affect the security of the Alliance by spilling over into neighbouring countries, including NATO countries, or in other ways, and could also affect the security of other states.[33]

Secretary of Defense Donald Rumsfeld's decision to decline proffered alliance assistance for the initial 2001 attack on Afghanistan on the grounds that the allies were insufficiently capable, produced a flurry of concern about what this portended for NATO's future. The United States then proposed that NATO create a rapid reaction force, which would be ready for future crises. This was agreed at the NATO Summit in Prague in November 2002. These proposals crept through the NATO bureaucracy and emerged in June 2003 as the NATO Response Force, or NRF. From the large number of military personnel serving in their militaries, the allies would endeavor to have ready at all times a force of roughly twenty-five thousand, including ground, air, naval, and logistical assets, able to begin deployment with five days' notice and sustain itself for a month.[34] Thus roughly 1 percent of all the military personnel in NATO's European member state forces would need to be highly ready at any one time. The force would be staffed on a rotational basis given the difficulty that any military unit quite reasonably experiences trying to sustain such high readiness.

On the whole, though varying levels of success have been claimed in this endeavor, this modest ambition has not been met. At NATO's Riga Summit in November 2006, the NRF was declared to be at full operational capability, with twenty-five thousand troops. A year later, however, lacunae began to surface, and the member states began to complain that coupled with peacekeeping missions in Kosovo and Afghanistan, they lacked the forces to sustain the NRF. Though the alliance could hit the twenty-five thousand personnel figure, it could not regularly produce the enabling logistic, medical, airlift, and helicopter units necessary. The alliance was also unable to generate an equivalent force that might be needed to relieve the initial troops if the contingency lasted as long as a year. Finally, the costs of missions underway meant that additional defense spending would be needed to buy the equipment to meet the NRF requirements. Though NATO formally remains committed to the NRF, the alliance pared its ambitions significantly, and the real current capability of the NRF is unclear.[35]

NATO's 2011 campaign to halt the depredations of the Gaddafi regime against a political and military rebellion appears as a logical extension of the vague but expansive set of regional and global political objectives to which the alliance has committed itself. It also revealed how little progress the European allies have made in acquiring the capabilities to implement the strategy during the intervening decade. Though Libya paled as a military power versus the European members of the alliance, an internal NATO report concludes that the operation was highly dependent on direct U.S. support for everything from precision guided munitions, to intelligence, surveillance and reconnaissance, refueling capabilities, and even key personnel.[36]

NATO in Afghanistan

Hours after the attack of September 11, 2001, NATO offered its assistance to the United States, consistent with Article V of the treaty. The United States accepted minor assistance, but declined the cooperation of NATO as an institution in the original offensives in Afghanistan of Operation Enduring Freedom. The Rumsfeld Pentagon believed that collaboration within the alliance command structures would produce an unwieldy operation, and the United States chose to involve allies only on an ad hoc basis.[37] NATO's offer was perhaps its finest hour, and Rumsfeld's rejection of its participation in Afghanistan was only the first of a series of strategic blunders.

Once the Taliban government was toppled, an international peacekeeping force was established to assist the United States in Afghanistan—the International Security and Assistance Force, or ISAF. It would help reconstruct Afghanistan while a separate U.S. command structure pursued Al-Qaeda and Taliban holdouts. Initially, this was an ad hoc operation, but it slowly became clear that only NATO had the organizational abilities to sustain such a large peacekeeping and reconstruction operation over a long period of time, and it assumed the mission in August 2003.[38] The mission grew from a Kabul security mission to a nationwide mission. NATO provides the command structure and many of the troops, though many non-NATO nations offer units to the operation. In 2007, ISAF and the U.S.-commanded Enduring Freedom were merged, and the U.S. commander in the theater was also designated the ISAF commander. The history of the command structure in Afghanistan illustrates the strange role that NATO plays. On the one hand, no other multinational organization in the world can run a mission like ISAF. On the other hand, NATO and its European members are insufficient on their own to sustain a significant effort, and U.S. capabilities are usually needed to make good the shortfalls. Ultimately therefore, to hand a problem to NATO, is simply to hand it back to the United States.[39]

ISAF is a major contribution to the effort to suppress the Taliban and Al-Qaeda in Afghanistan. It would be churlish to deny that NATO made this possible. The European allies bring significant capabilities to the fight and provide security in much of the country. Decades of experience preparing to fight the Soviet Union produced both habits and structures of military cooperation that eased the way for this effort. Afghanistan is divided into five regional commands, and the allies staff four of them. In total, some eleven hundred allied soldiers (European and non-European) had died in Afghanistan by the summer of 2013. The military forces of the NATO allies deserve credit for all that they have done and the price that they have paid. That said NATO European member states, as members of the alliance, are not holding up their end. The United States has some responsibility for this, as some believe that the allies would have been more deeply invested in the mission had they been included at the outset.[40] This mistake cannot be undone, but the alliance did commit itself to Afghanistan, and both quantitatively and qualitatively the allies have done too little.

Two of the most acute observers of the transatlantic relationship declared in 2009 that "NATO is now little more than a fig leaf in Afghanistan."[41] The United States then had perhaps 7 percent of its military personnel in Afghanistan. NATO Europe had perhaps 1.5 percent of its total personnel. As the situation in Afghanistan deteriorated, U.S. policymakers argued that additional troops were needed to prevent the unraveling of the country. President Obama decided to nearly triple the U.S. troop strength in country, from 40,000 to just under a 100,000 people, by autumn 2010. The Obama administration asked its allies to increase significantly their forces in Afghanistan but the Europeans did not offer much. NATO officials had a difficult time finding member states willing to contribute forces to the effort, which was unpopular in Europe.[42] The NATO allies promised to add 7,000 troops to the fight, but the total was deceptive: some of the troops were not from NATO member states; others came with caveats; still others were already there.[43]

The forces that NATO members sent to Afghanistan were neither as plentiful nor as useful as they should have been. As Secretary of Defense Robert Gates observed, "Despite more than 2 million troops in uniform . . . NATO has struggled, at times desperately, to sustain a deployment of 25[,000] to 40,000 troops, not just in boots on the ground, but in crucial support assets such as helicopters, transport aircraft, maintenance, intelligence, surveillance and reconnaissance, and much more."[44] In his view, these equipment shortfalls negatively affected operations.[45] Perhaps most critically, almost half of the Europeans sent their troops to Afghanistan with special constraints on their participation (termed "caveats").[46] These included limits on where they could be and what they could do. Many NATO member states preferred that their troops remain in somewhat quieter parts of Afghanistan, and many placed constraints on the use of their forces in offensive operations. Finally, the United States accepts that military operations require plus-ups to the defense budget, either through supplemental budgetary allocations, or within the normal defense budget; otherwise medium- and long-term defense programs will suffer.[47] The allies fund their military efforts out of the defense spending they have previously planned, and thus participation in the war suppresses long-term improvement plans. Moreover, the alliance deploys forces under a simple principle that each state pays the operational costs of its own troops. If they agree to risk their forces, poorer European countries are stuck with big bills, which they have a hard time paying. Richer members of NATO have not offered to underwrite their costs.

The European members of NATO made important contributions to the Afghanistan War, but as he completed his service in June 2011, outgoing secretary of defense Robert Gates noted that "though we can take pride in what has been accomplished and sustained in Afghanistan, the ISAF mission has exposed significant shortcomings in NATO—in military capabilities, and in political will."[48] The secretary went on to discuss his grave concerns about the future of the alliance if the members could not better this record.

Japan

Secretary of State Hillary Rodham Clinton observed in January, 2010, on the fiftieth anniversary of the U.S.-Japan Security Treaty that "the U.S.-Japan Alliance plays an indispensable role in ensuring the security and prosperity of both the United States and Japan, as well as regional peace and stability."[49] Such bromides are common at official meetings but obscure deep and obsolete inequities embedded in the alliance. Japan does far less for its own defense than it should or could. It contributes almost nothing, other than funds, to international peacekeeping or

U.S.-led military operations farther afield. Japan's promises of support even for potential U.S.-led military operations in Asia are lukewarm and preparations limited.[50]

The Japanese Constitution of 1947, written under U.S. tutelage, placed strict constraints on the country's ability to build military forces.[51] Article 9 banned any offensive military activity of any kind; by some interpretations Japan should not have military forces. Over the years, as a consequence of the necessities of the Cold War competition, and the frequent requests of the United States, many of the initial constraints have been reinterpreted or eroded.[52] Japan does have a large military and a large defense budget, roughly comparable to the budgets and force structures of France or the United Kingdom.[53] From 2002 to 2012 the budget fell every year, for a total reduction of roughly 6 percent over the decade.[54] Japan has purchased excellent equipment, and some of its forces can reach out hundreds of miles from Japan for purposes of defending the home islands. Nevertheless, Japan probably cannot defend itself on its own and is quite limited in its ability to mount even tactically offensive operations.[55] It should be noted, however, that the current Japanese defense program does orient future efforts on the "southwestern islands," the area around Okinawa where proximity to Taiwan, and to islands disputed with China, suggest the potential for conflict. A small amount of additional military spending has been authorized. Other than the near-term shift of a few radars, and the movement to Okinawa of a single fighter squadron, it remains to be seen whether more substantive plans for programs such as an expansion of the Japanese submarine force will be realized.[56]

The U.S.-Japan Security Treaty of 1960 commits the United States to defend Japan, but only commits Japan to assist in its own defense. The United States was granted the use of major military facilities in Japan, which it enjoys to this day. Perhaps fifty thousand U.S. troops are based in a dozen major bases, a third on the Island of Okinawa.[57] In practice, Japan has had little say over how those facilities are used. From the U.S. point of view, these bases are not merely for the defense of Japan but support the overall military effort of the United States in Asia and farther afield. Japan is well situated to support U.S. military operations in the area of Korea or Taiwan (see map 1). During the Cold War, Japan's geographic position also helped to bottle up the Soviet Pacific Fleet. That position would make Japan even more useful in constraining the operations of the Chinese Navy, should that ever become necessary. Japan contributes $3 or $4 billion a year to support U.S. forces on its territory and is contributing special funds to the reorganization of U.S. bases in Japan now underway. From the point of view of useful bases, and direct financial contributions, Japan does contribute to the U.S. regional and global strategic effort.

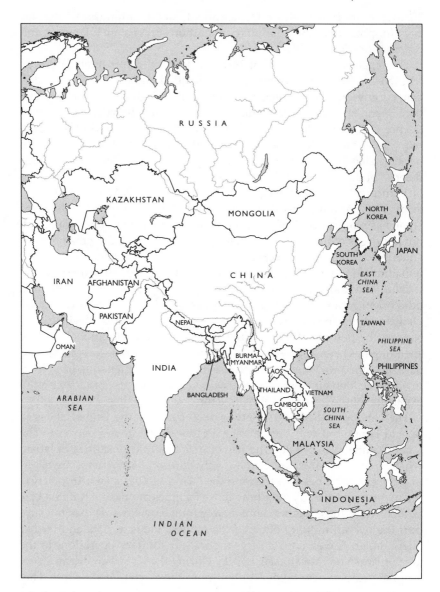

MAP 1 Political Asia

It is hard to argue, however, that Japan is contributing its fair share, or even what it ought to contribute, given its own defense needs. Japan, as a matter of domestic political agreement, does not spend more than 1 percent of GDP directly on its military. This reflects the antimilitary

[42]

orientation of its constitution, which has widespread public support. Given the per capita GDP of the country, the defense burden is very light. From the point of view of planning for the actual defense of Japan, cooperation between the two countries seems surprisingly sparse.[58] A recent report by longtime participants in the U.S.-Japan security relationship, Joseph Nye and Richard Armitage, declares that "the new environment requires significantly greater jointness and interoperability across services in both countries and bilaterally between the United States and Japan."[59] United States and Japanese units in Japan do exercise together frequently at the tactical level, and since 2005 some limited efforts have been made to develop command arrangements that would permit close coordination during actual combat operations, at least for air and missile defense.[60] On the whole, however, the persistence of exhortations to do more causes one to suspect that progress is slow. Moreover, Japan does not seek joint planning, apparently out of fear that if it did, the United States might ask it to commit more explicitly to real military action in its own defense.[61]

Since the end of the Cold War, the United States has unsuccessfully pressed Japan to make greater contributions to security operations farther afield. In 1992 the Parliament passed the International Peace Cooperation Law, which allows Japanese troops to participate in UN peacekeeping. The 1992 law was accepted in part to mollify the United States after Japan's absence from the 1991 Operation Desert Storm. Japan sent money, but no soldiers. Both the Clinton and the Bush administrations succeeded in eliciting formal commitments from Japan to enhance its capabilities and to intensify security cooperation. The Koizumi government found ways to participate a bit more in U.S. operations after the September 11, 2001, attacks: Japanese naval units provided logistical support to the United States in the Indian Ocean and one Japanese infantry battalion was stationed in a quiet corner of southern Iraq for several years providing reconstruction assistance. It is commonly acknowledged that they were so constrained from using their weapons that units from other members of the coalition were assigned to defend the Japanese. These troops departed before the United States did, and with the coming to power of the Democratic Party of Japan in 2009, the country's naval logistics units were pulled out of the Indian Ocean. On the whole, despite much intra-alliance diplomacy, agreed statements, and parliamentary laws, Japan still is inclined to participate very little in missions abroad. It is much more troubling, however, that Japan remains ill-prepared to contribute fully to its own defense.

Ironically, Japan's policymakers argue that the United States is not holding up its end of the alliance bargain. The election of President Obama and the launch of an internal review of the U.S. nuclear force

[43]

posture and the promise of new nuclear arms control negotiations, prompted concerns about the reliability of the United States extended deterrence commitment, so much so that a new consultative mechanism was established to discuss it.[62] The precise reasons for this concern were murky; nuclear threats to Japan that could emanate from North Korea or even China are far less than they were during the Cold War. Then, the United States could not prevent nuclear damage to Japan in a determined Soviet attack—it could only deter it. And the alliance was quite strong. Now the Japanese standard appears to be higher, although it is difficult to interpret. Some Japanese officials past and present seem to believe that there is a particular type, or a particular quantity of U.S. nuclear forces that would deter North Korea or China, and/or successfully prevent their ability to do any damage.[63] Against even modest nuclear forces, such assurance is simply not possible, and Japanese officials surely know it. The North Korean forces are small, and it is possible that ongoing Japanese and U.S. theater missile defense efforts will be able to shoot down a nuclear tipped missile. But this cannot be guaranteed. United States conventional or nuclear offensive operations might prevent a North Korean launch altogether, but this too cannot be guaranteed. Against a much larger Chinese nuclear potential, the odds of defensive or offensive success are extremely low. There is little that the United States can do about this. Deterrence of either of these actors depends on the credible threat to retaliate, which arises from the massive capability of the U.S. nuclear forces, and U.S. interest in ensuring an independent Japan. The presence of U.S. forces and the fact of the U.S.-Japan Security Treaty are the key indicators of U.S. interest.[64]

Reckless Drivers

Some U.S. allies do too little, but others do the wrong things. They take bold actions that may harm U.S. interests, or even their own. The United States has proven itself incapable of disciplining these allies, despite their small size and relative dependence on the United States. In part this is because of credibility concerns. In part it is because the United States, as a global power, is often preoccupied, and its allies can play while the cat is away. And finally it should be noted that small states and groups often find friends in the pluralist U.S. system, who will serve as their publicists.

Israel

The state of Israel may be the most problematic reckless driver allied with the United States. It is not the only one, but it is a revealing case. Particularly after September 11, 2001, and the entry of U.S. forces into direct combat with states and groups directly or indirectly associated with Al-Qaeda, the United States has tried to convince the Islamic world, especially the Arab world, that the enmity of the United States is narrowly focused on those who support terror. The United States has always tried, with some success, to balance its affection for Israel with its geostrategic interests in the Arab world. The struggle with Al-Qaeda and its friends has generated a new premium on such balance.

Policymakers believe that the United States has geostrategic and economic interests in the Arab world: most would place the free flow of oil exports from the Persian Gulf in the top tier of U.S. strategic interests. Suppressing Al-Qaeda and other potential terrorist groups is also a key U.S. strategic interest. To pursue these interests means that the United States is deeply involved in Arab politics. (I wish this were not the case and discuss some ways to reduce the U.S. profile in the next chapter.) And many Arabs care about the plight of the Palestinians. Thus, to ease the way for diplomacy in support of these interests, the United States has tried to show a moderate degree of concern for the Palestinian problem.

It is the considered view of many strategists that a settlement of the Arab-Israeli dispute, or at least sustained movement toward a settlement, is necessary to support U.S. diplomacy in the Middle East and Persian Gulf. Aaron David Miller, a longtime participant in Middle East peace negotiations, deserves quotation in full:

> We will be in the Middle East for generations. The Arab-Israeli issue will continue to rattle around out there, providing opportunities for our enemies to exploit. We can't do everything or be everywhere but on this issue uniquely, our national and moral interests combine with a demonstrated capacity, when we engage wisely, to make a bad situation better. To ignore or address ineffectively an issue that fuels so much rage and anger against us is irresponsible in the extreme.[65]

During the Cold War, centrists in the U.S. policy community believed that working for peace between Israel and the Arab states was necessary. An accord would help reduce Soviet possibilities in the region. Palestinian nationalism and Arab pan-nationalism were always one element in this calculation. United States allies in the Arab world could not abandon the Palestinian national cause. That said, the United States focused first on states, investing enormous resources in the Egypt-Israel peace treaty, and only turned seriously to the issue of the Palestinians' future as the Cold War was ending. Years of political organizing, and violent and nonviolent resistance by the Palestinians against the Israelis, convinced the United States, the rest of the Arab world, and even some Israelis that some kind of political settlement with the Palestinians would be necessary. The

United States has worked for this outcome, sometime energetically, and sometimes not, but if it intends to remain heavily engaged in the Persian Gulf region then working for Arab-Israeli peace, which now means a state for the Palestinians, is essential.[66] It also seems likely that the revolutions associated with the collapse of Arab autocracies will mean that across much of the Arab world the public will have more to say about policy, and these publics will likely have some sympathy with the Palestinians. If the United States must deal with these governments, it probably will not be able to ignore the lack of progress on a Palestinian state. Former secretary of defense Robert Gates concurs, "There is no question that the absence of Middle East peace does affect U.S. national security interests in the region."[67]

The seemingly unstoppable growth of Israeli settlements throughout the territories occupied during the 1967 war, settlements that the United States and indeed all members of the United Nations have deemed illegitimate, undermines the U.S. message of balance and helps the enemies of the United States portray it as an adversary of the Arab peoples. More than 500,000 Israelis now live in these settlements and though it is widely understood that many of them will remain after a peace settlement, their enlargement is corrosive.[68] This is reckless driving. To be clear, I do not attribute the lack of progress in the peace process to settlements alone, nor to the intransigence of either side alone. There are many obstacles to a negotiated end of the conflict. Here I make a different point. Settlements make the negotiations more difficult; settlements complicate other important policies that the United States is trying to pursue, and restraint on settlements would not detract from Israeli security in the slightest. The United States, in its own national security interest, needs Israel to cease the enlargement of existing settlements and East Jerusalem "neighborhoods," and stop the building of new ones across the occupied territories, including Jerusalem. A real freeze is necessary to support negotiations with the Palestinians toward a "two-state solution" to the conflict, which the United States and virtually all the rest of the states in the world, including the Arab League, have embraced.[69]

The negotiation of a two-state solution is not a simple matter and a settlement freeze in the West Bank and East Jerusalem is not a panacea.[70] It is however, a necessary condition, an important confidence-building measure.[71] It is unlikely that any Palestinian leader can conclude a negotiation while settlements grow. An agreement will need to be legitimate among the Palestinian people, and an agreement made under such duress will not be.[72] The provisions of a deal that seem pragmatically possible will be hard enough for Palestinians to accept. It is very likely that any arrangement will require the Palestinians to accept some large Israeli settlements in the West Bank and concede that real estate to Israel, and abandon the hopes of hundreds of thousands of refugees to return to their former homes inside the 1967 borders. The Israeli goal in Jerusalem, which is to hold the city and all its environs, directly contradicts Palestinian dreams, which is to have a piece of the city as the capital of their new state. The Al Aq'sa Mosque in Jerusalem is both a religious and a national symbol. It is unlikely that any deal will give Palestinians political control over the old city, but the look and feel of influence that a capital in East Jerusalem would provide is almost surely essential to a settlement. Enlargement of Israeli neighborhoods in East Jerusalem will make it harder to work this puzzle.

The United States has made its objections to settlements clear to Israel repeatedly. Yet settlements continue. Indeed, even before the "minor Israeli glitch" of announcing new building in East Jerusalem during Vice President Biden's March 2010 visit to Israel, a series of unfortunate coincidences had occurred.[73] Israel not only insists on building more settlements and more Jerusalem neighborhoods against U.S. wishes, it seems to announce new real estate deals just before, during, or immediately after the visit of U.S. officials. Secretary of State James Baker averred that "every time I have gone to Israel in connection with the peace process on each of my trips I have been met with the announcement of new settlement activity."[74] Similar coincidences occurred during Secretary of State Condoleezza Rice's visits to Israel, on January 15, 2007; April 1, 2008; and June 15, 2008.[75] Announcements of new construction just preceded a visit by President George W. Bush in early January 2008.[76] The announcement during Vice President Biden's March 2010 visit, and the subsequent "glitch" in which new building was announced in Jerusalem just minutes before Prime Minister Netanyahu was to meet with President Obama, suggests that there is something peculiar in this long-term pattern. Long time Middle East watcher and New York Times columnist Tom Friedman followed the first episode with the observation that the United States should strongly oppose new settlements, because settlements were not even good for Israel. He analogized to the public service commercial once widely seen in the United States with the theme that "Friends do not let friends drive drunk."[77] But the analogy is wrong. In this case the friend also buys the car and fills it with gasoline.

The Congressional Research Service notes that "Israel is the largest cumulative recipient of U.S. foreign assistance since World War II"[78] and reports that overall the United States has provided a total of about $90 billion (in 2009 dollars) in grants, and another $15 billion in loans to the state of Israel. About $70 billion of the total was for military purposes.[79] United States military assistance presently provides 18.2 percent of the Israeli defense budget.[80] A casual review of the Israel entry for the IISS Military Balance has for decades listed an Israeli arsenal that consists mainly of advanced U.S. weaponry, especially in the Air Force.[81] The United States has also contributed to the development of a domestic Israeli arms industry; Israel is the only country allowed to spend U.S. military grants on its own weapons. All of these resources help Israel to defend itself, which is a good thing. They also free up Israeli resources for its settlement effort in the occupied territories, which is a bad thing for Israel and for the United States. The United States subsidizes a reckless driver.

Iraq

States can drive recklessly in their relations with others, affecting the United States negatively. Governments and factions can drive recklessly internally and negatively affect U.S. projects. This is particularly the case when the United States is intensively involved in peace enforcement, state building, or counterinsurgency. The Maliki regime is a prime example of internal reckless driving.

President George W. Bush conducted a major review of the then failing U.S. effort in Iraq in 2006, which resulted in a change of policy and an intensification of U.S. efforts in Iraq. This review suggested a new, more focused effort to suppress the Sunni and Shia insurgencies in Iraq and included the "surge," which took troop levels from 130,000 to 160,000 troops (from fifteen to twenty brigades), and also focused military efforts somewhat more consistently on the problem of population control, a central tenet of counterinsurgency theory. In early 2007 it was also judged that Iraq would need generally to work toward political reconciliation among the various ethnic, religious, and political factions in the country, instill the rule of law, suppress corruption, improve administration, limit political interference with the military, and develop an independent logistics capacity in the Iraqi military that would permit it to operate without U.S. assistance.[82] The United States, by agreement between the Bush administration and the Maliki government, then stipulated that all U.S. combat forces would leave Iraq in December 2011. This was necessary to burnish Maliki's own nationalist credentials.[83] The Obama administration carried out this provision.

Nouri Al-Maliki has been the prime minister of Iraq since May 2006, so there has been nominal political continuity since the launch of "the surge." Though it is a fact that the security situation in Iraq improved mightily in 2007 (in a way that I did not predict,) the other elements of the project have shown little progress. According to the U.S. Department of Defense, these were all still considered to be significant issues in mid-2010, three and a half years after the commencement of the "surge": "Iraq remains fragile, primarily because many underlying sources of political instability have yet to be resolved. Once the new government is formed, it will need to continue to build legitimacy through the provision of basic services and improved security for the Iraqi people, the formulation of a solid plan for long-term economic growth and employment, and the creation of enduring solutions to lingering political, ethnic, and sectarian disputes."[84] No subsequent report on conditions in Iraq appears at the Pentagon web site, but these problems endure.[85]

Prominent Shiites did what they could to manipulate the national elections in 2010, which ensured that the government would enjoy little legitimacy. Prior to the national election on March 7, 2010, Iraq's Justice and Accountability Commission, banned five hundred aspiring candidates from running in the election due to their alleged past ties to the Ba'ath Party. Most of these candidates, Sunni and Shia, were affiliated with the less sectarian parties and the ban had the effect of eroding the campaigns of Maliki's challengers, and in particular prevented many prominent Sunni politicians from running.[86] The parties replaced these candidates, but the commission then tried to ban forty of these new candidates, which were only allowed to run provisionally. Once the election produced a tiny plurality for challenger Ayad Allawi's Iraqiya bloc, the commission set about disqualifying two of its successful candidates.[87] Shenanigans of this kind helped to destroy Sunni confidence in the new government. Sunnis overwhelmingly backed Allawi, but he could not find enough support from other parties to form a government. Eight months after the election Maliki finally formed the government that remains in power as of this writing.

Relations between the Iraqi central state and the Kurdish Regional Government, which welds the three Kurdish majority provinces into a semi-autonomous statelike structure (a construction permitted by the Iraqi constitution of 2005), have deteriorated since 2007.[88] Oil rich Kirkuk, as well as a good deal of other real estate, is in dispute, with the Kurds claiming that these areas were wrested away from them by Saddam Hussein. Sunni and Shia Arabs, and minority Turkmen, deny this claim. Political efforts to settle the land dispute have been anemic. The political game in these disputed areas is a rough one, with coercion of local inhabitants, politically induced in- and out-migration, and near-violent clashes between the Kurdish Pesh Merga militia and the security forces of the state.[89] Both sides appear bent on solving these issues by force majeure: the central government is more capable overall than the Kurds, but the Kurds probably have an important local advantage. If each side believes it can win the dispute by force, then compromise will appear unnecessary, and the odds of violence increase.

The surge must be judged by its strategic results; did it produce a stable, democratic, and functional Iraqi government, friendly to the United States? The answer is no.[90] Failures to reform the Iraqi government and address key political issues can be attributed to any number of factors and it is difficult to apportion blame. It is striking that having waged a vicious civil war, Iraqis did not during the U.S. occupation, nor do they now, feel any pressure to settle matters that could lead, indeed may already have led, to a resurgence of fighting. It is hard to escape the suspicion that the presence of U.S. forces permitted key actors to defer hard decisions, rather than providing a safety net to insure them as they made difficult compromises, which was the hope. It seems that the parties simply took advantage of the U.S. presence to rest and refit for fights to come. The extent to which the surge per se reduced violence in Iraq remains a matter of considerable debate.[91] But regarding the most critical political issues, passage of legislation on the distribution of the country' oil wealth, the integration of those formerly connected to the Saddam regime into Iraqi society and politics, the integration of Sunni Arabs into the security services—including those who fought as insurgents against the United States or the new Iraqi government—and the settlement of internal territorial disputes with the Kurdish region, little or nothing was accomplished prior to the departure of U.S. combat forces.[92] By mid-2012 close observers of Iraq turned deeply pessimistic, noting that "a badly conceived, deeply flawed political process has turned into a chronic crisis that could bring down the existing political structure."[93] In the first seven months of 2013, 4,137 civilians were killed in political violence in Iraq, the highest level in five years.[94]

IDENTITY POLITICS AND INTERVENTION

Presence and Pushback

Most U.S. uses of military power since the end of the Cold War have been occasioned by identity politics. The U.S. purpose has usually been to extirpate violent identity politics through the installation of liberal democratic structures that we believed would channel political energies in a more benign direction. The intervention in Somalia aimed to deliver humanitarian assistance to those immiserated by a war of all against all among heavily armed clan-based militias. Bosnia aimed to end a war among three groups, two of them well-established national identities— Serbs and Croats, and third, the Bosnian Muslims, aiming to build and consolidate a national identity. The war with Serbia over Kosovo was occasioned by the effort of the Serb state to suppress the national identity of the Albanians who constituted the majority of the citizens of the province of Kosovo. The September 11 attack on the United States originated in a particular, fundamentalist and reactionary, interpretation of Islam in a small group of mainly Egyptian and Saudi Sunni Arabs. These leaders believed that the Arab nation states were under the sway of the West, especially the United States, and had fallen into corruption as a consequence. The United States stood in the way of a renewal based on a return to religious orthodoxy. The U.S. intervention in Afghanistan, precipitated by the attack of September 11, pitted the United States against a deeply religious, mainly Pashtun Taliban government in Afghanistan. Pashtuns are found on both sides of the Afghan-Pakistan border, but are a majority in Afghanistan. They are certainly a very cohesive ethnic group, perhaps a nation. The United States sided with Tajiks and Uzbeks, also ethnic groups/cum nations to overthrow Taliban rule. The United States then invaded Iraq, this time for ideological reasons. Although the immediate case for war depended on faulty intelligence about vestigial weapons of mass destruction research and development programs, the more basic motivation was a fear that if such weapons existed, they would fall into the hands of the Muslim Arabs who had already attacked the United States. The only way to ensure a safe Arab world was to drive identity politics from it, by installing supposedly benign liberal democratic governments. Iraq would be the start. Ironically, cracking Saddam's grip on power released a violent political struggle between Kurds and Arabs, and Shiite Arabs and Sunni Arabs.

Since at least the French Revolution, nationalism has been one of the most potent forces in modern politics. National identities often integrate within them ethnic and religious roots but nationalism is a modern idea. It holds that a group, united by language, history, and culture, should be protected by the power of a state that it controls. As society and economy became more complex, the utility of literacy for survival became a reality. Individuals thus developed a strong personal interest in the language with which economic activity, including legal processes, would be transacted. The state will do its business in the language that the nation speaks. The state will protect the identity by consolidating it in schools and transmitting it to the young. Nationalism includes within it an egalitarian impulse. The state owes its people a certain amount of protection from the vicissitudes of modern life. The state is also expected to provide protection from threats that originate outside the society. If necessary, members of the nation will serve in its armed forces to protect the group. Nationalism has proven to be a powerful mobilizing force in adversity, most used as a way to elicit willing sacrifice in times of trial, especially war.[95] Nationalism has also proven a useful mobilizing tool for politicians who raise the specter of threats to the nation to secure domestic support. And occasionally it has provided a rationale for despoiling others of their lands or wealth, in favor of one's own nation.

Perhaps the strongest manifestation of nationalism is to be found in the resistance of modern peoples to occupation and governance by other nations.[96] On the eve of World War II much of the world was carved up among empires, mainly European, although Japan had managed to accumulate some spoils, as had the United States. The Soviet Union, even within its borders, was to some extent an empire, as ethnic Russians constituted less than half of the population. The Soviet conquest of Eastern Europe in the final months of World War II made it more of an empire. The striking fact of the twentieth century is that all of these empires collapsed, many in violence. Between a third and a half of the violent conflicts in the 1950s were rebellions against empires.[97] Even when the empires won antinationalist counterinsurgencies, they soon decided that the victories were unsustainable. To be sure, the metropoles had problems of their own, which reduced their ability to sustain their imperial projects.

Though the U.S. war in Vietnam was not aimed at establishing an empire, it collided with the nationalism that had been mobilized to eject France. Some 1.1 million North Vietnamese and Viet Cong soldiers reportedly died fighting the United States and its South Vietnamese client, making for the highest military loss rate of any belligerent in a twentieth-century war.[98] Nationalism deserves some of the credit for sustaining these sacrifices.[99] Vietnamese nationalism alone is not responsible for the U.S. loss of that war; the northern Communists were simply a more modern and better organized state than the U.S. client in the south, and both the southern communists and North Vietnam received heavy backing from the Soviet Union and the People's Republic of China. Nevertheless, without the sustained willingness of many Vietnamese people to sacrifice their lives, the United States would not have been stalemated.

It is equally striking that the death of empires was followed by separatist wars within the newly minted states. Most of the political violence in the post–World War II era has been "internal."[100] Between a third and a half of these internal conflicts were associated with nationalism.[101] Imperial boundaries were not drawn to be congruent with ethnic boundaries. Indeed the reverse was often the case. Imperial conquerors often tried to include many groups within an administrative unit in order to pursue divide and conquer strategies. When the empires left, these groups naturally competed for power. Some groups hoped to dominate the new states, while others wanted autonomy, or to secede and set up their own states. Nationalism alone ought not to be blamed for particular conflicts. As students of nationalism and war note, there is a lot more nationalism than there is violence. Each conflict has its own specific causes, but these causes often work in tandem with nationalism.

[52]

Nationalism is probably becoming an even more relevant political factor in much of the world. Globalization is one of the most important aspects of the last several decades, and it is likely a stimulant to identity politics.[102] Globalization means the extension of market capitalism to a global scale. It is more than mere trade; it involves direct and indirect investment, and global supply chains. It is enabled by inexpensive transport by sea, air, and land. It is also enabled by inexpensive and dense communications networks, which has facilitated the rapid movement of information. Businesses and governments can communicate in real time. It is also true, however, that individuals the world over know a great deal more about what is happening on a global scale. The world is also experiencing a significant population growth; most of this growth is occurring in cities. Because they concentrate people uprooted from the country, and involve intensive economic activity, cities are centers of political activity. Thus, even before the end of the Cold War, but more intensively since, people the world over are being socially mobilized for political activity. And where this occurs, nationalism is not far behind, because it provides a claim on the state and security for the future in a highly insecure environment.[103] Predictions about the pace of population growth and urbanization over the next several decades suggest that the developing world will see a steady supply of urbanized citizens at the lower end of the income scale.[104] They will experience acute economic and personal insecurity even as urbanization and modern communications technology make it easier to reach them with political messages.[105]

As noted above, U.S. forces are deployed around the world on the soil of other countries. Students of the local politics of U.S. bases find that this presence can produce negative views.[106] Most important for this discussion, bases that originate in a colonial or neocolonial relationship seldom survive for very long. Once autocracies transition to democracy, bases often become a political football, and the United States loses the base altogether, or accepts significant constraints.[107] These findings suggest that populations are irked by foreign military presence, even if that presence was not achieved through violence. They seem to attract opposition on nationalist grounds, though scholars have not investigated whether or not bases actually cause nationalist mobilization, or ultimately destabilize the autocratic regimes that often volunteer as hosts.

There is very strong evidence that anti-Americanism, systematically negative views of the United States, has become a sustained and powerful force in the Middle East. When the United States appears meddlesome, local nationalists are quick to respond, and the response has an anti-American flavor.[108] Diffuse anti-Americanism has been present for a long time, but the apparent deterioration in views of the United States during the George W. Bush administration precipitated new scholarship on the subject.[109] New scholarship suggests that there is a lot less anti-Americanism in the world than casual consumption of media accounts might lead one to suspect, and that it is very difficult to show that it impacts anything that truly matters. The exception to these two generalities, however, is to be found in the Middle East, especially the Arab World. The growing post–Cold War presence of the United States, and the policies that that presence has served, has produced markedly intense and sustained anti-Americanism.[110] These policies include the sheer ubiquity of the U.S. presence, perceived U.S. uncritical support of Israel, past meddling in the internal affairs of countries in the region, the effects of the post-1991 economic sanctions regime on Iraq, and the 2003 invasion of Iraq and subsequent counterinsurgency. These issues are processed through the twin lenses of Islamism, and resentment of prior colonialism, and then magnified again by the pan-Arab media.[111] Arab societies are unusual; each one has a national identity, but that national identity is loosely connected to the larger Arabic culture and language. Pan-Arabism, the notion that all Arabs share a national identity, was once a vibrant idea, and though less important in the region than it once was, it connects the twenty-two countries in the Arab League. It is thus relatively easy for U.S. policies that negatively affect some Arabs to be viewed as an affront by all Arabs.

MILITARY POWER AND INTERVENTION

United States policymakers have hoped that the West could find sustainable political remedies for violent conflicts related to identity politics. These remedies have gone under a variety of rubrics since the end of the Cold War. Military forces have practiced humanitarian military intervention, peacemaking, peace enforcement, and counterinsurgency. These were to be the precursors of nation building, state building, and the spread of democracy. Western militaries have done a competent if costly job suppressing violence. The political follow-up solutions, however, have been conspicuous by their failure. Political institutions are notoriously difficult for outsiders to transplant.[112] Onlookers should not confuse the fact of elections with the establishment of a stable functioning democracy. The question is whether elections are seen as a reasonable way to address the distribution of resources in the society, and whether the resulting governments can produce a state that functions effectively to deliver law and order, and essential services, in an honest and reliable way.

[54]

Bosnia-Herzegovina

The NATO intervention, and subsequent EU reconstruction of Bosnia Herzegovina is a good test of the hypothesis that liberal democratic institutions can be transplanted to societies that have been rent by nationalist internal conflict, and that these institutions can become self-sustaining barriers to the reemergence of violence. It was the perfect place for an experiment. Bosnia Herzegovina is right next to wealthy and liberal Europe, which agreed to take a hand in its social reengineering. It is a tiny place, with a pre–civil war population of only 4.5 million and a post–civil war population of 4 million. It had known little violence for the preceding forty-five years, because Tito and the Communist Party had kept order there. By the time NATO ground forces arrived in strength to enforce a peace negotiated with the interested regional powers, the Serbs had been crushed militarily, and the Croats and Bosnian Muslims ought to have understood that they only crushed the Serbs with the aid of the United States.

The solution in Bosnia Herzegovina was meant to create a democratic federation, in which the previously warring groups would cooperate on common issues but would be allowed a certain amount of autonomy to manage their own regional affairs. To ensure a safe launch of this project, sixty thousand NATO troops came into the republic and enforced the disarmament of military forces not connected to the new central state. A high representative from the European Union was assigned as viceroy to guide the local political reconstruction. This project was launched eighteen years ago. Though it is certainly true that Bosnia has not returned to warfare, evidence suggests that the effort to build a functioning multiethnic democracy has probably failed.[113] The three groups live mainly in their own regions; few internally displaced people have returned to their places of origin if those places are dominated by another group. The central government does not function well; the state still depends on significant international economic assistance; and some key political decisions are still made by the EU high representative.[114] Efforts by the international community to build a functioning multiethnic state foundered on the sustained resistance of nationalist politicians of every stripe, and the public support they were able to garner. Some would say that the original terms of the Dayton agreement allowed too much representation of these factions. But given that they were the principal players in the civil war, and the United States and other members of the "international contact group" aimed for a negotiated settlement, these players needed to be accommodated in the settlement. The alternative would have been an even larger, most costly, and entirely open-ended external administration of the country, for which the outsiders clearly lacked the political

[55]

will. If NATO and the European Union cannot bring democracy to a tiny, dependent, neighboring European state, the United States is unlikely to bring a stable democracy and a functioning state to Iraq or Afghanistan (or Pakistan should that prove seductive).[115]

"Humanitarian Military Intervention"

Somalia, Haiti, Bosnia-Herzegovina, Kosovo, and Libya were occasioned in part by the deliberately engineered suffering of civilians in those violent conflicts, which precipitated arguments about the need for "humanitarian military intervention."[116] The Grand Strategy of Restraint is chary of "humanitarian military intervention" to rescue victims of internal political violence, but it is difficult to devise hard and fast rules about the matter. The conflicts are complex and diverse, and the emotions in play in the United States are intense. It is impractical to insist that the United States never undertake such operations, and it is equally impractical to try to devise codes of U.S. conduct.[117] In the next chapter I offer an affirmative case for Restraint. Here I simply review the broad considerations it recommends to guide humanitarian intervention.

First, though war crimes and genocide are terrible things, they have little to do with U.S. national security. The United States may or may not be able to employ military power to protect the innocent in these situations, but this is philanthropy, not grand strategy. One, extreme, hypothetical illustrates the rule. If a country possessed of a secure nuclear retaliatory capability were violently oppressing its own people, it is unlikely that the United States would wage war on that country for their protection. Restraint argues that occasions for U.S. armed philanthropy be considered from the point of view of core U.S. security interests; would the costs or consequences of U.S. actions meaningfully harm the United States?

Second, Restraint advises that nonmilitary remedies should be fully explored? International humanitarian law provides for the punishment of individuals who order or commit the worst excesses. If American policymakers wish to do some good, they could do a better job creating a track record of prosecution. The United States could, for example, join the International Criminal Court. Similarly, the Refugee Convention commits signatories to provide refuge to those fleeing a country who have well-founded fears of persecution. The United States has signed this convention, and is rich enough to receive many individuals in such dire straits, though in the case of the Haitian boat people the United States evaded that responsibility. But much violence happens in the poorer parts of the world. When poor states honor their commitments

[56]

under the convention, or host refugees even though they have not signed the convention, the United States should make generous donations to assist. Though this kind of charity can seem expensive, it pales in comparison to the dollar costs of even a short war.

Third, if the United States considers military power as a remedy, the practical requirement of determining whether there is a way to employ military power effectively to address the problem remains as important as it would be if traditional security interests were at stake. It is difficult to bend military power to political purpose; it is also difficult to bend it to humanitarian purposes. For example, air power is quick to apply, and in some situations could cheaply fend off or deter some egregious threats to civilians. Air power might be able to prevent "safe havens" from being overrun, which protects those sheltering there from the worst. The Gaddafi regime's assault on Benghazi in March of 2011 was turned back with one or two days of air strikes against the advancing armored columns. The threat of air strikes probably deterred attacks on safe havens in Bosnia for many months. Air power could not have done much, however, to stop the genocide in Rwanda, where the killing was person-to-person, all over the country, often off the main roads. Only capable and tactically mobile ground forces could have prevented the murders.

Finally, Western intervention advocates often conflate the employment of military power for the narrow purpose of achieving a humanitarian end with the application of military power to eliminate the political problems that gave rise to the humanitarian problem. The political coalition for using military force is built not just on a humanitarian but on an ideological impulse. Reform by the sword is seen to be necessary and possible. Restraint finds these premises dubious. Rescue and reconstruction are different projects; the second is harder than the first, and often involves picking winners. Winners determined by outsiders may have neither the power nor the skill to rule. In the Libya war, the West did too much and not enough. Destruction of a political order was the purpose, but weary after two imperfect and costly reconstruction efforts in Iraq and Afghanistan, Libya was left to reconstruct itself. Success has proven elusive. Winners may not treat their former oppressors any better than they were treated, hardly a humane outcome. The West intervened ostensibly to stop Serb depredations against the Albanian majority population of Kosovo, but from the outset was intent on detaching Kosovo from Serbia. Once in the driver's seat, the Albanians repaid years of Serb unkindness, and the "rescuers" looked the other way. Restraint advises that those recommending "humanitarian military intervention" should have limited aims—deny or deter the worst excesses, and let the combatants work out their own end to the fight.

[57]

Iraq

The United States overthrew the Ba'athist government of Iraq in 2003, and then set about trying to find a suitable democratic successor. This proved the most militarily costly effort of the United States since the Viet Nam War. Counterinsurgency is typically a difficult project, and Iraq was no exception. Iraq is also a complicated case. There were two insurgencies against the United States, but there were other conflicts within the society, which the United States was ultimately able to turn to its advantage.

Iraq is not the most difficult counterinsurgency and state-building effort the United States might encounter. Though these data are at best indicative, they tell a disturbing tale of weak adversaries, who were nevertheless able to impose high costs on the United States for a long time. An insurgency emerged more or less spontaneously against the U.S. occupation in the summer of 2003. At the outset, this insurgency was based in the Sunni Arab community, about 5 million of the 25-odd million population of Iraq. The Sunni insurgency sustained about five thousand committed fighters and perhaps another fifteen thousand direct supporters for most of its active history. The Sunni did have some resources at the outset—weapons caches left by the regime, millions of dollars in the hands of former regime members, and large numbers of individuals with at least some military training. Al-Qaeda did adopt the Iraqi resistance, providing additional fighters and resources. By 2004, Shia factions began a parallel campaign against the Americans. By 2005, Sunni and Shia factions also fought each other with increasing ferocity. Large numbers of Iraqis, mainly Shia, joined the army and police to fight against the Sunni insurgency. Although they did not love the Americans, they loved the Sunni less. In 2007 and 2008, during the "surge," the insurgency contracted—many Sunni males were incarcerated; some were killed by U.S. special operations forces; and many more defected to the United States side out of pique at their Al-Qaeda jihadi allies and in the hope of balancing Shia power.

The U.S. campaign to suppress the twin insurgencies in Iraq and end the Shia-Sunni civil war was costly in human and dollar terms. Disorganized Iraqi nationalism proved no less potent an opponent than organized Vietnamese nationalism. The United States spent more in real terms on the Iraq war than it did in Vietnam, $784 billion versus $738 billion in fiscal year 2011 dollars.[118] Though many fewer U.S. soldiers were killed or wounded in Iraq than in Vietnam, this may be explained in part by the huge amount of money that the United States spent relative to its adversaries. In Vietnam the United States may have spent about 10 times what its enemies spent and achieved a kind of stalemate.[119] In

Iraq, the United States may have spent as much as 350 times what the Sunni insurgency spent.[120] In Vietnam, U.S. adversaries received lush assistance from the Soviet Union and the People's Republic of China. The United States lost thousands of helicopters and aircraft over North and South Vietnam to Soviet supplied antiaircraft weaponry. In Iraq, neither Sunni nor Shia insurgents had great power backing. Vastly superior United States spending in Iraq paid for a great deal of "force protection"—body armor, special armored vehicles, heavily defended bases, highly responsive casualty evacuation, Orwellian redundant electronic surveillance systems, and very high quality medical care, all of which helped keep casualties down. Casualty estimates for the insurgents are difficult to find, but twenty-five thousand dead seems plausible. This casualty rate is much less than the dramatic sacrifices of the Vietnamese communists, but measured against the Sunni Arab community would still amount to nearly 0.5 percent of the population.

Though military analysts believe that the Vietnamese were much more competent militarily than the Iraqi insurgents, the Iraqi insurgents appear to be twice as efficient killers. In Vietnam roughly 50,000 Americans and 250,000 South Vietnamese troops died versus 1.1 million communist troops.[121] The United States suffered about 4,400 dead in Iraq, and Iraqi security forces around 9,300 versus as many as 25,000 insurgents.[122] The exchange rate has deteriorated from 4:1 to 2:1, largely due to the cunning employment of command-detonated IED's to kill Americans and their allies without having to expose oneself to counterfire. Since Vietnam, the United States has invested heavily in military technology, which significantly lowered the personnel costs of the Iraq war relative to Vietnam and probably forced Iraqi insurgents to avoid the pitched battles with Americans that the Vietnamese sought. The Iraqi insurgents countered with their own technology—the improvised explosive device—and engaged in a seesaw innovation battle with U.S. detection and jamming gear.

The United States did ultimately stalemate the Iraqi resistance. The U.S. withdrawal of combat troops from Iraq was followed by much diminished but nevertheless sustained political violence, which has recently turned upward.[123] As noted earlier, the political results of this vast U.S. effort are unimpressive. The costs to achieve this outcome were quite high, however, and the more important fact is that as difficult a problem as Iraq proved to be, it could have been a great deal worse. A larger population, a better-organized resistance, a bit more external support with somewhat more sophisticated weaponry, and somewhat different demography and topography, and U.S. costs could have been a great deal higher. Given the low returns on these U.S. interventions and their high and probably growing costs, it makes little sense to continue. Indeed, efforts to do so may erode the U.S. power position.

[59]

The United States is uniquely well placed among modern great powers to misunderstand the political power of nationalism, ethnic identity, and religion. The founding documents extol the individual and view the group as a social contract, not as an organic historical entity. The United States was largely founded and peopled by settlers and immigrants. To some extent, they had agreed to leave a part of their identity behind when they came to the United States. Once here, the physical and social mobility of the U.S. economy and society further eroded these identities. For others, slaves brought to the United States, tribal identities were obliterated. Formally, church and state are separated in the United States, although many members of the society remain deeply religious relative to other societies. It is true that almost every generation has known some religious or racial or ethnic prejudice, but these are in conflict with the American creed and have gradually been beaten back. The United States fought one horrible internal war over competing identities, the Civil War, and though it took another hundred years of struggle to consolidate the Union victory politically, the war ended with the country as a whole, rather than the individual states, as the focus of political allegiance. Before the Civil War, many referred to "these United States;" after the war "the United States." United States elites thus continue to be surprised at the power of identity politics abroad.

OVERSTATED BENEFITS

Partisans of Liberal Hegemony might accept some of the factual statements above but would argue that the good the strategy has achieved far outweighs the bad. As noted in the introduction, partisans assume that liberal democracy, human rights, market economies, free trade, nuclear nonproliferation, middle and great powers that do *not* take responsibility for their own security, and U.S. political and military hegemony are all mutually causative, and all lead ineluctably to a vast improvement in the security and welfare of others, and hence to the U.S. security position.[124] They also posit that the world is fragile; damage to one of these good things will lead to damage to other good things, so the United States must defend all. The "fragile and interconnected" argument is politically effective. By accident or design, the argument derives an inherent plausibility due to the inevitable limits of our substantive knowledge, fear, uncertainty, liberal ideology, and U.S. national pride. Most targets of the argument do not know enough about the world to argue with experts who claim these connections; the chain of posited connections always leads to danger for the United States, and fear is a powerful selling tool. Once fear is involved, even low-probability chains of causation can be

[60]

made to seem frightening enough to do something about, especially if you believe your country has overwhelming power. It is pleasant to believe that the spread of U.S. values such as liberty and democracy depend on U.S. power and leadership. The argument does not stand close scrutiny.

First, it obscures the inherently strong security position of the United States, which I have already reviewed. The economic, geographic, demographic, and technological facts supporting this point are seldom discussed, precisely because they are facts. It takes very large events abroad to significantly threaten the United States, and more moderate strategies can address these possibilities at lower costs. Typical Liberal Hegemony arguments for any new project take the form of domino theory. One small untended problem is expected easily and quickly to produce another and another until the small problems become big ones, or the collection of problems becomes overwhelming. Whether these connections are valid in any particular case will always be open to debate. Even if the connections are plausible, however, it is unlikely given the inherent U.S. security position that the United States need prop up the first domino. It has the luxury of waiting for information and choosing the dominos it wishes to shore up, if any.

Second, proponents of Liberal Hegemony often elide the difference between those benefits of the strategy that flow to others, and those that flow to the United States. Individually, it is surely true that cheap-riders and reckless-drivers like the current situation because of the welfare, security, or power gains that accrue to them. United States commitments may make the international politics of some regions less exciting than would otherwise be the case. The United States, however, pays a significant price and assumes significant risks to provide these benefits to others, while the gains to the United States are exaggerated because the United States is inherently quite secure.

Third, Liberal Hegemonists argue that U.S. commitments reduce the intensity of regional security competitions, limit the spread of nuclear weaponry, and lower the general odds of conflict, and that this helps keep the United States out of wars that would emerge in these unstable regions. This chain of interconnected benefits is not self-evident. United States activism does change the nature of regional competitions; it does not necessarily suppress them. For example, where U.S. commitments encourage "free-riding," this attracts coercion, which the United States must then do more to deter. Where the United States encourages "reckless driving," it produces regional instability. United States activism probably helps cause some nuclear proliferation, because some states will want nuclear weapons to deter an activist United States. When the United States makes extended deterrence commitments to discourage

[61]

proliferation, the U.S. military is encouraged to adopt conventional and nuclear military strategies that are themselves destabilizing. Finally, as is clear from the evidence of the last twenty years, the United States ends up in regional wars in any case.

Fourth, one key set of interconnections posited by Liberal Hegemonists is that between U.S. security provision, free trade, and U.S. prosperity. This is a prescriptive extension of hegemonic stability theory, developed by economist Charles Kindleberger from a close study of the collapse of global liquidity in 1931 and the ensuing great depression.[125] Professor Kindleberger concluded from this one case that a global system of free trade and finance would more easily survive crises if there was a "leader," a hegemon with sufficient economic power such that its policies could "save" a system in crisis, which would also have the interest and the will to do so, precisely because it was so strong.[126] Subsequent theorists, such as Robert Gilpin, extended this to the idea that a global economic and security hegemon would be even better.[127] Robert Keohane, and later John Ikenberry, added to this theory the notion that a "liberal" hegemon would be still better, because it would graft transparent and legitimate rules onto the hegemonic system, which would make it more acceptable to the "subjects" and hence less costly to run.[128] A comprehensive rebuttal of hegemonic stability theory is beyond the scope of this book. But this theory has fallen into desuetude in the study of international politics in the last twenty years. Proponents did not produce a clear, consolidated version of the theory that integrated economics, security, and institutional variables in a systematic way that gives us a sense of their relative importance and interdependence, and how they work in practice. The theory is difficult to test because there are only two cases: nineteenth- and early twentieth-century Britain, and post–World War II United States, and they operated in very different ways under very different conditions. Finally, testing of narrow versions of the theory did not show compelling results.[129] These problems should make us somewhat skeptical about making the theory the basis for U.S. grand strategy.

The transformation of hegemonic stability theory into a foreign policy doctrine is problematical. First, if there is a gain to having a global hegemon, we do not know its magnitude, and we do not know whether the gains to the United States are commensurate with the costs to the United States. I argue they are not. It is easy enough to imagine that the Great Depression could have been avoided had there been a leader in the 1931 banking crisis; it could also have been avoided, as we saw in 2007, had the central bankers of a handful of major states had a better understanding of economics and banking. Second, the theory tells us that the hegemon must have both the power and the will to sustain the system. How much power is an open question; I doubt that the United States actually has enough power to fulfill its appointed role in this system, especially its appointed economic role. For example, theorists argue that the hegemon must be both the lender and the market of last resort to perform its stabilizing role in crisis. The United States can no longer do either. Third, the question of how much of the hegemon's power needs to be economic, and how much needs to be military is not a settled matter. This is particularly important given that the U.S. share of global GDP is destined to diminish; can the United States protect its hegemonic position by simply hyperinvesting in military power and deploying it around the world? Does the provision of military security provide a level of stability that inherently supports a global economic system, which would otherwise collapse? Is the existence of that global economy so central to U.S. economic power that if it did collapse, the United States would suffer disproportionately?[130]

Because U.S. economic performance is connected to U.S. power, a realist ought to be concerned if there is some strong connection between Liberal Hegemony, international trade, and relative U.S. economic power. Two points are in order. The United States does not depend very much on international trade; imports and exports made up about 29 percent of GDP in 2010, among the smallest shares of advanced economies.[131] Moreover, nearly a third of that trade is with Canada and Mexico, states the United States secures inherently by securing itself.[132] China, at 13 percent, ranks as one of the top three U.S. trading partners, even as the U.S. Department of Defense begins to view it as a near-peer strategic competitor. Another third of U.S. trade is spread among a dozen nation states across the globe, and the rest is scattered across many more. It would take an unusual series of capitulations, conquests, or just plain market closures to close down enough trade to affect greatly the U.S. economy.

A security hegemon is, in any case, unnecessary to insure international trade. Liberal Hegemonists worry that if states feel insecure, their concern about relative gains from trade, and the effect of those relative gains on relative power, will drive out trade. But states have traded with one another under a variety of power constellations. Though political scientists—especially hegemonic stability theorists—and historians view Britain as the global hegemon in the late nineteenth and early twentieth centuries, it was at best "first among equals" in a multipolar great power system, and its grand strategy looks much more like "offshore balancing" or Restraint than it does Liberal Hegemony. Britain was not the day-to-day global security provider. Rather it was the balancer of last resort. Peter Liberman notes that in this period, British-German trade climbed, despite the fact that each came to identify the other as their principal naval rival. Similarly, U.S.-Japan trade grew in the interwar period, even as U.S.-Japan relations deteriorated.[133] States trade with one another due

[63]

to mutual commercial interest; it seems to take quite a lot of fear and hostility to change the calculus. It is also likely, as Liberman suggests, that the existence of nuclear weapons has reduced whatever relative gains concerns there once might have been, insofar as great powers armed with nuclear weapons do not really depend on economic auton-omy for their military power and hence their security. It is therefore im-probable that a less militarily activist United States would lead to a collapse of international trade.

Some argue that a global military hegemon is necessary to secure peace and order in the global commons—sea, air, space, and cyberspace—to enable international trade and globalization. As a global naval power, Britain did bring a measure of peace and order to the global commons for most of the nineteenth century. But by the early twentieth century all great trading states had navies capable of securing their merchant ships against any predator who was not a great power. And the fact that other great powers might interfere with this trade did not prevent them from trading with one another, because such interference would have meant war. Mutual deterrence protected the global trade routes. In any event, as I will be argue in chapter 3, the military strategy of Restraint *is* commit-ted to maintaining what I have called "command of the commons." That is the bedrock military capability needed by the United States to influ-ence geopolitical events abroad, should that prove necessary. Whatever side benefits for world trade that might arise from the capability to keep order in the commons would still be present. The U.S. interest in main-taining command of the commons is premised on its contribution to U.S. national security, not its contribution to global trade.

Fifth, some might argue that the United States must remain the world's military hegemon, in order to preserve the dollar as the world reserve currency. The dollar as a world reserve currency is a handy tool if and when the United States needs to spend a lot of money fast on military preparedness, so one might be concerned if U.S. failure to serve as the world's gendarme would somehow erode the power of the dollar. But it is unlikely that the dollar enjoys its world reserve status because of the current grand strategy. Rather, it enjoys this status because the United States is a large and diverse economy, secure in North America, ruled by law, and possessed of very well developed capital markets. World trade seems to need a world reserve currency, and the dollar will likely keep this role until something better comes along. As noted earlier, the U.S. dollar had become a de facto world currency in the 1920s, when the United States eschewed a global security role.[134] We see that in most cases, when either the international political system or economic system is roiled, individuals flee to the dollar. In general, if the United States were somewhat less active militarily, and somewhat more committed to improving its economy and fiscal situations, and others were more worried about their security, one suspects that the dollar would grow stronger, not weaker, and its role as a world reserve currency would be more likely to persist.

PERSISTENT PROBLEMS

Liberal Hegemony is a costly, wasteful, and self-defeating grand strategy. The strong inherent security position of the United States makes it unnecessary. The United States has spent vast sums to sustain omnidirectional military superiority. The United States has endeavored to reassure wealthy and prosperous allies and to deter former, present, and potential future adversaries. It has waged war to reorganize the internal politics of other states, usually weak ones that constituted little threat to the United States or its interests. Liberal Hegemony is not making the United States more secure. The huge global military presence and the frequent resort to force produce several unfortunate outcomes.

First, the United States is causing countervailing behavior. The United States has stimulated actions great and small from the world's middle powers, which increase U.S. costs, or aim to erode U.S. advantages. Most of this activity has not quite risen to the level of true "balancing," but rather constitutes a kind of erratic but sustained obstructionism. China, however, is developing the underlying economic power to permit true balancing and is building up its military capability. It is the nature of a competitive anarchical system that what one side does to defend itself often has offensive potential versus others. So it is hard to tell how much Chinese military activity is balancing, and how much is the common phenomenon of a rising power developing sharper elbows. At the same time, Russia which is not a rising power, and which has reason to fear China, nevertheless often makes common cause with it. This looks more like old-fashioned balancing. So-called "rogue" states also do what they can to build their capability—some is for mischief but some is a search for a deterrent against future U.S. intervention. As other states grow in capacity relative to the United States, which seems to be in the cards, there will likely be more balancing if the United States remains so energetic. As others build their capabilities, the Liberal Hegemony project will become even more costly.

Second, the common response by U.S. allies to the U.S. project has been to "cheap ride" or "reckless drive." Most allies have cut their defense efforts since the end of the Cold War. This is understandable in Europe, where the direct threat from Russia is difficult to discern. Nevertheless, the continuing U.S. commitment to NATO makes this an easy choice for the Europeans. Japan is the more striking free rider. Its low defense spending is noteworthy given the oft expressed concerns of Japanese policymakers about the rise of China. Jawboning by the United States of its allies—asking for higher defense spending and more efficient defense efforts—has for the most part failed to elicit much cooperation. Advocates of Liberal Hegemony may argue that this makes the case for continuing the strategy. The liberal democratic allies of the United States are somehow unwilling to look after themselves, so the United States must, in its own interest. This ignores the fact that they make their defense decisions in the face of extravagant United States promises to defend them. They will not do more unless the United States credibly commits to doing less. And in the case of Europe, we must acknowledge that they may simply have gauged the security situation on their continent better than has the United States. Be that as it may, underdefended allies mean more work for the United States.

Reckless driving by U.S. allies is also a significant problem. Secure in the knowledge that the United States will serve as the military lender of last resort, they invest in policies that redound to the political disadvantage of the United States, which can ultimately precipitate real military costs. Israel is the easiest example; its policies in the occupied territories contribute to the negative image of the United States in the Arab world, complicating both the struggle with Al-Qaeda and now the effort to contain Iran. Many would argue that Israeli policies are not even good for Israel. United States military backing makes the costs of this policy low for Israel. Indeed the U.S. security subsidy probably demobilizes potential domestic opposition in Israel, because the financial costs are not fully realized by Israelis. It is not easy to translate these political costs into explicit security costs for the United States. We only have the testimony of U.S. diplomats and soldiers that these Israeli policies complicate efforts to cooperate with Arab states.

Another kind of reckless driving emerges among the domestic partners found by the United States in its counterinsurgency and state-building efforts in Iraq and Afghanistan. The U.S. relationship with the Maliki government and the Karzai government reveals a long-understood tension in counterinsurgency conducted by outside powers, waged on behalf of internal political factions. Counterinsurgency depends for its success on a combination of tactical "best practices" and political solutions. But the regimes backed by the United States mainly have an interest in perpetuating their hold on power. Moreover, these dependencies are slower to reform their own militaries, because the United States is there to take up the slack. If the United States is fighting their enemies, then they can focus on their internal friends. If negotiations with insurgents are launched, they have an equal interest in securing the most favorable deal for themselves. The politics of the arrangement works against internal reforms that would win "hearts and minds," and against negotiated solutions. This puts a heavier burden on the outside military effort, which in these cases means the United States. It also ultimately renders the military effort somewhat futile.

Third, Liberal Hegemony is insufficiently sensitive to identity politics. Nation, ethnicity, and religion remain strong forces in the world today, especially in areas experiencing rapid social and economic change. Identity politics has posed three large problems for the strategy of Liberal Hegemony. First, in some parts of the world there is simply great opposition to the very presence of the United States. This is particularly true in the Arab world. Second, a good deal of internal violence is associated with identity politics, which complicates the U.S. effort to install liberal institutions as part of a peace-making, nation- and state-building strategy. Power sharing is more easily mobilized in principle than in practice. Bosnia-Herzegovina and Iraq testify to the difficulty of installing a working "consociational democracy" as a solution to civil wars embedded in identity politics. Finally, the U.S. experience in Iraq and now Afghanistan demonstrates that small numbers of motivated militants with roots in local society can mount very effective violent resistance movements on thin resource bases. While many members of these societies, perhaps most, would rather sit out a violent insurgency, the local fighters nevertheless have a home court advantage. That the United States managed to suppress the Iraqi insurgencies, build a semicompetent Iraqi security force, and install a ramshackle system of governance should not blind us to the mediocrity of the outcome and the high costs in blood and treasure it took to get there.

The Expansionist Dynamic

Liberal Hegemony cannot rest on its laurels. It is inherently expansionist and seems destined to drift regularly into military action. According to one analysis, measured by months, the United States has been at war nearly twice as often since the Cold War ended as it was during the Cold War.[135] The United States has expanded its formal alliances, taking on new responsibilities in the former Warsaw Pact states invited into NATO. The geographic scope of U.S. security interests now encompasses most of the globe. The United States is very powerful, and the Cold War ended with U.S. alliances and forces far forward in the world. With the collapse of Soviet power, the areas just beyond the frontiers came to seem both unstable and open to U.S. action. Realist theorists have coined the phrase "imperialism of great power" to explain the consequences that arise from this opportunity.[136] Great states tend to dominate weak ones. To this basic dynamic is added an obsession with credibility, which arises in part from the sheer magnitude of U.S. commitments, and the fear that any sign of weakness could produce more simultaneous challenges than even U.S. power could manage. There is also a great fear that the power advantage, which is unusual, could prove precarious. So the United States goes to great lengths to preserve it; the obsession with nuclear proliferation and the consideration of preventive war to stop it flows naturally from this concern. Finally, because liberalism is embedded in the hegemonic project, both as purpose and source of legitimacy, the U.S. policy community feels obliged to take up the question of whether military intervention is necessary in the bloody civil wars that emerge from time to time beyond the borders of the U.S. alliance system, and which challenge liberal principles.[137] Involvement in each of these wars is far from inevitable, but involvement in some of them is all but assured. For all these reasons, Liberal Hegemony tends toward political expansion, high defense spending, and war. It is not a status quo policy.

[2]

The Case for Restraint

A Grand Strategy of Restraint must focus on vital U.S. security interests and at the same time reduce the pernicious consequences of the last twenty years of activism. The United States has an enduring geopolitical interest in maintaining the balance of power in Eurasia. The United States also faces threats to its safety: these mainly arise from the existence of nuclear weapons, though the potential threats are more complex than they appear at first glance. Some nuclear threats could arise from geopolitical competition with other countries. Other nuclear threats could arise from an unlikely, but nevertheless not impossible, loss of nuclear weapons to a violent nonstate actor. Thus the United States has a twin interest in managing the proliferation of nuclear weapons capabilities and in suppressing terrorist organizations that have global ambitions.

Below I develop elements of a Restraint strategy for four regions of the world. Restraint demands significant change to U.S. policies in Europe, East Asia, the Middle East and Persian Gulf, and South Asia. I will also discuss the special problems posed by nuclear weapons and the challenges posed by terrorist groups with unusually ambitious objectives. In the next chapter, I will treat the U.S. military strategy and force posture that supports the strategy, though of necessity there is some overlap between this chapter and the next.

THE GEOPOLITICAL INTERESTS OF THE UNITED STATES

National security is about the preservation of sovereignty, safety, territorial integrity, and power position. The last, power position, is both a means and an end. Power position—national capabilities relative to other key actors in the system—is a state's primary insurance in a world without a policeman. States are typically very concerned about their power position, so much so that it may become an end in itself. Power position depends on a state's own capabilities and the capabilities of others. States try to develop their own capabilities, and when possible, discourage the assemblage of superior capabilities elsewhere. Given the facts of the case of the U.S. strategic position in the world today, what are the threats to U.S. national security that grand strategy needs to address?

Though the United States is presently the most capable state in the world, its power position could erode over the next several decades to the extent that it would face a traditional strategic threat. This risk arises from two sources, one internal and one external. The internal threat is simply that the U.S. economy could lose its vitality through our own mistakes. It is difficult to tell whether the anemic growth, high unemployment, eroding middle class living standards, deteriorating infrastructure, and fiscal imbalances presently plaguing the United States are transitory difficulties or represent some deeper set of structural problems that will continue to erode our economic vitality, and hence our power. Either way, a solution is beyond grand strategy, which instead, can only contribute to domestic economic health by improving the efficiency of national resource allocation and avoiding what Paul Kennedy and others have referred to as strategic "overstretch." Restraint would contribute to the U.S. economy by saving significant amounts of money, which could be reallocated to restoring the fiscal health of the country, whether that is a short-term or a long-term problem.

Grand Strategy mainly addresses possible external threats to the U.S. power position. Historically the main concern has been that a power with resources superior to those of the United States could somehow arise on the Eurasian land mass, and then challenge the United States at home. Due to the oceans that separate the United States from Eurasia, and provide the United States with an extremely useful defensive barrier, and the U.S. nuclear deterrent, such a challenger would need to be very powerful indeed. Because many capable nation-states exist in Eurasia, and they have an interest in maintaining their autonomy, they tend to combine to prevent one of their number from achieving regional hegemony. They balance against the more ambitious and capable among them. Coupled with extant U.S. strength, this means that the United States has time to judge whether potential hegemons are truly emerging and to decide on how to contain them.[1]

Occasionally, because of the superior national power of particular expansionists, continental balancing has been impossible to achieve, and the United States has had to come to the rescue. This occurred three times in the last century during World War I and World War II versus Germany, and during the Cold War against the Soviet Union. This could occur again, and the United States must remain vigilant to oppose such an eventuality. Today there is no candidate for hegemony in Eurasia. China's capabilities are growing fast, but there are few easily conquerable resources in range that would tip the global balance in its favor. There are plausible balancing coalitions in the event that China proves ambitious: Russia is currently loosely aligned with China but could easily end up its target; Japan is capable of balancing though it prefers its comfortable free ride on the largesse of the United States; and India is rising quickly, though still lagging China. Two of these three states possess nuclear weapons, and the third, Japan, has the scientific and engineering capability, and the stocks of fissionable material to produce them in short order. That said, China bears watching and will be discussed at greater length below. At the western end of Eurasia, Russia is a shadow of the Soviet Union, although it is still heavily armed with nuclear weapons. A coalition of any two of the principal Western European powers—Germany, France, and Britain could easily balance Russia in terms of GDP and population. Thus the threat of the rise of a continental hegemon, against which the United States previously focused tremendous energy, is now muted. The United States should retain some capability to deal with such possible threats in the future, but they seem unlikely.

Generally, I propose a phased reduction in U.S. political commitments and military deployments. The ultimate goal is to place the responsibility for the security of major and minor U.S. allies squarely on their shoulders; the last vestiges of Cold War alliance organization and commitments should be ended. That said, for reasons of prudence and practicality I will argue that there should be a prior stage of much diminished but still significant United States overwatch of key regions. Getting there should take perhaps a decade. The United States and its allies can then determine whether or not they want the United States to sustain this limited role, or move to complete strategic autonomy.

NUCLEAR WEAPONS: DILEMMAS, DANGERS, AND OPPORTUNITIES

A threat to the safety of the United States arises from the existence of nuclear weapons. Advanced industrial states, even those with economies much smaller than that of the United States, can now assemble nuclear forces of sufficient size and sophistication to damage terribly, if not entirely destroy, the United States. There is no plausible combination of U.S. offensive and defensive systems that can alter this fact. The answer to this threat is partly technical and partly political. The technical answer is for the United States to maintain a large secure nuclear retaliatory force, which it does. Indeed the United States is the most capable nuclear power in the world. The political answer, subject to the need to oppose severe foreign threats that would upend the Eurasian balance of power, is not to threaten other states that possess such forces, and where possible to avoid confrontations with such states, lest the confrontation escape control, and end in a nuclear exchange.

The other problem with a strategy of nuclear deterrence is connected to the threat of large-scale terrorism. This is a threat to U.S. safety, not to sovereignty, or territorial integrity, or power position. Even a terrorist group with a nuclear device cannot threaten these values; it could, however, do painful damage. There are two ways this could occur. A nuclear-armed nation-state might consider giving nuclear weapons to hostile nonstate actors, and nuclear weapons states might inadvertently lose nuclear weapons or materials to hostile nonstate actors. The United States has an interest in keeping nuclear materials and completed weapons out of the hands of such groups. Suppressing terrorist groups, and ensuring that only states with return addresses possess nuclear devices, is a significant U.S. strategic objective.

Here to Stay

United States grand strategy today is fixated on preventing nuclear proliferation. The fear of nuclear proliferation helps to fix existing security commitments in place and to spawn new ones. It has already provided the occasion for one disastrous war and holds out the specter of a second one. This entire policy position requires reconsideration. United States commitments to NATO Europe and in Asia are justified in part due to the political difficulty of allowing Germany and Japan to get nuclear weapons. The United States fought a war against Iraq in part due to the concern that Iraq might still have a live nuclear weapons program. The Clinton administration nearly fought a war with North Korea to eliminate its nuclear weapons program. Efforts to disengage U.S. forces from the Republic of Korea (South Korea) will be met with arguments that this will cause the republic to acquire nuclear weapons to deter the North, which would in turn make it more difficult for Japan to deny itself nuclear weapons. Fears that Iran's nuclear energy project could be a Trojan horse carrying a nuclear weapons program prompted the United States to lead a sustained effort to force Iran to abandon the enrichment of uranium. The use of military force to forestall this possibility was regularly invoked. A nuclear or near-nuclear Iran is presumed to be dangerous to the United States, to U.S. interests in the gulf, and more generally so threatening to others in the region that they too would seek nuclear capabilities. As noted earlier,

Israel considers the possibility of an Iranian nuclear weapon to be a mortal threat, regularly pressed the United States to do something about it, and intimated that if the United States did not, they would.

President Barak Obama has asserted his belief that the world should move to the abolition of nuclear weapons.[2] Article VI of the Nuclear Non-Proliferation Treaty requires existing nuclear weapons states that are parties to the treaty—the United States, Russia, China, France, and Britain—to work for nuclear disarmament. This is, however, a fantasy. It is unlikely that a world of no nuclear weapons can be created, and it is unlikely that the emergence of new nuclear powers can be prevented. The present U.S. effort to do so, which assumes the risks and responsibility of defending other capable states around the world, and fights and threatens preventive wars to deny potential adversaries nuclear capabilities, is costly and risky, and ultimately futile.

Nuclear weapons are a fact of modern life: states that possess them will want to keep them, and some states that do not presently have them will probably get them. I say this for three reasons. First, nuclear technology is no longer exotic. Small countries such as Israel, and relatively poor countries such as Pakistan, have designed and deployed nuclear weapons and nuclear delivery vehicles, all despite the existence of the Nuclear Non-Proliferation Treaty, which prohibits its signatories from assisting these nonsignatories in the development of nuclear technology. Abjectly poor North Korea has produced a nuclear explosive device. Many countries could build and design weapons if they wished and nothing can be done about this. Indeed, the expansion of the nuclear power generation industry worldwide, which is currently under consideration, suggests that in the future even more countries will be able to produce nuclear weapons.[3]

Second, nuclear weapons are the great equalizer. Nuclear weapons are destructive, easy to hide, easy to package for delivery, and relatively inexpensive. They permit small states to defend their sovereignty against large ones. Wealthy nuclear powers can threaten to launch many more nuclear weapons than poor ones, but how many cities would a great power be willing to lose for the privilege of annexing or destroying a small country? Even the risk of the tactical use of nuclear weapons implies the possibility of high costs to a great power considering invasion of a small one. Thus states facing real security threats find nuclear weapons attractive. If they do not have them, they may want them. And if they already have them, they probably will not give them up. All it takes is one holdout to discourage all the rest from giving up their weapons. And it is all but inevitable that there will be one holdout, because short of the rise of a world government, at least one state will have sound security reasons for wanting nuclear weapons. Nuclear weapons permit Israel to insure itself against the more populous Arab states even if it lost the

[73]

support of the United States, Pakistan to insure itself against a much more populous and powerful India, and Russia to insure itself against a rapidly developing and more populous China.

Third, on close analysis, a world of zero nuclear weapons probably would not be more stable and secure than the present situation.[4] Concerns among strategists about how well this world could work would probably prevent any such agreement. We cannot disinvent the knowledge of making nuclear weapons, and so long as there is a nuclear power industry, resources will be available to support a breakout. Many existing conventional weapons, including aircraft, cruise missiles, and ballistic missiles, as well as space launch vehicles, can be turned to the task of delivering such weapons. Because the weapons are so effective, there would be a significant, "first mover" advantage for anyone who chose to cheat on the agreement. If a state (re-)developed the weapons in secret, and got a jump on all others, it would know that the advantage would disappear quickly, and hence it would be prone to exploit it, either as a cover for conventional aggression, or to destroy the capacities of others whom they fear. Advocates of disarmament will argue that very effective inspection regimes could eliminate this problem. It seems unlikely, however, that any regime of this intrusiveness can be devised that states would accept. Nor would they be willing to count on such a regime reliably to constrain others from cheating.

States party to such an agreement would not only want a way to detect defection early, but have a countermeasure against the completion of a program. One solution would be the maintenance of capabilities by most great powers to attack such programs with conventional weapons. These conventional weapons would, however, be ideal tools of conventional preemption, so a new kind of nonnuclear instability would be introduced into international politics, one that great powers will begin to understand as they attempt to negotiate nuclear abolition. Alternatively, all great powers would wish to retain their own compensatory breakout capabilities. The great powers would not be nonnuclear weapons states, but rather near-nuclear weapons states. While this arrangement would, on an average day, reduce the chances of an accidental nuclear war, it would not be a more strategically stable world for the reasons outlined above. Moreover, one has to ask about the potential risks of a nuclear accident that would arise if states suddenly decided all at once to rebuild nuclear weapons programs, and do so in haste.

What Is to Be Done

The first priority of U.S. national security policy must be to deter nuclear attacks on U.S. soil by capable nation-states. As I have argued above, the United States can rely on a secure retaliatory force to deter nuclear attacks on the United States by other nuclear powers. In principle, it does not matter much whether the United States faces a world of few or many nuclear powers: maintaining the ability to retaliate should deter any or all of them from attacking the United States. The ability to retaliate includes warning and intelligence to detect an attack and identify its origins, and long-range weapons that can penetrate adversary defenses after surviving an adversary's best efforts to prevent those weapons from being launched. Today and for the foreseeable future it is understood that submarines equipped with ballistic missiles are the best means to this end, and that they are extremely effective. By the end of the Cold War, the detection of a well-built, effectively operated ballistic missile nuclear submarine had become extremely difficult, indeed nearly impossible. If indeed the United States ever faces a world of many nuclear armed adversaries, the problem of maintaining warning and intelligence capabilities would grow in complexity. The United States would have to pay special attention to convincing others that it can identify the source of an attack for purposes of retaliation. The United States has secure second-strike capabilities today in surplus. Over time as threats change, or the number of threats grows, the United States would need to adapt, but these problems do not seem insurmountable. On the whole, it is not fear of deliberate nuclear attacks by other "normal" nation-states on the United States that motivates current policy in any case.

There are two problems with a strategy of nuclear deterrence based on the threat of retaliation: extending deterrence to others is difficult and risky, and it is difficult to deter a nonstate actor that gets its hand on a nuclear device. The major problem is extended deterrence, and it arose during the Cold War, when U.S. efforts to prevent Soviet hegemony in Europe exposed the United States to nuclear risks. The United States sought to extend nuclear deterrence to its weak and/or nonnuclear allies in Europe and Asia, and sought to use nuclear deterrent threats to convince the Soviet Union not to threaten them with nuclear *or* conventional attack. Under the circumstances, the United States did not have much choice but to assume this onerous obligation to prevent the risk of Soviet continental hegemony. The United States, for most of the Cold War, had no technical answer to the fact that had it used nuclear weapons first, the Soviets would have retained significant retaliatory capability. The United States and its allies resorted to many tactics to make the first use of nuclear weapons seem credible. The organization of NATO and the stationing of United States forces in Europe, both tools to demonstrate U.S. interest, were prudent and wise. But many methods associated with both the nuclear and nonnuclear forces were impetuous. The United States worked assiduously to get an advantage in a strategic nuclear exchange that would permit it to reduce the damage it would suffer. This would have required striking first, or early with ballistic missiles. The United States would have employed its nonnuclear forces to put pressure on Soviet nuclear forces; for example U.S. attack submarines would have hunted Soviet ballistic missile submarines well before any nuclear exchange.[5] Finally, the United States distributed seven thousand so-called "tactical nuclear weapons" across Europe, some under its own control, but many under the partial control of its allies.[6] In the event of a large-scale Soviet conventional invasion, keeping control over all of these weapons, and using them discriminately would likely have proved problematical. They were a kind of nuclear minefield. All these steps were taken to convince Russia of the credibility of the U.S. commitment to use nuclear weapons in ways that were manifestly dangerous to the U.S. itself. While on the one hand, knowledge of these various schemes may have helped keep the Soviet Union back from the brink, they encouraged a more intense peacetime military competition, and more importantly would have rendered the avoidance of escalation from intense crisis to war rather difficult.[7]

One lesson of the Cold War should therefore be that extended deterrence is a risky business, and the United States ought to have been glad to shed such commitments after the Soviet Union collapsed.[8] Instead, the United States retains extended deterrence commitments in Europe and in Asia. Discomfort with extended deterrence has of this writing helped move the United States to consideration of preventive war against nascent Iranian nuclear weapons potential. Presently good relations with Russia and China, the small size of China's intercontinental nuclear force, and the likely puniness and crudeness of Iran's force if and when it emerges, makes current extended deterrent commitments less risky than the Cold War. But extended deterrence commitments remain a plausible path to one or more nuclear weapons being used either against U.S. forces or the U.S. homeland. In contrast to the much discussed threat of nuclear terrorism by nonstate actors, these capable states will likely possess multiple nuclear weapons that would work.

The existence of irrational states is sometimes posited as a threat that defies deterrence. One cannot rule out that a singularly motivated state, ruled by religious or ideological fanatics, might attack other states with nuclear weapons or give nuclear weapons away to terrorist groups regardless of the risk. This should be very unusual, however, and the burden of proof should be on those who make the argument.[9] Nuclear weapons and nuclear retaliation are easy to understand; most rulers want to remain in charge of the states they lead, and it should be clear that attacks on other nuclear armed states are a sure way to lose all.[10] Strong statements to the effect that though deterrence may work with rational actors the actor in question is not rational, figure in many arguments for preventive war.[11]

The debate on what to do about Iran's nuclear enrichment program exemplifies the "crazy state" argument for preventive war and also teaches why skepticism is in order. In the present U.S. debate about the correct policies to deal with Iran's nuclear technology programs, statements by its then president, Mahmoud Ahmadinejad, led some to dismiss the reliability of containment and deterrence as policy options in the event that Iran produces nuclear weapons. Some proponents of preventive war argued that Ahmadinejad and other elements of the Iranian leadership seek national martyrdom as a mean to usher in the return of the Mahdi, Islam's version of the messiah.[12] To be sure President Ahmadinejad was a disturbing individual; and like many political figures in the Middle East no stranger to the political uses of violence. He denied that the Jewish Holocaust is a proven fact. He said, or implied, that Israel should disappear from the map of the Middle East, though he did not specify a means.[13] In particular he did not suggest that Iran should be the instrument of this crime.[14] We cannot know if these observations were simply offered to produce a certain emotional effect, or whether they were evidence of intent. He was president of Iran for eight years, and though Iran accepted meaningful economic costs to pursue its nuclear enrichment activities, he did not take bold measures to confront Israel.

The evidence that Iran is governed by religious fanatics bent on martyrdom does not stand up well to close scrutiny. Iran does indeed have a system of government that is difficult to comprehend, and religion plays a huge role in politics. Some analysts have built on these facts an argument that Iran cannot be deterred. Though widely parroted, this argument is not well supported. It depends on dubious interpretations of religious beliefs and the selective use of important facts. Yet, partly on the basis of these arguments, not only Israel, but the United States has contemplated preventive war. A careful examination of these arguments by Andrew Grotto reveals that few sources are cited to support them, that they are cited over and over, and charitably, they are misinterpreted.[15] Iran's religious leaders have in the past shown themselves sensitive to costs; the founder of Iran's revolution, Ayatollah Khomeini, ceased the war with Iraq in the 1980s when he determined that the casualties and economic damage were too great, and risked the survival of the Islamic Republic.[16] And the supreme leader Ayatollah Khamenei has issued a fatwa, revealed in August 2005, against the development, production, stockpiling, and use of nuclear weapons (although the purpose of this fatwa is opaque). The fatwa suggests at minimum some awareness that nuclear weapons are particularly destructive and terrible.[17]

The weakness of the "crazy state" arguments in the Iran case should cue us to be skeptical of arguments of this type. Given the damage nuclear weapons can do, critics are right to recommend that the United States and indeed the world should be vigilant about who is trying to get their hands on nuclear weapons, and why. At the same time, the argument that a prospective nuclear weapons state is too "crazy" to be deterred has the quality of seeming to "trump" rational debate on what to do about a new nuclear state. Nuclear weapons are incredibly fearsome things; the same things that scare us about them usually scare any statesperson. Preventive war as a proliferation solution will often be a risky, open-ended, and costly affair in its own right. We should demand a high standard of argument and evidence before acting.[18]

Nuclear weapons will also affect the problem of transition to a Strategy of Restraint. The two most economically capable U.S. security dependencies in Eurasia remain Germany and Japan. These two powers caused the Second World War and committed great crimes during that war. As a consequence, other states have not wanted them to have nuclear weapons, and as signatories of the Nuclear Non-Proliferation Treaty they have agreed not to acquire them. During the Cold War, and after, the United States extended its own nuclear deterrent to these states. NATO and the U.S.-Japan Security Treaty are essentially about the creation of political and military connections that would make this extension of nuclear deterrence credible, despite its risks to the United States. The question is what if anything replaces these extended deterrence commitments, and how quickly. If nothing replaces them, then these two states are then at least in theory vulnerable to coercion by nuclear weapons states.

Germany and Japan have four options: find new nuclear allies, develop their own nuclear weapons, ignore the problem and hope that it goes away, bandwagon with local threats. These are not entirely distinct, and some could be combined. Only the fourth is truly inimical to U.S. security interests, but it is the least likely. Capable states seldom bandwagon when threatened; they "buck pass" if they can, and balance if they must. Germany has potential nuclear allies: France and Britain. Though weaker than the United States, their interest in an autonomous Germany anchored in the European Union might suffice to elicit a commitment from them and render it credible, especially given Russia's comparative weakness. Japan is a more difficult case, because there is no other plausible nuclear guarantor. One can imagine a relationship with India or Russia, but the shallowness of Japan's present political, economic, and military relations with these countries would make alignment with them seem a weak reed. These alliance solutions to the German and Japanese nuclear deterrence problem would be less advantageous to them than the present relationship with the United States. Thus the possibility of nuclear-armed Germany and Japan is front and center.

If Germany and Japan did decide to become nuclear weapons states, they would face technical and organizational problems. Though they might successfully solve these problems rather quickly, a more deliberate pace could make sense. These states will have to design safe nuclear warheads of a size and shape that they can be placed on existing missiles or aircraft. This will be a second-best solution from the point of view of a secure and reliable retaliatory capability, so they would set about designing purpose-built delivery systems, capable of surviving a first strike and penetrating defenses to strike targets. A nuclear command and control system that prevents unauthorized launches and ensures authorized launches would be essential. All this requires planning. It could be rushed, but it would be better if it were not. German officials, having been tasked during the Cold War to receive control, under certain circumstances, of hundreds of U.S. "theater nuclear weapons," probably have a pretty good idea of how to organize this. For Japan, it would all be quite new.

Germany and/or Japan might consider some unconventional alternatives. Either or both could decide that national nuclear weapons programs would seem quite threatening to neighbors with long memories, creating more dangers than they would solve. Under present circumstances, with international conflict among great powers generally muted, it might make more sense for the two states to simply "ignore" the nuclear capabilities of their neighbors. Germany and Japan have highly developed nuclear energy capacities, and military industries, such that they can become nuclear weapons states quite quickly. "Near nuclear status" may be deterrent enough under some conditions. Were great power strategic arms control to progress over the next decade, "near-nuclear weapons" status could become even more acceptable to them. Great power nuclear arms control will not eliminate nuclear weapons but may so reduce the numbers, alter the readiness posture, and enhance the transparency of extant nuclear weapons states that the risk of imminent coercion will seem low. After reaching new global arms control agreements, the decision by any of them to attempt nuclear coercion would signal the rest that it was time to resume the competition. The first to make a coercive threat would be marked, and thus the object of others' buildup in the first instance. It is worth noting that true nuclear coercion of nonnuclear weapons states has not occurred, presumably because any effort to do so would elicit quite negative reactions from other nuclear powers.

Finally, accommodative policies toward possible threats could also be in the mix. Like the Cold War neutral states in Scandinavia, Germany and Japan could maintain a significant nonnuclear capability to resist at-tack and occupation, but avoid policies that would give offense. Implicit nuclear threats might induce appeasement, in which Germany or Japan did a favor for Russia or China from time to time. In the worst case, nu-clear coercion or fear of such coercion could conceivably cause a nonnu-clear Germany or Japan to bandwagon with, rather than balance against possible nuclear challengers. Successful nuclear coercion of these two significant states is perhaps the only way that they could be induced to contribute to the rise of a Eurasian superpower. These risks are limited in Europe, however, because Russia is not very capable and has little or no chance of reemerging as candidate European hegemon. Moreover, if Ger-many were unwilling to defend itself, it seems unlikely that it would contribute enthusiastically to the aggressive designs of another state. In Asia, China is quite capable, and growing more so, and a willing Japan would add significantly to its capability. The problem is similar, how-ever. If Japan were to bandwagon with China out of fear, it seems un-likely that it would then cooperate enthusiastically with ambitious Chinese projects. If China were clever, it might extract some useful eco-nomic contributions from Japan, which would in turn permit China to allocate more national resources to military purposes. The net gain would fall far short of what a true military alliance would provide, but could be significant relative to China's plausible continental adversaries, India and Russia. Of course, these states should understand this possibil-ity and offer Japan some kind of alliance relationship to keep it out of China's grip. If Japan were to bandwagon with China, this would nega-tively affect the U.S. military position in a different way, easing the path of China's navy to the open oceans.

The possibility of nuclear terrorism exercises many countries and ex-perts today because there is little confidence that terrorists can be de-terred. Some terrorists probably can be deterred, and some probably cannot. Terrorists are nonstate actors, which means by definition they do not control territory against which retaliation can be directed, though this problem is not as insurmountable as it seems. Many terrorists have normal political goals; they seek a state or autonomy within a state. The use of a nuclear device would disqualify them with most extant states from ever holding power—the use of the device would set back the ter-rorists' cause. Some of their supporters would distance themselves, and intelligence would likely be more forthcoming from others, further weakening the group. The group wants a state because it sees itself as the defenders of a nation; the nation is vulnerable even if the group is not. While most targets would be loath to retaliate indiscriminately against defenseless people, some might. In any case, that people would be marked for close surveillance for decades if not centuries. Political terrorists are thus unlikely to resort to the use of nuclear weapons. Such a group may, however, try to acquire a weapon and manipulate the threat of its use for bargaining purposes, but even this seems hugely risky. Groups *may* also emerge that are not strategically rational, which would simply use a nuclear device if they had it. They could be delusional; perhaps highly emotional, interested only in revenge; or eschatological, interested in playing a role in a culminating religious confrontation of good and evil. Groups of this kind do not seem to come along very often, thankfully. As of this writing, two groups are typically cited with these ambitions: Aum Shinrikyo (a defunct Japanese cult that did mount nerve agent attacks in Tokyo) and Al-Qaeda.[19] The number of groups that would attempt nuclear terrorism is probably low, but not zero. Concern for nuclear terrorism is motivated by the magnitude of a single event, not its probability.[20] Prudent measures to avoid the loss of materials or complete weapons therefore make sense, as do measures to survey borders and suppress known terrorist organizations.

Terrorists could acquire a weapon or the materials to make a weapon in one of two ways: a state could offer them as a gift, or the group could steal a weapon or nuclear materials from poorly guarded facilities. The solution to the first problem is straightforward and relies on nuclear deterrence as traditionally and successfully practiced. States with nuclear materials need to understand that if they give them away and they are used, retaliation will be directed to the source. All states that believe they could be victims of a nuclear device provided as a gift need to work on the problem of attribution. Once an attack occurs, intelligence agencies the world over will be reviewing their databases looking for patterns of information on activities that could have led to the attack. One hopes that intelligence agencies can connect the dots ahead of time to forestall an attack, but they might indeed fail, as they have in the case of nonnuclear terrorist attacks. There have, however, been many successes connecting the dots after the fact.[21] The process would be aided by the fact that there are only a handful of plausible potential sources of nuclear materials. They would all be assumed guilty until they can prove their innocence. A victimized country and its friends are likely to be as ferocious as the United States was after the attacks of September 11, 2001, indeed much more so. At that time, even sworn enemies of the United States such as Iran and Iraq were surprisingly cooperative.[22] All suspects will probably not cooperate, but at that moment the risks of noncooperation will look absurdly high, and many will help. Indeed, I suspect that under present circumstances, even enemies of the United States that came into the possession of intelligence on possible nuclear terrorist attacks against the United States would share this intelligence just to ensure that they would remain above suspicion.

[81]

The problem of nuclear security from theft arises in two situations: the daily operations of civilian and military nuclear establishments, and situations of state collapse. Under normal circumstances, security can be addressed most efficiently through the sharing of best security practices among states with nuclear industries, weapons, or research and development (R&D) facilities. In 2010, President Obama launched a four-year international effort to secure nuclear materials.[23] Most attention to the International Atomic Energy Agency (IAEA) is centered on its ability to negotiate and supervise the "safeguards" agreements that monitor whether the nonnuclear-weapons-state signatories are diverting civilian materials to clandestine nuclear weapons programs. The IAEA's Department of Nuclear Safety and Security is, however, a leader in helping states ensure that their nuclear energy programs are as safe as they can be from both accidents and theft.[24] Nevertheless, the Non-Proliferation Treaty (NPT) signatories, and the UN Security Council could do more to strengthen this organization, and its rights and responsibilities.[25] Physical security from theft should be as important to the IAEA and its safeguards agreements as is the surveillance of materials against state diversion to weapons programs. IAEA safeguards only address civilian systems, however.

The possibility that normal security measures could break down in periods of domestic political unrest, permitting nuclear weapons or materials to fall into the hands of criminals or terrorists, is one of the most disturbing possibilities of the nuclear age. There can be no hard and fast rule to address this risk. As we have seen since the late 1980s, political instability can come even to heavily armed, modern nuclear powers such as China or the then Soviet Union. A small nuclear power, South Africa, experienced a complete change of regime. Three successor states to the Soviet Union possessed large numbers of nuclear weapons for several years, before giving them up. North Korea possesses nuclear devices, and its government is entirely opaque. Pakistan experiences violent political unrest. Nuclear powers great and small have experienced or are experiencing considerable political change, and we have been fortunate that no weapons have been lost in the process.

The nuclear arms control community has proposed solutions that ameliorate these risks both in the realm of nuclear weaponry and nuclear energy. All nuclear weapons should have coded devices on them that render them useless to those without the codes, as is presently the case in the United States. Privately, the United States and other advanced nuclear powers should do what they can to help all states in possession of nuclear weapons improve the security of their devices, regardless of whether or not they have signed the Non-Proliferation Treaty.[26] Arms control experts have long advised against the use of plutonium in the nuclear power industry, because of the ease of diverting the material to weapons production. Highly enriched uranium was once widely used in research reactors; efforts are now under way to remove these materials and to convert research reactors to less dangerous fuels. These are all prudent policies that help reduce the risks.

States undergoing rapid political change have a strong interest in maintaining control over their weapons. Whether for the "old" or the "new" regime, the loss of nuclear weapons to independent actors creates grave internal and international risks, which range from radiological accidents, through unintended or intended detonations on one's own soil, to preemptive conventional or nuclear attacks from fearful neighbors. The military, scientific, and police professionals with custody of nuclear weapons understand these risks particularly well. Following the collapse of the Soviet Union, outside powers engaged diplomatically to remind the successor states of the importance of control and to offer key actors help in ridding themselves of the weapons. This is the preferred mechanism. Finally, it is clear from press reports that the U.S. intelligence services and military do work on ways to get control over weapons in chaotic situations, or disable or destroy them.[27] Such options probably only exist in some cases where the number of weapons is small, intelligence is good, and access can be achieved. It is probably the case that some other advanced states also have made these kinds of preparations. None of these are foolproof, and some require international cooperation if they are to be successful. These are policies that the United States should pursue regardless of its grand strategy.

THE STRUGGLE WITH AL-QAEDA AND THE ENDURING RISK OF INTERNATIONAL TERRORISM

On September 11, 2001, a well-organized and effective terrorist organization, Al-Qaeda launched a terrible attack on the United States. At that time the organization linked together relatively small numbers of angry fundamentalist Muslims of many different nationalities to direct violence against the West. This organization was led by Osama bin Laden, a once wealthy Saudi who organized assistance to, and occasionally directly took part in, the Afghan rebellion against the Soviet occupation of 1979–89.[28] Ayman al Zawahiri, a veteran of violent struggle against the Egyptian government, was bin Laden's principal deputy and may have inherited leadership of the organization after U.S. forces caught up with bin Laden and killed him in Pakistan on May 2, 2011.

The rise of Al-Qaeda, the damage it was able to do, and the mistakes made in combating the organization provide valuable lessons for the

[83]

future. Though the organization did egregious damage using prosaic weapons, the possible nexus of a skilled and motivated terrorist organization with a nuclear device added special energy to the U.S. response and indeed led that response into excess. Though acquiring nuclear materials or a functioning nuclear bomb, and mounting an attack with those resources, would be no easy task for a terrorist organization, the materials exist, as does the motive for using them.

The first lesson of this experience is that an omnipresent United States makes it too easy for others to blame the United States for their problems. Al-Qaeda grew out of unsuccessful efforts by insurgents in the Arab world, mainly in Egypt and Saudi Arabia, to affect change in those countries. It turned its attentions to the United States because of its failure to make revolution at home. The change they desired was essentially reactionary—to put in place governments that would enforce a particularly stern vision of how a Muslim society should be organized. These societies should, as much as possible, be detached from the liberal and democratizing West. United States influence in particular was seen as excessive and detrimental. Egyptian and Saudi rebels had no luck changing their societies in their preferred direction through political organization or by violence. True or false, they explained their failure by the support that the United States provided to these regimes. Thus key leaders such as Bin-Laden and Al-Zawahiri gradually came to believe that success depended on pushing the United States out of the greater Middle East, from North Africa to the Persian Gulf.[29]

The second lesson is that the Western world is inherently vulnerable to small violent groups, whether domestic or foreign. Liberal democratic Western societies are on the whole quite open; individuals are free to travel within these societies and can rent cars, hotel rooms, and apartments. In the United States in particular, weapons and explosive ingredients are easily obtained. International travel and redundant electronic communications are part and parcel of globalization. Thus there are many opportunities for individuals or small groups of individuals intent on harm to penetrate the Western world and do damage. The advanced countries have been struggling to plug the gaps in their defenses, while at the same time protecting the rights of individuals. This is a work in progress.

The third lesson is that a mix of defensive and offensive means is needed to fight terror, but finding the right mix is quite difficult. Defense speaks for itself, but offense forces the terrorists to spend time and energy defending themselves that they might otherwise use to plot and prosecute attacks. In 2002 I devised a strategy to address the Al-Qaeda threat. I concluded that the United States probably could not achieve the rapid annihilation of Al-Qaeda. Instead, the United States could "aspire to reduce the terrorists to desperate groups of exhausted stragglers, with few resources and little hope of success."[30] It seems that this has been achieved; the original core structure of the organization has suffered egregious damage and lives as fugitives.[31] On the other hand, like-minded groups, which self-identify with Al-Qaeda, and occasionally assume the label, seem to have emerged across the Middle East and North Africa, in Iraq, Syria, Yemen, and the Maghreb. Al-Qaeda and its "affiliates," are small, hardened, conspiratorial, and elusive organizations. There are more than 200 million Arabs, and many more millions of Muslims, from whom they can potentially draw support, for reasons of political, national, or religious sympathy. In the Arab world, and in Afghanistan and Pakistan, it is embedded in populations to which the United States only has limited access. Al-Qaeda members usually know these populations and countries better than the United States does. Depending on the ebb and flow of other political events, these populations provide varying levels of support to Al-Qaeda. Because the organization is small, it probably does not need much material help, and only a few new recruits are needed to replace casualties. It is thus difficult through offensive means to crush these organizations; indeed an excess of offense probably brings them just enough recruits and support to replace the losses the United States can impose. The director of national intelligence, James Clapper, made this very point in congressional testimony on January 31, 2012, "A key challenge for the West during this transition will be conducting aggressive CT [counter terror] operations while not exacerbating anti-Western global agendas and galvanizing new fronts in the movement."[32]

The fourth lesson is that the basic nature of Al-Qaeda and its environment make intelligence the lynchpin of the battle. Defense and offense depend on intelligence. The United States and other states must place as many barriers as possible between Al-Qaeda and Western society. Borders, airports, and seaports must be observed and guarded. Dangerous individuals must be identified and denied access to Western facilities such as civilian airliners or nuclear reactors, which provide by their very nature the ingredients for destructive attacks. Within the limits of what is possible in a democratic society, internal security services need to be proactive in searching out potential conspiracies. In the United States since September 11, efforts have been made to reorient and strengthen the internal security services. The FBI in particular has undergone significant structural change, though it remains to be seen whether these prove effective.[33]

Offense is also central to the campaign against Al-Qaeda, and this too depends on intelligence. In a perfect world, offense would be so effective that the organization would be destroyed. The best kind of offense is directed by governments abroad against Al-Qaeda elements in their midst.

Diplomacy is central to creating the political conditions that permit the organization of intelligence cooperation—"intelligence liaison," with the foreign police forces and intelligence agencies that are best equipped to gather intelligence in their own countries. International intelligence cooperation has been a hallmark of the campaign against Al-Qaeda; to its credit the Bush administration did recognize its importance.[34] The United States can supplement local efforts with its own advanced technology— especially signals intelligence and satellite and drone imagery. Failing local cooperation, the United States should operate from a distance, with the least amount of force consistent with some success. Small special operations units or air and drone strikes should be the preferred option. The Obama administration turned increasingly to these in its first term. Finally, diplomacy must be part of the mix. Diplomacy is needed to organize cooperation with other governments and to affect the attitudes of publics. For diplomacy to be successful, the United States must show by its actions that it is not the enemy of the Islamic world. As Al-Qaeda peddles a tale of U.S. domination and U.S. violence, the campaign against them must take care not to put more evidence into their hands. The invasion of Iraq, and the subsequent extended counterinsurgency campaign, did exactly that. A Grand Strategy of Restraint would contribute directly to the goal of counterterrorism. I argued in 2002 that the United States would need to exercise more discipline about its goals in international politics and its means.[35] In particular, the United States would need to compromise more and to avoid any military actions that were not essential, in order to convince other governments that the United States was not bent on expansion. This kind of diplomacy would help to exploit Al-Qaeda's own violent excesses, which have done more political harm to the organization than any argument that the United States has been able to make.[36] Diplomacy also means lending a helping hand where that can be efficient and effective. Disaster relief is one such opportunity. Although not a magic wand, the U.S. military's relief efforts after the Asian tsunami on December 26, 2004, seem to have been somewhat effective in developing more positive views of the United States, although similar efforts in Pakistan did not produce meaningful results.[37]

The price of free markets, open societies, and globalization is often social dislocation abroad and vulnerability at home. The United States, indeed the rest of the world, must maintain vigilance to minimize the risks of terrorist attack. Defense is more important than offense in this effort, but against known terrorist organizations carefully focused offense also has a role. The offensive side of the struggle with Al-Qaeda or future terrorist groups must be extremely sensitive to the law of unintended consequences. Identity politics based on religion, ethnicity, or nation must be taken seriously. Large-scale U.S. military presence in some regions energizes political opposition; large-scale U.S. military operations energize even more intense opposition. A Grand Strategy of Restraint, with more limited deployments of military forces abroad, and more limited employment of U.S. military force, minimizes these political risks. That said; Restraint is no panacea. From time to time the United States will indeed have to employ military force, which is all the more reason to be very careful about when we do.

IMPLEMENTING RESTRAINT IN KEY REGIONS

Europe

United States policy in Europe since the end of the Second World War and the beginning of the Cold War has been a crashing success, and it is past time to realize the dividends. European economies have been rebuilt and democracies have flourished. The Soviet Union was contained and ultimately collapsed, as the architect of containment George Kennan recommended and predicted. The Eastern European states annexed by, or occupied by, the Soviet Union are free, and are now members of NATO and the European Union.

Europe should be the easiest region to implement a Strategy of Restraint. For those who doubt the viability of the strategy, but who are concerned about the sustainability of the current U.S. effort and are willing to test an alternative, there is no safer place than Western and central Europe to run such an experiment. When the Cold War ended, some argued that NATO's work was done and that it would or should have been wound up. Others, including me, believed that it was more prudent to leave NATO in place to ensure stability, particularly since the trajectory of Russia was unclear. This policy was correct then, but is wrong now. We know what Russia is—a somewhat bumptious middle power concerned with its prestige, security, and economic development. Its conventional forces are weak and its economy cannot support anything like the legions of the Soviet Union. Russia cannot threaten the principal powers of Europe, and if Europeans small and large choose to hang together, Russia cannot do much. It certainly can make no bid for hegemony.

First, Europe is inherently stable. There are only four independent nation-states in Europe with any significant military capability and economic potential: Russia, Germany, Britain, and France. They do not seem poised for a renewal of their sanguinary past. Russia is the only plausibly unsatisfied power among the four, but is also the weakest. Germany, Britain, and France are all liberal democracies, and belong to the European Union, a sui generis political and economic organization that joins twenty-seven countries—all democracies, with a total GDP of $16 trillion in 2009, and a population of 495 million, into a single market, with aspirations toward a shared society with agreed standards and rules for a range of economic, legal, and social activity, and an alliance aimed at ensuring against military competition among its members and aiming for political peace on its frontiers. Eighteen EU members as of January 2014 also share a common currency—the euro—after the U.S. dollar, it remains perhaps the most important currency in the world.[38] Most students and members of the EU would find it laughable to talk about the possibility of reemerging security competition among its key members. Even in the absence of the European Union, however, the facts of the case do not suggest a Europe poised for a hegemonic competition either among Western Europeans or between them and Russia.

None of the four states are economically or militarily strong enough to mount a bid for hegemony in Europe. All but Germany possess nuclear deterrents. Because Russia's economy is much weaker than the others, its conventional forces have deteriorated. It is doubtful that Russian ground forces could even reach Western Europe. Germany has the strongest economic base, but at present lacks a nuclear deterrent. Germany is a liberal social-democracy, with deeply antimilitarist public attitudes; even the limited role of its military forces in Afghanistan is very unpopular. Germany's military spending is presently the lowest of all four states as a share of GDP. Were Germany to return to its old ways, it would quickly find itself the object of balancing, but such an eventuality is unlikely. France and Britain are economically and technologically capable states,

TABLE 4. Capabilities of the principal European states

Country	2011 GDP[1] (trillion USD)	2011 GDP at purchasing power parity (trillion constant international dollars)	2011 defense spending share of GDP[2]	2011 defense spending (billions USD)	Active military personnel[3] (2011)	2011 population (million)
United Kingdom	2.43	2.29	2.60	63.60	178,000	62.64
France	2.77	2.30	1.93	53.50	239,000	65.44
Germany	3.57	3.22	1.34	48.18	251,000	81.73
Russia	1.86	3.03	2.80	51.60	1,046,000	141.93

[1]GDP and population from World Bank, "World Development Indicators."
[2]Defense spending and GDP share from IISS, *Military Balance, 2013* (London, 2013), 549–50.
[3]IISS, *Military Balance, 2011* (London, 2011), 471–72.

with advanced militaries, and more ability to project power at great range than any other states in the EU. The capability is still limited, however, and dwarfed by that of the United States. Their ground forces are now professional; as a consequence of the cost of a professional soldier and of modern equipment, each can barely muster eight brigades. (The world wars required these states to put hundreds of divisions, each consisting of two or three brigades, in the field.) All four states suffer demographic issues; Russia and Germany have rapidly aging populations while Britain and France are both dealing with the challenges of creating genuine multiethnic societies. They would have a difficult time mobilizing large numbers of citizens for adventures abroad.

Second, the EU provides a good base on which Europeans could build an autonomous defensive capability. If the EU could efficiently concert its economic, diplomatic, and military forces these would suffice to support a bid for European hegemony but it is not a single country. It is an unwieldy, though heavily institutionalized coalition of culturally, political, and economically similar nation-states welded into a single market. To the extent that it has a collective security ambition it is to have peace within its borders and a placid immediate neighborhood. It is the quintessential status quo power. At present the EU has only limited ability to act collectively with military force. The European Union Common Security and Defense Policy (formerly the European Security and Defense Policy, or ESDP) was developed since the end of the Cold War, largely as an insurance policy against the possibility of a future with less U.S. engagement.[39] The fact that the EU members built this insurance policy demonstrates that they can look after themselves, even if they do not want the United States to believe it.[40] At present the purpose of EU military efforts is the stabilization of the European periphery; it is not defense against external threat. The United States and several EU members, most notably Britain, have been insistent that the EU not compete with NATO for the defense mission. The orientation of EU military efforts to actual defense of the member states would be an innovation.

The European Union now maintains a skeletal military command structure and long-term force planning apparatus. This does not mirror NATO, but by design is much smaller, and depends on the member states to provide in crises the kinds of command structures necessary for action. Nominally, the purpose is to organize and manage peacekeeping and peace-enforcement missions that NATO (read the United States) declines. The key organs are a Political and Security Council of civilian officials from all the member states and a Military Staff that both reside in Brussels. A military council of the chiefs of staff of all European Union member states meets from time to time; a senior officer from a member state is appointed to represent the group in Brussels. The union also has several

[89]

different ways to manage large operations. These efforts provide a foundation for Europe to build and manage an independent defense organization. Indeed, given that the largest EU member states are also NATO members, it would be a simple matter to pass these NATO institutions to the EU as the United States disengaged militarily from the continent.

Third, nuclear deterrence helps further to stabilize European politics. Though Britain and France retain small independent nuclear deterrents, these are not yet integrated in any way with the EU. The connection of British and French nuclear forces to the security of all EU member states would be a significant innovation. Nevertheless, Anglo-French nuclear cooperation has been discussed by analysts and policymakers in the past, even in the EU context.[41] Nothing much has occurred, but we can see that the option is not inherently out of the question.[42] The European Union, though hardly a popular institution in European populations, is deeply embedded in the daily economic, social, and political life of Europe.

The European Union provides as good a foundation for U.S. disengagement as the United States will find anywhere in the world today. It is possible that it would fall apart in the event of U.S. disengagement but this seems unlikely. The reverse seems more probable as Europeans seize on the union as a necessary replacement. The first step in U.S. disengagement from Europe is to accustom Europeans to managing their own security affairs. Traditionally, a U.S. four star general or admiral is the Supreme Allied Commander Europe, or SACEUR. A European civilian is appointed to be the senior political figure in NATO, the secretary-general. The United States should propose that SACEUR be a European. This can be implemented quickly and easily.

There is nothing in the original North Atlantic Treaty that requires the existence of an institutionalized command structure.[43] This was an artifact of the Cold War problem of deterring potential attack by large Soviet ground forces based in Eastern Europe. Because the Soviet Union and its massive forward deployed ground and tactical air forces are gone, the practical necessity for the command organization is also gone. The United States should withdraw its operational forces from Europe over a ten-year period, starting with ground forces. Toward the end of that decade, NATO institutions could gradually transition to EU control and management if the Europeans desire or the Europeans can sustain them as a separate entity. Otherwise, they can be allowed to lapse. Depending on what the members can agree, the North Atlantic Treaty can be amended, rewritten entirely, or permitted to lapse. The EU would remain an important concentration of military and economic power on a big piece of valuable real estate. The United States and the EU would have many shared interests and would profit from regular consultation. My own preference would be to replace the North Atlantic Treaty with a new, limited security cooperation agreement between the United States and the EU in which the two parties would consult regularly on matters of mutual concern and would concert action in the event of threats to either. This would be a weaker commitment than that found currently in Article V of the North Atlantic Treaty, which commits the United States to defend any NATO member state suffering attack from any quarter.[44] This change is necessary for the disengagement effort to serve its purpose of encouraging Europeans to take up responsibility for their own security. Presuming that there is a treaty relationship of some kind, U.S. officers could remain in the Europe for liaison purposes, either with national armed forces, or with the EU, but not as functioning members of a command structure.

NATO has involved the United States in three significant military actions on Europe's periphery, in Bosnia, Kosovo, and Libya. NATO infantilizes the Europeans, leaving them militarily dependent on the United States. The United States touchingly participates in endless reform efforts to make NATO more relevant to the "new" security problems, but the bottom line is always the bottom line. Modern military power costs a great deal of money. Using it costs even more money. The Europeans have little interest in providing any more resources than are required to keep the U.S. happy. And the United States has proven easy to amuse.

East Asia

Asia exhibits more geopolitical dynamism among middle and great powers of any region in the world, and therefore is the most problematical region for the implementation of a Grand Strategy of Restraint. Table 5 provides a snapshot of the existing power balance in the region. At present, the United States is the major power; strategically it can offset Chinese power with little help from regional actors, other than bases. China's recent growth story is well known, but in a purely arithmetical sense, a coalition of three regional powers, Japan, Russia, and India could also offset Chinese power, though just barely. This is probably set to change over the next several decades. The United States will find China a greater challenge, and a coalition of regional powers may have a difficult time remaining competitive. The locals may need the United States, and the United States may need the locals.

According to the U.S. National Intelligence Council's *Global Trends 2030*, indices of aggregate international power suggest that China's share will grow significantly over the next twenty years, surpassing the United States between 2030 and 2040. Though the U.S. share will decline, it would remain a close number two to China. India will lag but its share of global power would also grow significantly, making it the number 3

TABLE 5. Capabilities of the principal Asian states

Country	2011 GDP[1] (trillion$) at market exchange rates	2011 GDP at purchasing power parity (trillion constant international dollars)	2011 defense spending share of GDP[2]	2011 defense spending[3] (millions 2011$)	Active military personnel[4] (2011)	2011 population (millions)
China	7.32	11.3	1.24	90,221–[5]136,700	2,285,000	1344.13
India	1.87	4.53	2.54	36,115	1,325,000	1241.50
Japan	5.87	4.30	1.02	59,834	248,000	127.82
Russia	1.86	3.13	2.78	51,594	1,046,000	142.96
ROK	1.12	1.49	2.54	28,335	655,000	49.80
Australia	1.38	.93	1.71	25,444	57,000	22.32
Indonesia	.85	1.12	0.69	5,844	302,000	242.33
U.S.	15.09	15.09	4.56	687,000	1,564,000	311.59

[1]GDP, population, and defense share of GDP from World Bank, "World Development Indicators."
[2]IISS, *Military Balance, 2013* (London, 2013), 549–50.
[3]IISS, *Military Balance, 2013* (London, 2013), 549–50. Official Defense budgets in local currency converted to dollars at market exchange rates.
[4]IISS, *Military Balance, 2011* (London, 2011), figures do not include internal security forces, which are very large in China and India.
[5]IISS, *Military Balance, 2013* (London, 2013), 255–56, The lower figure is the official defense budget; the higher figure estimates the costs of defense activities that China does not report in its official defense budget, including some internal security expenditures.

power by mid-century, at roughly two-thirds the capability of the United States. Japan and Russia, starting from a low base will decline to such an extent that even if they were allied, their total capabilities would be less than half of India's.[45] An analysis confined to projections of GDP at market exchange rates projects a similar evolution (see table 6). These changes might not occur for any number of reasons: political mismanagement can derail an economy; natural disasters can set it back; and as we have learned, flaws in financial systems can produce near depressions. And these macroindices may mask stubborn debilities of the rising powers and persistent strengths of the United States, which could slow the actual pace of geopolitical change; most notably the United States would still have the highest per capita GDP in the world by a wide margin, more than twice that of China, which would support a very high level of consumption of the most advanced goods and services and thus continue to provide a base for a very advanced military.[46]

The trends, however, suggest that the unipolar moment is fading fast. Perhaps two or three decades from now, the United States and China will look like true peers. At the same time, a handful of other states would likely have sufficient capability to "tip" the balance. This would contrast with most of the Cold War, where individual states had insufficient economic and military capability to affect significantly the superpower balance. If the latent and actual capabilities of other states matter, then alliance diplomacy will also matter. Though some anticipate a "bipolar" world centered on a U.S.-PRC competition, a multipolar world of shifting alliances is equally plausible.[47] Either power constellation demands a different strategy than Liberal Hegemony. A replay of the U.S. Cold War strategy is equally unattractive.

China's intentions remain opaque, in part because they themselves probably do not have consensus on their purposes, which range from official statements about a "peaceful rise" to a position of responsible, but influential stakeholder in an accepted global system to demands for full and timely implementation of all of China's various official and unofficial territorial claims on land and sea. One can craft from China's claims, actions, and its surprisingly fractious strategic discourse, an assessment that China aims for regional hegemony.[48] Given that it is generally the case that a state's ambitions, even if modest, grow as their capabilities grow, it is to be expected that China will want changes in the existing order. Its neighbors and the United States will need to consider carefully how much change they are willing to concede, and conversely which Chinese demands might be worth a fight, even if "only" a diplomatic standoff. Without going into details, it will not be wise, given China's growing power, to insist that no change is possible.[49]

Restraint must be responsive to the growth of China's power, but simple application of a Cold War model does not provide good guidance. As noted earlier, some aspects of the competition with the Soviet Union were risky in ways that we should not wish to repeat. China could prove a more difficult problem than the Soviet Union in certain respects. First, China is likely to be much closer in overall economic capability to the United States than was the Soviet Union. China will likely achieve parity with or surpass the United States in terms of total economic potential at international market prices; the Soviet Union never had more than about half of U.S. economic capacity measured at "purchasing power parity," perhaps even less. China's GDP by this measure is already 75 percent of the United States. Second, because China has embraced capitalism and participation in international trade, its economy will be much more dynamic and innovative than was that of the Soviet Union. China will be connected to all the global developments in advanced civilian technology,

TABLE 6. A future multipolar world? Projections of GDP at market exchange rates (billions of 2011$)

Rank	2011 Country/GDP		2030 Country/GDP		2050 Country/GDP	
1	U.S.	15,094	China	24,356	China	48,477
2	China	7,298	U.S	23,376	US	37,998
3	Japan	5,867	India	7,918	India	26,895
4	Germany	3,571	Japan	6,817	Brazil	8,950
5	France	2,773	Brazil	4,883	Japan	8,065
6	Brazil	2,477	Germany	4,374	Russia	7,115

John Hawksworth and Danny Chan, *World in 2050, The BRICs and Beyond: Prospects, Challenges and Opportunities*, "Appendix B: Additional Projections for GDP at Market Exchange Rates," Price Waterhouse Coopers, January 2013, 23. http://www.pwc.com/gx/en/world-2050/the-brics-and-beyond-prospects-challenges-and-opportunities.jhtml.

management techniques, and higher education that provide the foundations for modern military power.

Some aspects of the situation will likely make China a less potent competitor than the Soviet Union, especially on a global scale.

First, China faces a geopolitically more problematic environment than did the Soviet Union. The Soviet Union after World War II faced immediate neighbors exhausted by war, and hence vulnerable. The opposite is the case today; global prosperity has been growing since the end of the Cold War. China has two nuclear neighbors—India and Russia. One of them is potentially as dynamic economically as China. Two other neighbors, the Republic of Korea and Japan could easily become nuclear weapons states. China's own population near its land borders often consists of ethnic minorities, restless under governance from Beijing. China cannot afford war on those borders.[50] Many neighboring countries are separated from China by bodies of water, which would make it difficult for China to apply military pressure, if it ever came to that. Finally, at least for the immediate future, China's economic prosperity is inextricably bound up with global trade, which leaves it vulnerable in extremis to blockade. United States naval, air, and space power allow it to dominate the open oceans. So long as this remains the case, in the event of hot war, the independent nations on the edge of the East and South China Seas would all have access to the outside world, while China would not.

Second, and related, China's geography makes it at most an Asian land power. The Soviet Union spanned Eurasia and thus it had inherent potential to be a global power: it had ports and airfields that allowed it to project at least some power in almost any direction, and it could move resources from one theater to another overland or through its own controlled airspace. China's naval geography, even in Asia, helps hem it in. Independent countries with their own nationalist sensibilities sit astride China's route to open waters.

Third, China does not have ideology working for it. The colonial empires were collapsing as the Cold War opened. In part due to resentment of the capitalist system of their former colonial masters, and in part due simply to the moment in history, communism was an attractive ideology and social system in the early Cold War. It served as a legitimating force for Soviet activities worldwide. Local nationalisms in the developing world were more suspicious of the West than they were the Soviet Union, creating opportunities for Soviet political penetration in the emergent countries. Nationalist sentiment today seems to be omnidirectionally suspicious, which would make Chinese penetration difficult, and leave Chinese influence vulnerable to constant local attack. China does not have an ideology or social system that travels, in any case. Authoritarian capitalism with Chinese nationalist overtones and communist trappings is not much of a brand.

The United States has a strategic interest in preventing a single state from dominating Eurasia, and to do so it must preserve its access to Eurasia. China will probably become a very capable state, even if it does not politically dominate any other powers. Its internal capabilities may ultimately be very great relative to those of the United States, and there is very little the United States can do to prevent this. If, however, China were also to leverage its own capabilities to achieve political dominance over a significant number of neighboring states and break out of the geographic barriers that constrain it, China's capabilities could grow even more. China might then become tempted to expand its influence farther afield. The United States would incrementally find its own options narrowed.

How should U.S. interests be defended? The answer provided by the U.S. foreign and defense policy establishment is already clear. The Obama administration's "pivot to Asia" is an effort to initiate a Cold War style containment strategy of China, one based on U.S. political and military leadership of an opposing coalition. The contemporaneous announcement of a new military concept "Air-Sea Battle," which is easily read as an offensive military strategy to deny China the ability to defend itself against U.S. air, sea, and nuclear attack through sustained offensive operations against the Chinese mainland, has a distinctive Cold War flavor.[51] Even the Asian states whose expressed concern for the growth of China's capabilities and its increasing assertiveness are likely to be chary about U.S. policies that look like a new Cold War.[52] The emerging pattern of U.S. behavior is both premature and wrong. China is not yet the equal of the United States; it faces many internal obstacles on its path to growth;

[95]

and it may even stall. The day for containment may come, but it is not here yet.

Restraint, by contrast, reminds one and all that the U.S. strategic position permits it to take a cautious approach to China's rise. The United States is inherently strong, so a very great shift in China's regional and global influence is necessary to affect the United States. Nuclear weapons make aggression against major powers very difficult, so India and Russia are inherent bulwarks against Chinese ambitions. Nationalism is a strong force across Asia; if China grows too willful, leaders and peoples will balk. Even if the United States did very little to oppose it, China would have a difficult time achieving a high level of strategic success because of all of the debilities discussed above. Out of an abundance of caution, however, the United States ought not run this experiment.

The United States should pursue a balance-of-power policy in Asia, but it should do so with full knowledge that it starts from an inherently secure position. China must overcome many obstacles to realize its own power potential, many more to achieve hegemony in Asia, and still more to become a global threat. China is not so strong now that the United States must rush to build a ring of containment, which seems to be its current purpose. Moreover, the interactive nature of Chinese and U.S. power and purpose needs to be accommodated. Our debate is about their future capability against us and our allies. Their debate is about our current capabilities against them, and our apparent interest in having even more. Though some students of China worry that the United States is doing too little, others worry that the United States and its allies are doing too much.[53] China's extant suspicions may be confirmed and heightened, helping to fuel a spiral.[54] United States efforts do reassure its allies, but this is not an unalloyed benefit, as there is little evidence that they are inspired to do more in their own defense.

If the U.S. intelligence community projections are correct, China may ultimately prove too strong for the United States to oppose with the Cold War model, where the United States carries most of the military weight, takes huge military risks, and treats allies as wards. Restraint advises that the United States take advantage of the present moment to encourage its allies to assume more responsibility for their own defense. Moreover, should China prove very strong, the United States should not wish to replicate the extended nuclear deterrence commitments of the Cold War in any case.

Allies and Potential Allies

The principal and middle powers in Asia will have a strong interest in protecting themselves against an expansionist China, if it should emerge.

[96]

Some of them have, or soon will have, the capability to contribute a lot to this effort. Others have less capability, but their geographic position makes them an asset. The regional actors have a strong interest in convincing the United States to do any heavy lifting that is required. The United States, for reasons discussed above, has a strong interest in ensuring a more equitable distribution of costs and risks, though the current administration is yet to realize this.

India, even without much encouragement from the United States, will likely pose an important obstacle to any global ambitions that China might ultimately develop. The United States is tempted to imagine a role for India in Asia that would be similar to its own World War II and Cold War relationship with the united Kingdom. This is implausible and unnecessary. India is growing economically and is projected to grow quite a lot more by mid-century. Demographically, it has a younger population than China, so it should continue to grow at a high rate as China's own growth rate begins to taper. Though the border with China is long, the terrain is favorable to defense. And India enjoys excellent naval geography relative to China. It can easily block the exits from the straits of Malacca and China's trade routes to Africa, and oil routes to the Persian Gulf. India has the basic wherewithal to oppose the projection of Chinese power, if it sees an interest in doing so. It has had limited, if long-standing territorial conflicts with China, including one disastrous border war, and has seen China assist Pakistan militarily. Thus there is a legacy of mistrust, which causes India to be wary. The important caveat is that India is a very nationalistic country and suspicious of the United States.[55] The United States has been courting India since the George W. Bush administration, because U.S. strategists can see the future limned above, and India is of obvious strategic utility. But India will act only when it sees its own interests threatened, and they are not eager to start a conflict with China.

India has the military basis to oppose China should it choose to do so. India is a nuclear power with a small arsenal, which can be expected to grow if necessary. The Indian military is one of the largest in the world measured in personnel, and though undistinguished in any major military engagements, is stolidly competent. It is moderately well armed and embarked presently on a major modernization campaign. The budget has risen steadily, though not as fast as China's, so overall it spends only about a quarter to a third as much.[56] Indian strategists benchmark themselves against China and are not happy with the current state of affairs. At the same time, India's priority is economic growth. If China plays its hand cautiously, India will likely not seek confrontation but will remain on guard. If China becomes more energetic, then it is quite likely that India would counter. Depending on when this occurs, India might want

[97]

and need external military assistance. Insofar as the United States has been selling some arms to India recently and the two countries have had many joint military exercises, China probably understands that the closeness of India's strategic relationship with the United States is in its hands; lack of moderation will prove inimical to China's interest. At the same time, the United States ought to understand that India will not cooperate in what seems to be the present U.S. disposition to initiate a containment strategy against China, and to give India an important role.

Russia, though a superpower no more, has rebounded from the nadir of the post-Soviet years. It is not a global superpower, but it does have sufficient economic and military capability to be a player in balance of power politics. It often makes common cause with China against the United States, but geography ultimately may make it wary of China's growing power, especially if China grows more energetic, and the United States pursues Restraint. There is nothing much of an affirmative nature that the United States can do to hurry this process along. Present U.S. grand strategy probably delays a falling out between the two states.

Japan

The security of Japan has been the principal U.S. strategic interest in Asia. Japan has the odd property of being weak enough that it could be vulnerable to coercion, and rich enough, at least in the near term, to be a valuable strategic prize. Commencing in the mid-1980s and until 2010, Japan had the second largest GDP in the world. It is easy to forget that as the Cold War ended, some were predicting a new bipolar competition between the United States and Japan. The crash of Japan's stock and property markets, the political mismanagement of its economic recovery efforts, and the inability of Japan to create a truly dynamic domestic market to supplement its initial successful export-led growth strategy has left it with a slow growth economy.[57] Japan's population is aging, and the country does not welcome immigrants, so the population will likely diminish precipitately in the coming years, further retarding the growth potential of the economy. Finally, Japan suffered grievous economic losses and human tragedy associated with the earthquake and tsunami of 2011, as well as the accompanying nuclear reactor failures. Nevertheless, Japan still has one of the most formidable economies in the world. It produces and exports billions of dollars' worth of advanced products each year including electronics, heavy machinery, automobiles and trucks, and machine tools.[58] Japan also has a moderately well-developed defense industry, which produces both domestic and U.S. designs. Though under stress, Japan can contribute more to its own defense than the 1 percent of GDP to which it has limited itself.

[98]

The United States has a more narrowly military interest in the security of Japan that arises from Japan's position in the nautical geography of Asia. The Japanese home islands, including the Ryukyu island chain that stretches southwest to Taiwan, constitute a defensible barrier to Chinese exit to the open waters of the Pacific. If this barrier were to disappear, either due to conquest or to Japanese realignment with China, the U.S. Navy would have a more difficult job preserving United States access to Eurasia. Easy access to the open oceans would also allow China to interfere with the ability of its maritime neighbors to trade with the rest of the world. This could in turn permit China quietly to coerce its neighbors.

China, on the other hand, has become a trading state. Thus the line of island or peninsular states from Japan through Oceania, the Indonesian Archipelago, and Indochina amounts to a defensible palisade that puts limits on China's global ambitions, should these ever emerge. This palisade is made durable by the fact that it consists of independent nation-states with strong commitments to their own sovereignty. So long as these states remain autonomous, the United States would be able to choke off China's seaborne trade, in extremis, if China were to threaten anyone in the region. Chinese strategists surely understand this. The present situation should make them cautious, but it is no surprise that they bridle at the U.S. position.

Japan's military geography is mainly favorable to defense. As a large island nation, it is very difficult to invade. The U.S. invasion planned for 1945–46 would have been a massive affair, despite the fact that Japan was already greatly weakened by years of bombing, blockade, and the strain of supporting land and naval warfare across its collapsing empire.[59] It is difficult to see how any possible challenger in Asia would be capable of such a thing. Unfortunately, Japan is relatively close to China as the crow flies, which creates a *mutual* vulnerability to air and rocket attack. Tokyo is 750 miles away from Chinese military air fields near Harbin; the U.S.-Japan Sasebo naval base on the southern island of Kyushu is 500 miles from Shanghai, and even Tokyo and Beijing are only 1,300 miles apart. The two states do not need particularly expensive military systems to threaten harm to one another, and in the case of ballistic missiles to do so quickly. On the one hand, if they are not careful about how they base their military forces, proximity could be a seduction to preemption in an intense crisis. On the other hand, if they are careful about how they base their forces, then each would easily be able to retain retaliatory capacity.

Japan suffers from one major strategic vulnerability, however, which it tragically attempted to solve through conquest in the 1930s and early 1940s: it has almost no domestic sources for the raw materials or energy resources necessary to power its industrial base or support the population.[60] It is not self-sufficient in food, and probably could not be. Thus

Japan has a great interest in secure sea lanes regionally and globally. It probably has just enough naval power presently to secure its home waters, and protect the movement of critical materials by sea in waters proximate to Japan.[61]

Though Japan is potentially vulnerable to an extended attrition war with China, the reverse is also true; China's wealthy coastal areas are reciprocally vulnerable, as is its burgeoning global trade. Assuming military attentiveness and the commitment of reasonable fiscal resources, neither China nor Japan should be able to develop high-confidence capabilities quickly to strangle the other, and neither should fear that the other has much of an advantage so long as each remains militarily prepared. Fear of blockade can also be ameliorated by the maintenance of large domestic stocks of oil, and if need be raw materials. Japan already maintains stocks equivalent to six months of oil consumption.[62] China appears to be starting a stockpile. Any conventional war between China and Japan would thus probably not be settled quickly. As China's naval and air and missile power grows, Japan will need to improve to sustain its ability to defend itself. Given Japan's wealth, and present low level of defense spending, this challenge should not be insurmountable, so long as the United States carries the burden of defending the open ocean sea lanes.

A different political understanding with the United States, and the withdrawal of significant numbers of U.S. troops is necessary to convince Japan that it must take responsibility for its future and invest more in its own defense capabilities.[63] Japanese policymakers also need to do more on the diplomatic front to convince others in Asia that it is a worthy ally in its own right, and not a militarist amnesiac that could suddenly recover its former taste for empire. To accomplish the goal of greater Japanese responsibility two measures commend themselves, one political and one military. First, the U.S.-Japan Security Treaty should be renegotiated. As noted earlier, this is a very strange treaty between sovereign countries, which makes the United States the prime defender of Japan, and leaves the Japanese military with ancillary duties. This must be changed. Japan should have principal responsibility for its own defense; the United States should agree to assist; and for the sake of balance Japan should also commit to help the United States in certain circumstances. Second, the United States should also alter its military deployments in Japan. The degree is a matter of judgment. At minimum, forces that make no contribution to resilience against surprise attack, and to the combined United States and Japanese ability to keep the sea lanes open, should be removed. Japan can invest in bare bases to support U.S. reinforcements in the unlikely event of war, and the use of these bases can be exercised regularly, as the United States did with the successful "Reforger" exercises in Europe during the Cold War.

[100]

The nuclear deterrence problem remains difficult. It is easy enough in theoretical terms to recommend that Japan develop its own secure nuclear retaliatory capability in order to forestall the possibility of coercion by other nuclear powers, most notably by China. Given historical antipathies and Japan's difficulty convincing other states in the region that it has abandoned militarism and imperialism, the nuclear issue must be handled with great care.[64] Japan is a "near nuclear weapons state" due to its highly developed nuclear energy sector.[65] It also manufactures a variety of advanced conventional weapons, and space launch vehicles, which could provide the basis for a nuclear delivery system.[66] Were the nuclear powers to negotiate their way to small nuclear forces, organized around the principal of stable deterrence based on the threat of assured retaliation, then even a near-nuclear power such as Japan might believe that it possesses deterrent enough. Were international politics to turn ugly, this capability could be actualized.[67] This is for the more distant future, however. In the medium term, some kind of extended nuclear deterrence relationship will probably remain necessary, and the continued presence of some U.S. troops in Japan will be an important index of the U.S. commitment.

The political situation in Asia is sufficiently unsettled that the United States will need to go slow on its disengagement, and this will make it more difficult to shock Japan out of its odd complacency.[68] Any U.S. effort to change radically the U.S.-Japan security relationship and endow Japan with much more responsibility for its own defense will precipitate a great deal of unease in Japan and in the region.[69] The kind of arrangement outlined above preserves many of the stabilizing qualities of the present relationship but changes the distribution of costs. It is also a bit less comfortable for Japan than the present system, in which the United States regularly turns handsprings to reassure Japan. Japan's alternatives would be to go it alone entirely and develop its own nuclear deterrent immediately, a policy that many within the country will oppose and that many neighbors will advise against.[70] I support such an outcome ultimately but suspect that Japan would find it safer to approach security autonomy deliberately with United States help rather than precipitately.

Japan's alternative to the steady assumption of greater responsibility for its own defense would be to "bandwagon" with the most powerful Asian state, which at this moment appears to be China.[71] It is difficult to see how this leaves Japan better off. Once in China's embrace, it is not clear how Japan would get out, or what would be the long-term costs of the romance. For this reason, bandwagoning is generally the last resort of states, especially capable states. Japan is not that weak. Japan could also consider a policy of very heavily armed neutrality. If Japan is willing to become a very heavily armed neutral, however, it might as well become

[101]

a better armed and more responsible ally of the United States.[72] Little about the Japanese national security debate suggests that willing subordination to China would be popular.[73] The arrangements proposed above are better for the United States and ultimately better for Japan than the present ones. They are more sustainable over the long term and provide Japan with a sound platform from which to become a normal power in international politics. It is difficult to see why the other alternatives would seem more attractive to a winning coalition in Japanese politics.

The United States has two other major security commitments in Asia, which implicate the United States in major military action: Taiwan and the Republic of Korea. They are largely legacies of the Cold War, and secondarily related to the security of Japan due largely to the geography of the region. The peaceful or the forceful reintegration of Taiwan into China, which is quite likely, or the reunification of Korea as a consequence of North Korean attack, which is quite unlikely, would both affect Japan's security. (The United States also has commitments to other states, most notably Australia, but these other commitments are more sensible and less costly.)

China and Taiwan

The U.S. commitment to Taiwan is simultaneously the most perilous and the least strategically necessary commitment that the United States has today. Taiwan is not a great power: it has a population of 23 million, a land area of thirty-two thousand square kilometers (less than Maryland and Delaware combined), a GDP (PPP) of $718 billion, and no important natural resources. It has some geographic utility in a naval war, but it is also a liability. As an island it *is* quite defensible in a tactical sense from Chinese invasion, and to the casual observer provides a potentially useful base for the United States only a hundred miles from China. Taiwan is a link in the palisade that contains Chinese naval power, and the loss of that link would require some expensive adaptation by the United States and the other Asian states. Unfortunately, proximity favors China, which can attack Taiwan easily with short range aircraft and missiles, and efficiently harass with submarines and naval mines the seaborne trade on which Taiwan depends.

The structure of the U.S. commitment to Taiwan is uniquely dangerous.[74] China is a nuclear power; though its forces are limited, some can reach U.S. soil. Thus the U.S. commitment implies a risk of nuclear escalation. Despite the evidence that China does not have an itchy nuclear trigger finger, we should understand that the confrontation could turn into one of relative will.[75] The U.S. commitment to risk nuclear war over Taiwan is inherently not credible. First, China believes Taiwan to be a lost province. Taiwan's independence is recognized by fewer and fewer states, so its view is internationally legitimate. Second, though indirectly, the United States has conceded that Taiwan is a lost province.[76] Third, the United States can convey no strong strategic interest to China because there are no strong interests. And fourth, the United States eschewed many years ago the principal physical move that one can employ to convey interest—the basing of U.S. forces. For now, China probably would expect the United States to fight for Taiwan and the nonnuclear balance of forces may still favor the United States. This probably induces caution. Nevertheless, Chinese planners probably believe that as their current efforts to improve their conventional capabilities bear fruit, the likely costs of such a war to the United States will rise. They may expect that Taiwan or the United States would tire of such a fight. China may thus become more willing to press its claims in a crisis. If an actual conventional military clash occurs, however, it could go badly for either side, and the temptation to make nuclear threats and invoke nuclear risks will arise. There is reason to suspect that China will care more, or will believe that it cares more. This situation is ripe for miscalculation and escalation.[77]

Because of the disparity in size, and Taiwan's proximity, China's conventional capability is inherently strong and will get stronger. This too erodes the credibility of the already tenuous U.S. commitment. Due to the obsolescence of its forces, China's conventional options versus Taiwan have been limited, but as its economy develops, its military will improve. China has already developed the air, naval, and missile capabilities that will permit it to impose high costs on Taiwan, and significant costs on any U.S. forces that would try to come to the rescue. It will probably not be long before such a rescue effort is extremely dangerous for U.S. conventional forces. As its navy grows China should be able to sustain a submarine campaign against Taiwan's trade with ease, because these warships would not have far to go and could thus remain on station for long periods. Taiwan, with U.S. assistance, would likely avoid conquest, because amphibious landings are tremendously difficult. But a war could easily degenerate into one of attrition, and Taiwan would find it hard going, even with U.S. assistance. Taiwan would not avoid privation. Given China's relative size, and its emergence as an important player in the global economy, one suspects that after such a war Taiwan could not return to its former life as a prosperous trading state, even though it might avoid outright conquest. Most Asian states will be interested in their future relations with China and will shy away from renewed trade with Taiwan. At best Taiwan would be a kind of ward of the United States, the Cold War Berlin of the twenty-first century.

United States domestic politics has made it very difficult to back out of the commitment to Taiwan. Fortunately, Taiwanese domestic politics is moving away from the confrontational stance of its former high-rolling nationalist leader, Chen Shui Ban. The current regime probably understands the facts outlined above. It is also keenly aware of the increasing economic integration of Taiwan with China. It is said that a million Taiwanese now live on the Chinese mainland. Taiwan is a trading state, and China has become the major economic power in Asia. Through indirect means, many Taiwanese invest heavily in the mainland. A significant percentage of the population of Taiwan is at best only weakly committed to the idea that Taiwan must formally assert a status as an independent country. Events seem slowly to be moving China's way. At present China seems willing to accept this situation. We should not be complacent, however. Either a resurgence of nationalism in Taiwan's domestic politics, or the growth of China's power, or both could produce a confrontation. Unless the ground has been prepared in U.S. domestic politics, and Asian regional politics, U.S. policymakers will find it difficult in a crisis to defuse a confrontation that it may not be able to win with military threats. Even if politics in Asia were to move in a way that makes a strategy of containment necessary, Taiwan is probably not the best place to make a stand.

The United States has been the military hegemon of the Pacific, including the Asian littoral, since the end of World War II, but this situation is destined to erode. United States military R&D, acquisition, and planning will continue to pursue the capability to prevail in a Taiwan war. This is probably a losing proposition, however. Due mainly to China's proximity, its growing economic capability can be efficiently translated into effective military power for a Taiwan clash. In Europe at the turn of the nineteenth century, the Royal Navy was pushed back from the coastline by similar kinds of factors; distant blockade replaced close blockade. During the Second World War, it took years of U.S. and British mobilization and hard fighting to wrest control of Europe's coastal waters from Nazi Germany. The United States can remain the most potent military power in the Pacific, but it will need to accept that the littorals will be a truly "contested zone" and adapt its grand strategy and associated military strategy accordingly.

The Korean Peninsula

The Republic of Korea (South Korea) is a prosperous and militarily capable country, well able to look after itself. The Democratic People's Republic of Korea (North Korea) is the principal threat, but on close inspection one wonders why the United States retains any significant forces in South Korea. At 49 million, South Korea has double the population of the North's 23.5 million, and we know that many residents of the north are tragically malnourished. The economy of North Korea is tiny, backward, and disengaged from the rest of the world. Meanwhile the economy of the South is over $1.3 trillion. South Korea now exports advanced electronics and industrial goods to major markets the world over, which are fully competitive with the products of Japan or the United States. It produces many of its own advanced weapons.

The geography of the Korean peninsula is well suited to defense because the "front" is relatively short (a hundred miles). The ROK army now has twenty-four active and an equal number of reserve divisions. These forces possess much better weaponry than their opponents and would be operating in well-prepared positions, on terrain that favors the defense. The ROK should be able to create such a dense defense that the DPRK army would find itself ground to pieces. There are essentially no flanks so clever offensive maneuver is not an option. The North is reported to have roughly twice as many men under arms, combat units, and major items of combat equipment as the ROK, and can surely launch what would be a brutal and destructive war. Nevertheless their odds of success are slight. Finally, if the present military balance is uncomfortable for the ROK, absent United States help, it can find more resources for its military, as it presently spends just under 3 percent of GDP on defense.

The DPRK's possession of a handful of nuclear explosive devices is the principal strategic inequality between North and South. It is not clear that the North can deliver these devices on an aircraft or missile, but the inequality is real and must be acknowledged. As in Europe, I recommend a transition period for passing responsibility to South Korea for its own defense. The United States should first withdraw all of its ground forces from South Korea. Air force elements can remain longer. During the drawdown, it may be possible to convince the North to forgo its nuclear weapons, as it claims that they are necessitated by a U.S. threat. The PRC might apply considerable additional pressure to the North to forestall the plausible nuclear consequences of U.S. disengagement. South Korea would likely consider becoming a nuclear weapons state; it has the technical wherewithal to do so. If this occurs, some Japanese analysts and policymakers will ask why they hew to their NPT commitment to abjure nuclear weapons capability while a smaller state next door proceeds with a program. Alternatively, the North may simply collapse in the interim.

In the near term, U.S. fundamental strategic interests in Asia are not greatly threatened. China is not perched on the edge of regional hegemony. The United States should use the time available before China is projected to grow very strong to change its relationships with its Asian partners. The United States should reduce, not increase, its current military presence in Asia. Rather than rush to reassure allies when they claim

[105]

a fear of China, the first question the United States should ask is what do they propose to do about it? What are they prepared to contribute and when? The United States should make clear that it values the sovereignty of the Asian states, but if China grows as much as is currently predicted, it will simply not be possible for the United States to offer the kinds of conventional and nuclear guarantees it once did. In the worst case, the contributions of all those in the way of an expansionist China will be necessary to contain it. If China does not grow as predicted, then the Asians will be able to look after themselves with limited U.S. help. In the near term, the United States can continue extended nuclear deterrent commitments to cap escalation temptations in local disputes, so long as these do not depend on an open-ended nuclear counterforce competition. China needs to be alerted to the likelihood, however, that should it embark on a genuinely expansionist foreign policy of its own, the United States will instead stop guarding against nuclear proliferation in the region and would support independent national nuclear deterrents.

The Greater Middle East

The United States has three major interests in the area from North Africa to Iran. Two of those interests, energy and nuclear nonproliferation, are traditional national security interests, which fall comfortably into the realm of grand strategy. A third interest, the security of the state of Israel, is often treated as a traditional security interest, but it is more complicated than that. During the Cold War there was a fourth interest, opposing the extension of Soviet influence throughout the region, which was in part driven by military geography, and in part by the interest in oil. Having addressed proliferation earlier, below I discuss energy security and Israel. United States interests in Israel, in energy, and in nonproliferation are interconnected, and sometimes contradictory. Presently the most difficult contradiction is the Israeli occupation of the "West Bank," the expansion of Israeli settlements and neighborhoods in this real estate, and the absence of a Palestinian state. Across the Arab world there is sympathy for the plight of the Palestinians; the salience of this sympathy is variable, and other issues are currently more important. Nevertheless, the United States is implicated in a policy that Arabs do not like, even as the United States relies on cooperation with Arab states to secure energy.

The Persian Gulf

The U.S. interest in the Persian Gulf arises from the energy resources concentrated there.[78] Fifty percent of the planet's proved oil reserves are found in the Persian Gulf. Twenty-three million barrels a day of oil,

[106]

or 30 percent of world liquid fuels, were produced in the gulf in 2012.[79] Perhaps 20 million barrels a day was exported, nearly 90 percent through the Straits of Hormuz.[80] The gulf states produce perhaps 40 percent of all the oil that is regularly traded on international markets, the rest having been tied up in long-term contracts. It is the presumed strategic value of the resources that drives the U.S. concern. War machines run on oil; the revenues from oil and gas can be used to generate military resources; and conceivably control over the supply of oil and gas could be wielded to achieve political leverage. The U.S. economy does not in any narrow sense depend on the energy resources of the Persian Gulf, which was the source of only 20 percent of U.S. oil imports as of 2012.[81] United States dependence on energy imports more generally is gradually falling, due mainly to the invention of new technologies to extract natural gas and oil in the continental United States. The market for oil is global, so if gulf oil were to disappear from the market, the price of oil worldwide would increase, and the United States would pay more for energy. This would harm the U.S. economy, but the level of harm does not rise to the level of a national security threat.

The U.S. military divides the world for purposes of military command, and U.S. CENTCOM (created in 1983), which oversees twenty-five countries across the greater Middle East and South Asia, and managed the wars in Iraq and Afghanistan, is now the largest. Since the end of the Cold War, the U.S. presence in the region has increased significantly. The United States built up a large force for Operation Desert Storm, but removed most of those troops after the liberation of Kuwait. Some remained, however, as did a significant infrastructure to receive reinforcements. Operation Iraqi Freedom in 2003 saw the return of nearly 200,000 U.S. troops to the Persian Gulf, though most of these were withdrawn by the end of 2011. The United States spends a great deal of money

TABLE 7. Persian Gulf oil production and proven reserves

Country	Oil reserves (billion barrels, 2011)	Share of world reserves (2011)	Liquids production (2009, mbd)
Saudi Arabia	260.1	17.68	9.6
Iran	137.0	9.31	4.1
Iraq	115.0	7.82	2.4
Kuwait	101.5	6.90	2.5
UAE	97.8	6.65	2.8
Qatar	25.4	1.73	1.2

Source: U.S. Energy Information Agency, *International Energy Outlook 2011* (Washington, DC: U.S. Department of Energy, September 2011), 38, 250.

to prepare for war in the region. Though efforts to assess these costs usually founder on the opacity of Pentagon accounting, and the shifting domestic political rationales for U.S. force structure, it is reasonable to attribute between 15–20 percent of U.S. annual military spending, as much as $110 billion in Fiscal Year 2010, to the maintenance of forces for military action in the gulf.[82] Billions spent on the war in Iraq are not included in this estimate.

There are four possible security threats connected to the oil resources of the Persian Gulf that could warrant U.S. concern: an oil hegemon could arise within the region through conquest or coercion, which would achieve significant control of revenues, supply, and price, which it would then use to damage U.S. interests; a regime could come to power in a single oil state that could nevertheless do similar damage; a general war could occur that would so damage the oil infrastructure of the region and/or so restrict the shipment of oil that there would be a worldwide economic shock of significant proportions, with knock-on security implications; or finally, the failure of the United States to guard against all these possibilities would cost it general influence that it somehow derives from its role as the gendarme of the gulf.

Because most of the Arab oil producers are relatively small countries, they are vulnerable to conquest by a greater power. On paper only two gulf states could bid for regional hegemony—Saudi Arabia and Iran. Iraq is no longer a viable candidate; it tried under Saddam Hussein and was trounced first by Iran and then by the United States, and still faces major internal divisions.

Saudi Arabia has not considered striving for dominance of the entire gulf. Because it has so much domestic oil, the value of conquest must appear low. Saudi Arabia's ability to mobilize significant military power, despite its high defense spending, is also suspect. It probably can mount a decent defense against a range of possible attacks, but it depends greatly on foreign advisors and technicians to maintain its advanced equipment. The Saudi Army has not shown particularly well in the few engagements it has had. The regime seems to fear its own armed forces, so it maintains at least two distinct ground forces of roughly equal size, the army and the National Guard, presumably so that each can check the other.[83] Saudi Arabia is thus an unlikely candidate for regional hegemony.

Iran possesses the ingredients for regional hegemony. Its population is equal to that of all the Gulf Arab states combined; it has a real, if rickety, industrial base, and a large, if poorly equipped military. With only 2–4 million barrels a day of oil production, and 1–2 million barrels a day of exports, political influence over the production and pricing of the others could appear a juicy target. To the extent that Iran has regional ambitions,

[108]

influence rather than control is thought to be their objective.[84] Under some circumstances, one could imagine a temptation to conquer others' resources outright, although there is no evidence that Iran's leaders entertain this kind of ambition. A significant expansion of Iranian control over the energy resources of the gulf would not be in the U.S. interest. If Iran had more oil to sell, or Iran could drive up the price of oil, it could improve its military capabilities, and perhaps then make even more mischief. If it could manipulate supply or price, it might get political influence with countries farther afield. None of this would shake the foundations of U.S. security, but if gains proved cumulative, they could be problematical. Given that Iran's actual ability to project force beyond its borders is limited, the cost to the United States of insuring against Iranian conquest or coercion of its neighbors is not particularly high. With some combination of naval presence, and the ability to reinforce quickly, any Iranian ambitions could be thwarted, at least for now. It is prudent, but not essential, to pursue this policy.

A second security problem arises from the possibility that an extremely hostile regime could come to power in another oil producing country, a regime as hostile, or more hostile, than the regime in Iran. Most of the gulf states are small powers and small producers, so, this would only matter because it would allow the new government to make a lot of money, and use it to support terror, or subversion of other governments, or the supply of weapons to allies. The United States and others could probably thwart such a threat. Because none of the other producers possess a particularly large share of gulf exports, their ability to turn that share into geopolitical influence would be limited at best, as would the ability to precipitate an oil shock to Western economies.

The biggest potential problem, however, is the possibility of a hostile regime in Saudi Arabia. Its proven reserves and large production would provide a hostile regime with significant financial resources to make trouble. It could purchase even more armaments, and with a different kind of political organization perhaps build a genuinely capable military. It could fund subversion and/or terror in the region and elsewhere and give favors to friendly nations farther afield. Conceivably it could also impose costs by withholding oil supplies, though the international oil market is probably flexible enough to cope with actions of this kind.[85] Though all these problems are plausible, recent experience in Iraq and Afghanistan suggest that it is not possible for the United States to cheaply and effectively prevent a hostile regime from emerging in Saudi Arabia.

The United States fought a costly and painful war in Iraq to assure the emergence of a semblance of stability: a war in Saudi Arabia might be even more difficult. The United States would make many enemies if it intervened militarily in Saudi Arabia. A greater share of the population

[109]

than in Iraq is likely to oppose the United States, and the wider Arab and Islamic world would be even more hostile. Medina and Mecca, the holiest places to Muslims the world over, are in Saudi hands. The presence of infidels would be a red flag. Though the Saudi oil industry is located in less-populated parts of the country, it is unlikely that military occupiers could efficiently lift the oil. Insurgents managed to do quite a lot of damage to the Iraqi oil industry during the recent U.S. counterinsurgency and concomitant civil war.[86] These seem like significant risks to run, and costs to incur, for the sake of a lower oil price. On the whole, therefore, despite the discomfort a hostile Saudi regime would cause, the United States probably has no direct cost-effective military option to prevent one. If such a regime emerges and is hostile, the United States will have to deal with it the old-fashioned way—diplomacy, containment, deterrence, intelligence and covert operations, economic pressure, and perhaps even conventional military operations designed to defend others, or to limit the options of the new and hostile regime.

The third key reason the United States maintains its presence in the gulf is to ensure the "free flow" of oil. It is feared that war in the gulf would substantially reduce exports and precipitate a price shock that could seriously damage the global economy. The United States therefore aims to ensure against blockade or damage to facilities. The necessity for U.S. action is premised in part on the geography of the gulf oil states and the key export routes. Oil production is concentrated close to the shores of the gulf nations, and thus it is efficient to ship the oil out by tanker. The gulf itself is small enough, however, to permit many of the local powers to harass the export by sea of the others' cargoes, even with primitive means such as armed motor boats, as occurred during the Iraq-Iran war. More important, all the cargos must go through the Strait of Hormuz, which is quite narrow, and thus lends itself to harassment by those controlling the shore; Iran in particular has options to wage a war of attrition against oil exports. More generally, there is also a concern that a general war in the region might cause the combatants to attack one another's production facilities, further limiting exports.

A war among the gulf states would surely roil oil markets, but the odds of major effects on the world economy are low. At present, it would be very difficult for any of the gulf states to shut off the exports of the others, whether or not the United States intervened.[87] During the Iran-Iraq war the straits were not closed; despite harassment of one another's tanker traffic and oil production, both Iran and Iraq (and its Arab allies) managed to export quite a lot of oil.[88] There are several reasons why cutting off the flow of oil is hard. First, tankers are more resistant to mine and anti-ship missile attacks than are warships, because of their size and the physics of the cargo, which tends to absorb explosive shock.[89]

Second, though alarmists often talk about the two-mile width of the tanker channels leaving the gulf, the tankers can use more of the sea space; the strait is thirty-four miles wide at its narrowest. Mining the strait with sufficient density to "close" it is thus a significant challenge. Third, the tankers could use parts of the sea space more distant from Iran's shore line, further complicating the problem of cruise missile and small boat attacks. There is therefore a persuasive case that gulf exports are in less danger than many suppose. Even if the United States did nothing, the local powers and the tanker owners could probably find a way on their own to export oil by sea if Iran or any other gulf state attempted to close the gulf, though the price of insurance would surely rise. If they are truly worried, Arab states could also invest in additional mine hunting vessels to ensure against future mine campaigns in the straits, and in supporting forces to protect their mine hunters while they are at work.

The world economy is also buffered from gulf combat by massive government and private stocks of oil presently held by industry and governments, nearly 2 billion barrels. This would buy time for consumers to adjust. It also buys time for external military intervention to succeed. If the United States chooses to intervene directly, analysis suggests that a force of moderate size would presently defeat decisively an Iranian campaign to close or constrict the straits, though depending on Iranian tactics and other uncertainties, this could take one to four months.[90] Some Persian Gulf oil can also move overland because pipelines lead eastward and northward.[91] The most capacious pipeline belongs to Saudi Arabia, and runs to the port of Yanbu on the Red Sea. Its capacity is at least 5 million barrels/day. A second pipeline leads from the northern Iraqi oil fields through Turkey and can carry roughly 1.65 million barrels per day. Two pipelines—Saudi-Lebanon and Iraq-Syria—are not presently in use, as a consequence of past wars and present political disputes, but depending on politics these routes could be revived. If the gulf states were truly concerned about threats to the Straits of Hormuz, they could invest in additional pipelines to the Red Sea or the Mediterranean.

Direct conventional threats to oil wells and production facilities are the final problem that could arise from wars in the gulf, if those wars were allowed to run their course, but these threats seem limited at the moment. Saboteurs with plenty of time and explosives, and a good understanding of the production system, *can* destroy wells and other production facilities, and reduce production. The Iraqi demolition of many Kuwaiti wells in 1991 and the insurgent sabotage campaign in northern Iraq during the U.S. occupation both demonstrate the damage that can be done. Very effective modern air forces with large numbers of precision guided munitions could presumably also do great damage, but no gulf state presently possesses such an air force: Iran's air force is obsolescent;

[111]

Saudi Arabia and the UAE have impressive air forces on paper but it is doubtful that they could sustain campaigns for very long without Western help. Experts on targets typically look for critical nodes; a recent analysis of the most obvious critical nodes in Saudi Arabia—tanker berths and sulfur separation facilities—suggests that these are redundant target sets, with considerable capacity. They are also small targets, so accurate strikes are needed. Simulations of missile attacks by Iran with its present inventory suggest that it could not do much damage. This is probably by design; Saudi Arabia has wisely purchased redundancy. If the threat grows, Saudi Arabia and others could purchase more redundancy.[92]

The U.S. commitment to the Persian Gulf probably arises from the belief that regional hegemony there matters to the U.S. global power position.[93] How might this work? Though the threats outlined above are on the whole not particularly impressive, or not amenable to military power, the U.S. military does make it seem that they are even less likely to occur, and if they occur, less likely to do serious damage. This may make oil prices lower than they would otherwise be to all Persian Gulf customers. The United States gives the world a little gift and perhaps it gets some respect or favors in return.[94] I have seen no evidence of this benefit, however. The United States can also create the impression, which to my knowledge has never been tested, that it could politically influence the supply of oil to other states.[95] Perhaps the United States could, if it wished, convince Saudi Arabia and other states simply to squeeze quietly a particular consumer.[96] Finally, the United States may fear the ramifications globally if others began to doubt the stability of the gulf as a supplier. For example, Japan and China depend heavily on gulf exports. If the supply became unreliable, these two states might become more aggressive in their search for more secure supplies, producing new conflicts. These arguments are not often made in public, and have not been subjected to critical analysis. Policy discussions of the role of U.S. military power in the gulf often seem like one hand clapping. Most threats and benefits that are usually invoked are not compelling or cannot be dealt with efficiently by military power. The massive U.S. effort seems better explained by some seldom invoked "factor x." I suspect that global prestige and influence is this factor x, but even this argument is not self-evidently strong.

Restraint argues that the United States has only limited interests in the Persian Gulf, mainly in preventing consolidated control over the region's wealth, an unlikely occurrence in any case. The secure flow of energy from the region by sea is a related interest. The United States can pursue those interests from offshore. United States diplomacy should make clear that the U.S. military is there to help nations protect themselves from invasion or coercion by others, not to help regimes defend themselves.

[112]

Arab peoples are neuralgic about Western presence for both nationalist and religious reasons. The United States should cut its shore presence in the gulf to the lowest level possible. Though there is no reason to state it publicly, U.S. policymakers should understand that they will not intervene in a civil war in Saudi Arabia under any circumstances. Naval power would be the principal forward-deployed U.S. force in the region. The gulf states could maintain extra capacity to host Western forces in the event they were invited back to assist in their defense, just as was done in the 1980s, and as is surely done today.

The Israeli-Palestinian Dispute

Israel is a small country, but in contrast to much of its history, it is now quite secure. Israel is much more populous than it was at its birth; the Jewish population has grown almost sevenfold since the founding of the state, to almost 5.5 million. Israel is prosperous by global standards, ranking forty-fourth in per capita GDP (PPP) not far behind the EU average, which ranks forty-second.[97] Israel has built a high-technology economy tightly enmeshed in the global economy. Its scientists, engineers, and entrepreneurs are world class. Israel has a small but quite advanced domestic arms industry, which exports weapons even to NATO countries. The Israeli Defense Forces are the strongest in the region, by a wide margin, when measured quantitatively and qualitatively.[98] Israel is widely agreed to possess a powerful nuclear deterrent.

Israel faces three potential security threats: attack by a traditional Arab military alliance; some combination of harassment or terrorist attacks from territory on its immediate borders, including land in dispute with the Palestinian nationalist movement; and possible attacks by long range weapons tipped with biological, chemical, or nuclear warheads. The first threat is presently remote, the second would profit from a combination of traditional security and political diplomatic remedies, and the third is soluble over the long term only by deterrence, for which Israel is well equipped.

In contrast to past decades, there is little potential for a significant military coalition against Israel. Israel rightly feared the combination of Soviet weapons factories and the Arab population advantage. The "frontline" states have, however, lost their most reliable arms supplier. The Soviet Union had a vast arms industry with a huge annual output of weapons. The advanced industrial states, including Russia, simply do not produce weapons this way anymore. The frontline states are busy with other things. Egypt, is officially at peace with Israel, and now embarked on a major political transformation. Though the overthrow of the Mubarak regime may make Egypt a less enthusiastic peace partner than

[113]

it was, there is little evidence that the movement for political change in that country has an appetite for war. The military coup that ejected the Islamist leaning government of Mohamed Morsi from power in July of 2013 did not bring calm to the country, and has provoked a reduction in U.S. military assistance. Egypt is less prepared for war than ever. Egypt would find it quite difficult to wage a war that the United States opposed, even if it wanted to do so, because it now depends on the United States for modern weapons.

Syria, the other major frontline state, is as of this writing, in the midst of a serious rebellion, which will weaken its conventional fighting power regardless of the outcome. It remains dependent mainly on Russian arms imports, but Russia now asks for cash and no longer has the large production runs of the past. Some munitions are imported from Iran but it does not produce large numbers of tanks and fighter aircraft, and thus has few to share. Syrian forces have modernized little since the end of the Cold War, though some advanced air defense, antiship, and antitank missiles have been acquired. Whether the present regime remains in power, or is replaced, either government would need to worry about internal security. Syria is already a much reduced conventional threat to Israel. Even if a future regime has an Islamist bent, it will not be very strong militarily.

Other states farther afield are also out of the game. Iraq was once a threat, but its mechanized forces were destroyed by the United States. Saudi Arabia possesses a significant inventory of Western weapons but also depends hugely on foreign technicians to make all this equipment work. Moreover, Saudi ground forces are far from Israel, and the lines of communication to Israel's borders are not good. Finally, Saudi Arabia seems quite concerned with the threat from Iran. Iran's ground forces would be lucky to reach the Israeli border, even if they faced no opposition whatsoever. Their equipment is old, and the logistical problem is massive.

Israel does face threats to its security, mainly to its safety. Because the state is small, the national and nonstate military actors along its borders can shell the country with cheap low-technology weapons—artillery, mortars, and especially rockets. Israel has answers to these threats but they are not perfect. Deterrence is the first; anyone who wants to engage in this kind of duel with Israel, or even hosts those who do, will be severely punished, as was Hizbollah and Lebanon in 2006, and Hamas in Gaza in 2009 and 2012. Israel has also developed a direct defense system, Iron Dome, capable of shooting down some incoming short range rockets, that is partially effective against attacks of limited size.[99] Finally, Israel also has the capability to attack these threats directly, though not always successfully, through counterbattery fire and air strikes.[100] If

[114]

necessary, Israel can invade these countries to push back these kinds of weapons from its borders. These are all costly answers, but they have for all intents and purposes been tested and have worked.

Israel is also vulnerable to terrorism, though this is much reduced in recent years. Many Arabs live inside Israel's pre-1967 borders, and though most of them are not involved in violence against the state, their presence makes it possible for violent outsiders to blend in for the minutes or hours needed to launch an attack. The "security fence" and other measures have reduced terrorism inside these borders. Israeli settlements in the occupied territory of the West Bank are more vulnerable to terrorist actions by Palestinian locals but this is a vulnerability that the settler movement willingly assumes, and the settlers themselves sometimes attack Palestinians. Between January 2009 and June 2013, Israeli civilians have killed five Palestinians in the West Bank, while Palestinians have killed sixteen Israeli civilians.[101] Though those Palestinians who turn to terror have a range of demands, much of the Palestinian violence against Israel is connected directly to the failure of Israel and indeed the rest of the world, to do much to satisfy the aspirations of the Palestinian people for statehood. Israel cannot now satisfy all the grievances of the Palestinian people. Most descendants of those who left or were pushed out in the 1948 war will not be allowed a "right of return." It would destroy Israel as a Jewish state, which is its purpose for Israelis, a purpose that is accepted by many in the United States and elsewhere. An agreement for a Palestinian state in the West Bank and Gaza would leave some aggrieved Palestinians, but it would also leave many with a stake in peace.

Farther afield, the possible beneficial effects of an agreement are more speculative. Iran uses Israel and the Palestinians as propaganda tools to make it more welcome in the Arab world. They are Persians among Arabs, a relatively strong power among relatively weak ones, and Shia among Sunni. They are also ambitious. The natural outcome is for Arab states to coalesce against them. Reports that Saudi Arabia and Qatar support the rebels in Syria, helping to weaken the Assad government, Iran's only ally in the Arab world, demonstrate the depth of this antipathy. Iran cloaks its ambitions with a great show of concern for Palestine in the hopes of weakening the tendency of Arab states to fear it and balance against it. Iran would still do so after an Israel-Palestine agreement, but the tactic might not work as well if there were a Palestinian state. Hizbollah, the Shiite state-within-a-state in Lebanon, probably would not give up its posture of hatred toward Israel. An accord, however, would leave even fewer Lebanese who will accept or support their maintenance of a private army postured versus Israel.

Israel faces a more egregious threat to its safety, the diffusion of the capability for the manufacture of weapons of mass destruction, especially nuclear weapons. Because the state is small, even a single weapon would do terrible damage. For many reasons Israel decided years ago that it needed its own nuclear deterrent and now is estimated to possess between a hundred and two hundred fission weapons. It can presently deliver those weapons by aircraft or ballistic missile to targets at least as far away as Iran and the Caucasus.[102] Israeli missiles are "road mobile" and thus difficult to target preemptively. Israel may ultimately be able to deliver nuclear armed cruise missiles from its growing flotilla of advanced diesel electric submarines. For all intents and purposes, therefore, Israel has a secure second-strike capability against the primitive regional nuclear powers that could emerge, but which do not yet exist, with Iran the most likely candidate.

Israelis, however, do not wish to rely on the threat of retaliation to deter nuclear attack. They would rather not face any risk of nuclear attack. Who can blame them? The United States did not like being in the Soviet gun sights during the Cold War. President Ronald Reagan drew huge domestic support for the Strategic Defense Initiative, a technologically quixotic effort to find a way to destroy sufficient incoming nuclear weapons to limit damage to the United States. The United States also worked throughout the Cold War on the possibility of limiting damage by striking first (or early.)

As strong as Israel is, however, it will not have the capability to limit nuclear damage to itself. Unless Iran decides, or is forced, to give up its nuclear enrichment program, Israel will need to rely on nuclear deterrence. Deterrence is rendered more uncomfortable for Israel by two other factors. As discussed earlier in this chapter, Israelis fear that Iran may have unusually malevolent goals, and also that its leaders may not fear the horror of nuclear war. A dispassionate analysis of Iranian rhetoric and behavior (as reviewed earlier in this chapter) suggests that most of this is posturing. The regime has shown itself aware of what it must do to survive. It has compromised on strategic goals in the past, and it has been careful about how much political violence it practices abroad.

Israel also shares U.S. concerns about the risk of nuclear terrorism— the possibility that a hostile regime could convince itself that it could give a nuclear weapon to a nonstate actor and not have the weapon tracked back to them in the event of its use. Given the Israeli nuclear deterrent, this is a risky scheme for the giver, which would need a very high level of confidence in its ability to elude detection. The Israeli nuclear deterrent should work against this possibility. The risk also exists for Israel that a neighboring state with nuclear weapons could lose control of them in the event of political unrest. Most states have an interest in forestalling such an eventuality, especially the United States. Israeli interests are best served in cooperation with others in this endeavor.

Israel may wage one or more successful preventive attacks in order to assure that no other state in the region ever poses any kind of nuclear threat, but this may prove costly for them, and for the United States. Moreover, it simply may not work.

The United States would find its way eased in the Middle East and Persian Gulf if there were a peace agreement between the Israelis and the Palestinians. Many friends of Israel believe that Israel would also find the security problem associated with attrition attacks, or terrorism, originating in bordering states and territories, ameliorated by such an arrangement. Such an agreement would have to be based on a "two-state solution," which would create a Palestinian state on the West Bank of the Jordan and in Gaza. This would remove a source of tension between the Arab world and Israel, remove a potentially incendiary issue from Arab domestic politics, would take an argument away from Iran, and would remove a source of resentment toward the United States. It would also ensure that Israel remain a liberal democracy.[103] The parameters of a plausible agreement are well known: the Palestinian state would encompass most of the West Bank and Gaza, with some adjustments for the very large Israeli neighborhoods and settlements that have been unfortunately permitted to grow up in the West Bank since the 1967 war. Furthermore a Palestinian state would be substantially demilitarized with the demilitarization provisions supervised by outsiders, and Palestinian refugees from the 1948 and subsequent wars would get citizenship in the new state, and would be compensated for their losses, but would not have a right to return to Israel. Also the new state would agree that these were its final borders and that these arrangements would constitute a final settlement of the dispute. Israel would be fully recognized by the new Palestinian state, which would also agree to suppress violent activities directed from within its boundaries toward the state of Israel.

Despite ample exploratory diplomacy, Israel, Palestine, the United States, and other interested parties have been unable to achieve an actual agreement. There seem to be three main reasons for this and one cannot say that any of them enjoys priority. First, one of the key actors in Palestinian politics, Hamas, which controls Gaza, simply does not agree with this solution; they still aspire to the destruction of Israel. Second, Israeli conservatives simply do not want to see a Palestinian state under the conditions outlined above. It is clear that whether for reasons of nationalist ideology, or national security, a Palestinian State can at best be one or more self-governing "statelets" within a larger territory controlled by Israel. This argument continues to be a winner in Israeli domestic politics. There is a third obstacle, which may or may not be as strong as it appears; even the Palestine Liberation Organization, which controls the West Bank, will not yet give up the "Right of Return" for several

[117]

million refugees who left, or were driven from, their homes in 1948 or 1967, presumably because the PLO believes it would lose power if it admitted that this is a necessary condition to any deal.[104] That said, there are signs that this obstacle could be more of a bargaining chip than a true barrier, to be traded for generous Israeli territorial concessions, and financial compensation that might ameliorate the passions of refugee descendants and create the economic foundation for the new Palestinian state.

The United States is viewed by many as the only player that could conceivably break the logjam. It has long been hoped that the United States would put its own peace plan forward, and bribe, cajole, and pressure the two parties into making the necessary compromises. This has not occurred and is unlikely to occur. The hypothesis has been tested in Republican and Democratic administrations and has failed. There are several reasons for this. The first is that Israel has many politically active friends in the United States, not just American Jews but also evangelical Christians. The second is that Israel has a good and in many ways very American story to tell in the United States. Israel is a Western country, with a pioneer history, a high-tech economy, a democratic government, and a generally successful military. These are qualities greatly admired in the United States. The third is that the Palestinians have only a mixed story to tell. True, many Americans, including many American Jews, are now impressed with the justice of the Palestinian cause. But the Palestinians are disunited, and more important have from time to time been seduced into outright terrorism. Finally, the Palestinians suffer for their associates in the wider Arab world. Even their sometime Saudi friends, with whom the United States has a longstanding alliance, are not much loved in the United States. Americans are unsympathetic to the group that fills its gas tanks at prices that seem vaguely extortionate when compared to the golden age of U.S. gas guzzlers. This was true even prior to the attacks of September 11, 2001, in which fifteen Saudi citizens collaborated. These affective elements would not be dispositive if the United States were a weaker country. But the United States is strong, and so it has been able and willing to accept the downside of its partnership with Israel. The United States has pursued its interests through the sustainment of peace processes that keep hope alive, but U.S. presidents have seen no reason to go beyond process to pressure.

I have no expectation that the United States will move beyond its present policies, but perhaps it can and should distance itself from regional feuds. Lieutenant General Sedky Sobhy, the chief of staff of the Egyptian armed forces, wrote in his thesis for the U.S. Army War College, that "nothing defines better the ideological struggle that the United States has to overcome in the Middle East than the hostility and negative perceptions that exist in the region because of the United States unique and one-sided strategic relationship with Israel."[105] Secretary of State John Kerry managed to relaunch negotiations between the two sides in July of 2013, but there is no apparent new factor overshadowing the talks that leads one to expect a different outcome than in the past. Interested parties in the Middle East, and outside, are now wise to the peace process industry, and seem to view it as a kind of palliative.[106] The "Arab Spring," which has brought to power governments that seem more connected to, and more responsive to, public sentiment, also complicates negotiations. These governments probably do prefer stable relationships with Israel, but they may not be willing to participate in diplomacy that goes nowhere. United States presidents are unlikely to take big domestic political risks to push a process through to fruition. The path of least resistance is to support Israel and encourage diplomacy, and not worry too much if the diplomacy is unsuccessful.

Within the terms and purposes of a Grand Strategy of Restraint the status quo would be a contradiction. The United States ought to reduce its salience across the board in the greater Middle East, including the Israel-Palestine dispute. As part of that policy, the United States should reverse course, returning to its policies prior to the 1967 Arab-Israeli War. Israel then competed militarily with the Arab countries largely on its own nickel. The United States provided little military assistance, and that was in the form of sales of military equipment. After the 1967 war, it appeared that the Soviet Union intended to bury Israel in arms provided to her Arab enemies, and the United States necessarily stepped in, but this risk is gone. Israel is now a rich and successful country. Soon, Israel will enjoy an immense new infusion of wealth from offshore gas fields in the Mediterranean, so much that the country has already set up a sovereign wealth fund.[107] The United States, through its military assistance to Israel, now indirectly subsidizes policies that are not in its interests. I believe that they are not in Israel's interests either. Thus, the United States should move deliberately to reduce this subsidy. The United States can and I believe should sell Israel the weapons it needs to deter attacks from enemy states. The United States should reduce both its grants and sales of arms to other countries in the region as well, depending on the specific internal and external security situation of each of them. Stable Middle East military balances at lower force levels are in everyone's interests. The purpose of reducing military assistance to Israel is not to make the country vulnerable, it is to energize Israeli democracy. The United States should not subsidize, even if indirectly, an ever more deeply rooted system of Israeli political domination in the West Bank and Gaza. Arab populations and elites will not be overjoyed by this fine grained distinction, but it would distance the United States somewhat from these Israeli policies. It would also create the conditions for a more pointed democratic debate in Israel about resource allocation. It might make Israeli decision making more judicious, if Israeli decision makers were to develop some doubt over whether they have essentially a blank check from the United States. Change might even affect the Palestinian negotiating position, because they would have less confidence that the United States would somehow deliver Israel. A continuation of present policies means that the United States is enduringly implicated across the Arab world in the repression of the political aspirations of several million Arabs. That the Arab world is presently busy with other matters, including democratization, the Shia-Sunni conflict, and the threat of Iran, should not lull interested parties into complacency. The Palestinian issue can and probably will resurface.

South Asia: Afghanistan, Pakistan, and India

The main purpose of U.S. policy in South Asia since Al-Qaeda's September 11, 2001, attacks, which were ordered and planned in Afghanistan, has been to eliminate the possibility that this could occur again. Though understandable, this was probably too ambitious, and efforts to achieve this maximalist goal have become counterproductive. A related, and longer-lived interest has been in managing nuclear proliferation in the region. Pakistan and India are both nuclear armed states, and though United States policy probably helped delay this development, it could not stop it, and both tested several weapons in May 1998. Since then, the United States has mainly tried to stop Pakistan from exporting nuclear weapons technology and quietly to ensure that Pakistan secure its weapons from theft. Pakistan did export technology to Iran starting in the late 1980s and to North Korea in the mid-1990s, but it seems to have been induced to stop this activity. The United States also has had an interest in acting through diplomacy to do what it can to reduce the odds of a nuclear war between India and Pakistan, a war that would not threaten the United States directly but would surely be considered an unwelcome precedent. The United States played an active role in limiting the potential for nuclear escalation in the 1999 Kargil crisis.[108] Finally, the United States has an interest that arises from the larger geopolitical changes in Asia: ensuring that India is in a position to play a balancing role as China rises. Insofar as India is jealous of its autonomy, the first rule for U.S. policy should be to do no harm to U.S.-India relations.

Operation Enduring Freedom, launched by President George W. Bush in response to the Al-Qaeda attack on the United States, had the twin purposes of destroying Al-Qaeda, and overthrowing the Taliban government of Afghanistan that had harbored them. The mission initially failed in the first goal. In subsequent years the United States continued to press on Al-Qaeda through neighboring Pakistan, to which it fled. The United States had some success during the Bush administration, much more in the Obama administration, though as noted earlier, it cannot be assumed that Al-Qaeda is finished. There is no disagreeing with the original intent of the U.S. intervention in Afghanistan—the destruction of Al-Qaeda. Even the death of Osama Bin Laden at the hands of United States special operations forces in May 2011 seems not to have entirely finished off the organization. At present, the best the United States can hope for is to keep the pressure on Al-Qaeda on an open-ended basis. This is a reasonable goal, and an important one, but less emotionally satisfying than ringing calls for complete victory. At the same time, efforts to reconstruct Afghanistan and Pakistan as self-sustaining bulwarks against violent extremism are proving futile.

The overthrow of the Taliban regime was intended to deny Al-Qaeda a sanctuary and send a deterrent message to other governments that might consider hosting Al-Qaeda. This was initially a success. Unfortunately, the Afghan Taliban were allowed to reorganize in both Pakistan and Afghanistan and launched an insurgent war of resistance against the United States and the government of Hamid Kharzai, which continues as of this writing. By the time President Obama was elected the Taliban had enjoyed sufficient success to convince U.S. policymakers that they stared catastrophe in the face, so President Obama twice ordered significant reinforcements, more than doubling U.S. troop levels. At its peak, in the summer of 2010, the United States had almost 100,000 troops in Afghanistan. The combined United States and NATO ISAF mission in Afghanistan is scheduled to end in 2014, although some U.S. and other troops are expected to stay behind in a support role for ten more years. The Afghan War is already the longest in U.S. history and may continue in some form.

President Obama announced in 2009 that the U.S. objectives were "to disrupt, dismantle, and defeat Al-Qaeda in Afghanistan and Pakistan, and to prevent its capacity to threaten America and our allies in the future." The second objective included the construction of an Afghan government that could command the loyalty of the population, and which would not give sanctuary to Al-Qaeda. The United States would also organize and train indigenous security forces able and willing to defend the state. As U.S. reinforcements arrived in 2009 and 2010, military operations intensified with the purpose of so weakening the Taliban that it could not threaten the Afghan government. It was hoped that military and political losses might induce the Taliban to negotiate an end to the war, with a visibly strengthening Afghan regime. As of late 2013, this strategy has been unsuccessful: the Taliban remain very strong, the

Afghan regime is fairly weak, and though negotiations are under consideration, they have not commenced.

President Obama also acknowledged in 2009 that Al-Qaeda had installed itself on the other side of the border and insinuated itself into Pakistan's deep internal conflicts. Thus the United States also committed itself to help Pakistan develop its economy, administration, and democratic processes, and to assist its security forces as they battle their own Islamic extremists.[109] Cooperation with Pakistan on these objectives is, as of this writing, characterized by friction and mistrust. Other than on tactical matters, it is doubtful that the United States can have any influence whatsoever in Pakistan's internal politics.

U.S. objectives are probably unachievable. Afghanistan is a desperately poor country, ravaged by thirty years of war, with a government known for corruption. Afghanistan is the world's largest producer of opium, and thus hosts a flourishing and profitable illegal drug trade, which is a source of cash for the Taliban. Despite much U.S. and NATO instruction, the military and police remain poorly trained, inadequately armed, sometimes corrupt, and only intermittently motivated. They are too few to truly control the vast and rugged spaces of Afghanistan.[110] The population of some 29 million is made up of several ethnic groups, and two major strands of Islam, all at odds. The most numerous group are the Pashtuns, of whom some 12 million live in Afghanistan, mostly in the south and east of the country, along the border with Pakistan. The Pashtuns are a warlike people and believe that they are entitled to rule Afghanistan. The Taliban are largely a Pashtun organization and are deeply rooted in the Pashtun population, even if the they are not much loved due to their puritanical and often violent enforcement of an originalist version of Islam. The remaining groups—Tajiks, Uzbeks, and Hazeras—disagree. Hazeras are mainly Shiites and were viciously persecuted by the Sunni Taliban. Given these antipathies, a strong central government is probably unachievable.

Pakistan

When the Obama administration first focused its attention on the resurgent Taliban movement in Afghanistan, it quickly concluded that Pakistan was a closely related problem because nearly 30 million more Pashtuns live in Pakistan, many just across the border, in parts of Pakistan barely under government control. The Taliban thus has millions of additional potential supporters in sanctuaries on the other side of a twenty-five-hundred-kilometer border that is too long and too rugged to police. These Pashtuns give aid and comfort to the Afghan Taliban in exile, and to Al-Qaeda. The Pashtuns on both sides of the border feel

[122]

strong kinship for one another, and it is probably true that many simply view the border as an abstraction. Pakistani Pashtuns often fight alongside their brethren in Afghanistan. Neither the Afghan nor the Pakistani Taliban have any difficulty raising money, acquiring arms, or training and motivating new fighters.[111] The border itself, the Durand Line, is not recognized by Afghanistan, a sore point with Pakistan because in the past, there were Pashtun efforts to secede from Pakistan. These have been quiescent in recent years. Instead, Pashtuns on both sides of the border have supported Pashtun control of Afghanistan, and at the same time struggled to preserve Pashtun autonomy in Pakistan. The Pakistani military, most notably its intelligence service, the ISI, has also supported the Afghan Taliban, even as it has often fought against its own home-grown version. Members of the Pakistani Taliban have at various times made common cause with the Afghan Taliban, though the movements appear at present to have different aims, with each engaged in struggles with its own nominal government. The U.S. strategy in Afghanistan has thus included a major effort to transform Pakistan.

The Pakistani Army identifies Afghanistan as a vital interest. They assert that a friendly Afghanistan provides them with "strategic depth" in their conflict with India, though inhospitable terrain and poor roads makes this argument seem silly if taken literally. Instead Pakistan probably has two interests. First, "Strategic Depth" is probably code language for another problem—forestalling the rise of a unified Pashtun nationalist movement, which could precipitate the further dissolution of Pakistan, indeed potentially its final dissolution.[112] The Pakistani military wants to keep state-oriented Pashtun nationalism focused on Kabul. The Afghan Taliban were and are a vehicle for this policy. The generals also fear that if India were friendly with Afghanistan, it could use it as a base to foment rebellion, especially in Balochistan.[113] The Pakistani Army thus prefers a pliant regime in Kabul and was very satisfied when the Taliban controlled most, but not all of Afghanistan. The Taliban war with the "Northern Alliance" of Tajiks and other ethnic groups kept the Taliban busy and dependent. It is thus very likely that the Pakistani Army will continue to support, even if secretly, the Afghan Taliban.[114] The leadership of the Afghan Taliban has been comfortably ensconced in Quetta in Balochistan since its escape from Kabul.

Pakistan was the majority Muslim country forged out of the British exit from India, but it is a deeply fissured society—ethnically, religiously, economically, and geographically. Roughly half the population is Punjabi, and the Punjabis have the lion's share of the power in the society and dominate the army. For historical reasons, the army is the strongest institution in society; occasionally it has taken power and ruled directly, though at present there is a civilian government. The army is committed to policies that preserve its influence in society. Pakistan's problems are as immune to outside intervention as Afghanistan's. The population of Pakistan is huge; at nearly 190 million people, the sixth most populous country in the world, size alone militates against the success of foreign reformers. Much of the land is still controlled by a small, semifeudal elite, resistant to reform. Pakistan is also one of the most corrupt countries in the world.

Though Punjabis "rule," they face competition. There are some 30 million Pashtuns, of which perhaps two-thirds live in the loosely governed Federally Administered Tribal Areas (FATA) and Khyber Pakhtunkhwa Province (formerly the Northwest Frontier Province) along the border with Afghanistan.[115] The Pakistani Taliban is strong in these areas, and it opposes even the traditionally weak writ of the central government. Recent offensives and terrorist actions suggest that it may wish to drive it entirely from these areas or even to topple the state altogether. The province of Balochistan in southwestern Pakistan is thinly populated, but Balochis are presently the group most committed to secession. The Pakistani military suppresses secessionist tendencies brutally in Balochistan. Finally, in southeastern Pakistan, including the port city of Karachi, are the Sindhis. In the past they too have shown dissatisfaction with Pakistan's government, and exhibited secessionist tendencies.

Pakistan is also riven between the two major strains of Islam; some 20 percent of the population is Shiite; violence against Shiites is common, including deliberate, organized, large-scale terrorist attacks. Among Sunnis there are two major tendencies, Barelvism which is politically rather benign, and Deobandism, which has since the late 1970s become puritanical and violent, and quite similar to the religious views of Al-Qaeda.[116] The Pakistani Taliban are Deobandis, though Deobandism is common throughout Pakistan. There are other violent fundamentalist Punjabi movements in Pakistan, most notably Lashkar e Taiba, which follows a religious tradition akin to Saudi Arabian Wahhabism, which some consider to be more "fundamentalist" even than Deobandism.

Islam is nevertheless the main idea holding Pakistan together, and the Pakistani Army has been very supportive of fundamentalist Islam as a unifying tool. The sum of these ethnic and religious fissures, however, is that from a purely internal point of view Pakistan is deeply insecure. The perception of insecurity is magnified by the history of the state, which once encompassed the now independent country of Bangladesh, formerly "East Pakistan." Despite sharing the Muslim faith, the people of Bangladesh tired of rule from Islamabad and rebelled; with the help of India they achieved independence. This example troubles the Pakistani military, who fear that this pattern could repeat itself. It also raises the issue of the threat from India, and the closely related conflict in Kashmir.

Kashmir and India

Since its birth, Pakistan has been in an unequal conflict with India, and it is falling further behind. The countries have fought four wars, three of them directly over disputed Kashmir. With nearly 1.2 billion people, India is the second most populous country in the world. Though predominately Hindu, some 160 million Muslims live in India. The division of the British raj was accompanied by wholesale confessional violence and what today we would call ethnic "cleansing." Hundreds of thousands of people were murdered as Hindu and Muslim populations were pushed or pulled across the borders of the two new countries. Some members of the Indian political class doubted the wisdom of the separation; some analysts still do. The violence of the partition, the disparity in size, and suspicions about India's ambitions, combined to make Pakistan insecure from birth. Pakistan's geography magnifies its insecurity; it is comparatively long and narrow; from the point of view of conventional warfare Pakistani soldiers have long feared that India could cut it in two. Pakistan's perception of vulnerability is getting worse despite its acquisition of a nuclear deterrent, because, in contrast to India's Cold War economic somnolence, it is now a fast-growing economy and widely viewed as a candidate great power, whereas Pakistan's economy is relatively stagnant. Pakistan cannot compete in most domains; its nuclear deterrent is its only defense against external attack.

The enduring dispute over Kashmir serves to keep Pakistani-Indian enmity energized. At the time of partition, Kashmir was one of many independent princely states in India. These states were meant to be able to choose whether to join Pakistan or India. The maharaja of Kashmir was a Hindu, but the majority of the population was Muslim. Pakistan and India schemed to get control; Pakistan supported Kashmiri militants, and India supported the maharaja. War ensued and Kashmir was quickly divided with Pakistan controlling about a third and India two-thirds of the territory. Muslims are the bulk of the population even in the Indian zone. In subsequent years, Pakistan supported Kashmiri insurgents in the Indian zone, and India repressed this insurgency with great brutality. Pakistani intelligence has made common cause with its own violent fundamentalist groups such as Lashkar y Taiba to recruit and train foot soldiers for this war. In the 1999 Kargil war, Pakistan mixed militants from these groups with its own "special operations" forces to cross the line of control in Kashmir and alter the status quo. India counterattacked and essentially drove them out, though U.S. diplomacy did finally help push the Pakistani president to order a withdrawal.[117] At present, though the insurgency is at a low ebb, India maintains nearly a half million troops in the area. In the last decade the two countries attempted "track two" negotiations to find a settlement of the dispute, and some analysts believe that progress was made. Nevertheless, nothing has come of it, and there is good reason to believe that nothing will, in part because the Pakistani Army is committed to the struggle.[118] Observers often argue that the United States should help settle this dispute, in order to focus Pakistan's energies on its internal security problems. India does not want the United States involved in what it perceives to be its business, and the United States has complied because it highly values the relationship with India.[119]

There is little reason to believe that the Pakistani Army would sanction any accord over Kashmir short of complete victory. The army sustains the conflict with India over Kashmir as a tool to mobilize Islamic solidarity in Pakistan. Islam is the ideological glue that helps hold Pakistan together, and the army is the institution that applies the glue. The conflict over Kashmir keeps the larger conflict with India alive, which in turn provides the overarching political reason for army dominance of Pakistan.[120] Given that India is an emerging great power, which has fought to retain Kashmir since partition, it is unlikely that it would make sufficient concessions to permit the Pakistani Army to claim victory. Thus this conflict will likely endure.

Pakistan offers a nurturing environment for Islamic extremists. The Pakistani Army protects its homegrown militant Islamists as foot soldiers for the Kashmir conflict, especially the Punjabi ones, so long as they do not threaten the state directly.[121] Leaked NATO documents suggest that the Pakistani security services continue to support the Afghan Taliban and Pakistani militant groups such as the Haqqani network and Lashkar Y Taiba.[122] These groups seem to have close, if complicated, relationships with the Pakistani Pashtun fundamentalist groups, and also with Al-Qaeda.[123] Al-Qaeda fled Afghanistan in 2002 as the United States took over the country. Once in Pakistan, Al-Qaeda appears to have found succor from every militant quarter—the Afghan Taliban in exile, various Pakistani Pashtun sympathizers of the Afghan Taliban (some of whom have since organized themselves as the Pakistani Taliban), and finally the other fundamentalist armed groups, especially Lashkar y Taiba.[124] Though Pakistani intelligence has often helped the United States to apprehend Al-Qaeda elements, it has until recently tended to look the other way so far at its homegrown militants are concerned.[125] Some Pakistani Pashtun elements became uncontrollable in the last several years, and the Pakistani Army then turned on them violently. That said, the Pakistani Army operates at its own speed. Some parts of FATA are still safe areas for militants as of this writing.[126] Based on past experience, one suspects that the Pakistani Army will be unable or unwilling to sustain sufficient presence even in those areas it has pacified to truly finish off the Pakistani Taliban, other extremist elements, and their Al-Qaeda guests.

A Change of U.S. Policy

The ambitious U.S. plans to build stable governments in Afghanistan and Pakistan that are able and willing to resist both foreign and domestic violence by Islamist militants is unlikely to work because of the complex web of militancy, fear, ambition, and even hatred embedded in the Afghanistan-Pakistan-India relationship. The large U.S. troop presence in Afghanistan, and the visible U.S. meddling and hectoring in Pakistani politics, energized individuals against the United States.[127] While enemies of the United States will hang on in these countries even if the United States were to depart, the current U.S. effort injects more energy into the opposition than is necessary. What then is to be done?

The United States first needs to remember why it is in this part of the world and what it is reasonable to expect. Al-Qaeda is the principal problem. Annihilating them would be the preferred outcome, but the facts suggest that this level of success is unlikely. Al-Qaeda has enough friends in the region that it can probably survive, if only as a fugitive. Thus the United States will need to moderate its goals. The objective should be to keep the pressure on, subject to wise conservation of U.S. resources.[128] This means ratcheting down the U.S. counterinsurgency, nation-building project in Afghanistan at the earliest possible time. The president has stated that all U.S. combat troops will be withdrawn from Afghanistan by the end of 2014; he should stick to this plan, no matter what develops. The United States has had little if any success separating the Pakistani military from its Afghan Taliban Pashtun proxies. Unless this occurs, defeat of the Taliban in Afghanistan is improbable. Thus the United States must simply accept that the Taliban will have an important role in Afghanistan. The United States should signal this understanding to Pakistan. The Afghans must solve their own internal political problems; the only U.S. requirement is that Al-Qaeda not have free run of the country. Promises are insufficient, so the United States should essentially restore the Northern Alliance that once resisted the Taliban, which allied with the United States to overthrow them. The United States should support non-Pashtun Afghans with money, weaponry, training, and political support. The United States should also continue to support any Pashtuns who wish to resist Taliban domination. With the U.S. backing its favorite factions, and Pakistan backing its favorite factions, the best that external powers and internal factions can hope for is a stalemate. Inclusion of all factions in a weak coalition government is the most plausible solution. The United States should make clear that the migration of Al-Qaeda elements into Afghanistan will be met with the same kind of targeted killings that the United States now directs at Al-Qaeda in Pakistan.

The United States should limit its own objectives in Pakistan to the suppression of Al-Qaeda. A firm stand against them by the Pakistani government will be easier if the U.S. war in Afghanistan winds down and if U.S. military activity in Pakistan is reduced. The United States may wish to continue aid to the Pakistani Army and internal security forces, but this aid should focus on improving their internal security capabilities and should only be proffered if there is evidence that Pakistan is indeed suppressing dangerous militants. The United States is now extremely unpopular in Pakistan, and U.S. military activity is one cause of this unpopularity.[129] The Pakistani people apparently blame the U.S. war in Afghanistan for radicalizing their homegrown militants. To the greatest extent possible, the United States should try to take this argument out of Pakistani politics. Unfortunately, this will be difficult because targeted strikes on Al-Qaeda in Pakistan may need to continue, if Al-Qaeda elements are permitted to remain in Pakistan. If so, these strikes should be tightly focused on Al-Qaeda and its closest supporters. Admittedly, even limited U.S. military activity will probably continue to irritate Pakistani citizens. At the same time, the United States should target some aid to Pakistani civil society simply in order to make a few friends and to demonstrate that U.S. intentions are not malign.[130] The United States should have no illusions about this aid; in and of itself it will not eliminate radical politics from Pakistan, nor stabilize democracy, nor change the balance between civilian and military authority in the country. It has already proven difficult to provide effective assistance, in part due to widespread corruption in Pakistan.[131]

The United States will need to accept that Pakistani help in Afghanistan and against Al-Qaeda may be partial and grudging. On the other hand, free of some of the U.S. pressure emanating from Afghanistan, and free of the Afghan Taliban who may return home, the Pakistani Army may find it easier politically to suppress some of its homegrown militants and their Al-Qaeda allies. That said, the United States faces a more enduring problem in its relations with Pakistan. United States leaders have been trying to improve relations with India since the Cold War ended. This has become more pressing with the growth of Chinese power and its likely future trajectory. If Pakistani military leaders and politicians find it in their interests to sustain the conflict with India, they will find the United States increasingly unsympathetic. Conversely, the United States will find it ever more difficult to appear evenhanded.

[128]

Three sets of possible risks could attend the transition to a policy of Restraint: geopolitical risks, "windows" risks, and great power nuclear proliferation risks. Below I assess these risks and recommend tactics to mitigate them.

Geopolitical risks are often highlighted by advocates of an alternative grand strategy advanced during the 1990s—Selective Engagement.[132] United States disengagement would create a "multipolar" Eurasia, with several relatively equal powers. International relations theorists and statesmen have not seen such a system for two-thirds of a century, and what they remember they do not like. First, such systems are subject to collective action problems. In the face of one state growing its power through internal efforts, and/or external expansion, the potential victims may hope that one of their number will step forward to do the heavy lifting of containment. Balancing is sometimes tardy and often inefficient. Despite a nominal balance of power, the ambitious state may develop a lead. Tardy and inefficient balancing behavior was a hallmark of the wars against Napoleon, and the initial efforts to stop Nazi Germany. An aggressive state can therefore sometimes upend a nominal balance of power system and threaten to establish hegemony. Second, the ambitious state will typically pay a lot of attention to its military because it is looking for opportunities. They occasionally develop major or minor military innovations that permit them to exploit their initial advantages to further improve their power positions through conquest. Revolutionary France invented and Napoleon perfected the mass conscription army; the German Imperial Army concocted the Schleffen Plan; and the Wehrmacht was the first military organization to master mechanized warfare, including the close integration of tactical aviation. Exploiting such innovations may give these states a military edge for a period of time. Finally, initial conquests are sometimes cumulative. Conquests are not perfectly additive, and this propensity varies across time and space. Sometimes the gains are geographical, improving the reach of one's military. Neither the German Luftwaffe nor the German submarine force was in a strong position to threaten Britain in World War II until the fall of the Low Countries and France. Sometimes they are material; in World War II the Germans were quite adept at integrating conquered economies into their war machine.

None of the forgoing problems is inevitable and the odds of these events occurring presently seem quite low. Nevertheless, it is possible that conquest might "pay" for a hostile state, further increasing its incentive and capacity for aggression. In the past, both of the principal offshore powers of modern international politics, Britain and the United

[129]

States, have paid a high price to reverse the early gains of an aggressive and skillful hegemon. This includes the Napoleonic wars, and the First and Second World wars. The United States needs to be sensitive to the possibility that a U.S. Strategy of Restraint could leave Eurasia open to such events in the long term. It is worth buying some insurance against them. Most of this insurance is military; the United States should retain capabilities that permit reengagement if necessary. These are discussed in the next chapter. United States diplomats and intelligence agencies also would have a role to play.

A second and related set of risks arise from the possible pace of change. United States disengagement requires that U.S. security dependencies develop capabilities to defend themselves and their interests—otherwise, windows of opportunity and vulnerability may emerge. The allies will need to increase and diversify their armed forces, and develop mechanisms of cooperation that do not depend on U.S. leadership. As discussed at the outset of this chapter, they will also need to arrange for nuclear deterrence or adapt to its absence. Practically speaking, I doubt that they can make this transition quickly. Efforts to force too quick a pace could backfire and involve the United States in exactly the kind of trouble it is trying to escape. First, these are all democracies and are accustomed to spending little on defense. They will need to have political debates about how much more spending they need and of what kind, which will wend their way slowly through their national institutions. Given the weakness of their plausible adversaries, states such as Germany, France, Britain, and Italy, are unlikely to view U.S. disengagement as meriting extraordinary measures. On the other hand, they are already quite well placed to meet the challenges of security autonomy. The Japanese polity, on the other hand, is simply unaccustomed to thinking about defense as a national responsibility. A jump in defense spending is politically unlikely even if the United States is packing up. Second, the military organizations of even the largest U.S. allies are deficient. Most U.S. allies have limited strategic intelligence, command and control, and power projection capability, and maintain only small stocks of advanced munitions and spare parts. Third, the allies are accustomed to the United States serving as the political and military leader of any large enterprise. In Europe the allies would need to work out new relationships, though the European Union experience gives them a leg up. In Asia there is no experience of cooperation among the principal powers. Fourth, and perhaps most important, Germany and Japan do not have their own nuclear weapons. A weakening of the United States extended nuclear deterrent commitment means big decisions for them, which I have discussed above.

Given these problems, rapid U.S. military disengagement could create windows of opportunity or vulnerability tempting some to engage in fait accompli diplomacy, land grabs versus states too weak to defend their interests, or even preventive war. If any or all of these problems were quickly to emerge as the United States was trying to disengage, the United States might not beat them out the door, or would have a difficult time following through with its plans, because of the appearance of emerging chaos. The larger point, that conflict in Eurasia would not produce a major threat to the United States, and the principal states of Eurasia are capable of managing their own security affairs, could be lost. Any relaxation of U.S. commitments involves uncertainty and risk. This is an important reason why analysts are chary of great change. There is no perfect way to ameliorate these risks. I favor a deliberate transition that would likely take a decade. The United States needs to credibly commit to a reduced presence if the allies are to step up. To make this commitment credible it needs to withdraw forces. To give the allies time to adapt, the transition ought not to happen quickly.

INTEGRATED REFORMS

More than twenty years after the end of the Cold War, the United States remains intensively engaged around the globe. This effort is costly—economically, militarily, and politically. Though some engagement is warranted, this effort is excessive. Above I have suggested how the most important U.S. interests can be adequately protected at lower costs. Though policymakers could pick and choose from the reforms outlined in this chapter, they are mutually reinforcing. If wealthy or unusually bold allies are to be encouraged to take responsibility for their fates, then the evidence that the United States is changing its policies in one region makes its intentions more credible in other regions. Because one purpose of the strategy is to make the United States a less attractive target for violent political entrepreneurs motivated by identity politics, it makes sense to reduce the U.S. profile as much as possible, in as many politically riven regions and societies as possible, and to avoid taking on new commitments in such places. I remind the reader that these changes should be accomplished deliberately but not precipitately. Change needs to come fast enough to free significant resources for other U.S. projects and to be credible to others so that they adapt. It needs to be slow enough to permit our allies to prepare themselves for their new responsibilities.

In Europe and Asia, the United States presently devotes excessive resources to the protection of states wealthy enough to defend themselves entirely or to make much greater contributions to their own security. United States treaty relationships, and concomitant military commitments, can and should be revised to change the balance of responsibility with these coalition partners, so that they are in the first instance responsible for their own fates. Asia is the more dynamic region, and a linear extrapolation of present trends could imply a significant threat to U.S. interests. I argue that the present situation is conducive to more local responsibility, and if the future turns out to be as challenging as some predictions suggest, then the United States will not be able to oppose Chinese power with the same alliance strategy that it used during the Cold War. Allies will need to step up; the time to endow them with responsibility is now. Moreover, the United States will have to face squarely the issue of extended nuclear deterrence. In my view, should China prove powerful and ambitious, then more nuclear proliferation, not less, will be part of the answer.

In the Persian Gulf, the United States needs to be much clearer in its ambitions and more candid about what military power can achieve. The United States can defend the flow of oil from the gulf; it can help defend gulf states from one another. The United States should not maintain military power to intervene in the internal politics of these countries. And the U.S. military should keep a low profile in order to avoid arousing nationalist and/or religious antipathy.

The United States should acknowledge that the Zionist project, to which it has contributed significantly, is a success; Israel is now a capable and secure country. There is presently no viable Arab war coalition against it, even if the Arab states cared very much, which does not appear to be the case. The remaining issue is with the Palestinians, who will require a state of their own if they are ever to become quiescent. The "two-state" solution is in the U.S. interest. If this does not occur, Israelis may remain secure against traditional foreign threats, but their lives will probably never be normal—they will face constant low level violence from Palestinians and their sympathizers. And the United States will face constant hectoring from Arab politicians and political entrepreneurs about its subsidy of a political arrangement that is inherently unfair to the Palestinians, and over which it is willing to exercise little influence. Perhaps these are just nuisances, which both Israel and the United States can manage. But the persistence of the ill will, and occasional bouts of violence, occasioned by the Palestinian problem, suggests that benign neglect has its own costs and risks. As part of a Grand Strategy of Restraint, the United States should reduce, if not eliminate altogether its military subsidies to Israel. The United States should sell Israel the weapons it needs to remain secure from foreign threats but should distance itself from the occupation.

In South Asia, the United States is simply in too deep. A punitive war against the Taliban in Afghanistan in 2001 was necessary; a war of political reconstruction was not. Given the negative consequences that often

[132]

arise from large-scale military presence, the United States should be moving toward the lowest possible commitment of military force to the region consistent with keeping Al-Qaeda on the defensive. The United States should help those who are willing to cooperate in this endeavor, but be prepared in extremis to bypass those who do not cooperate, or who actively help Al-Qaeda. The United States simply must not take on additional commitments that are unlikely to bear fruit.

The lessons of fighting Al-Qaeda in South Asia should be applied elsewhere. The United States and other states will need to cooperate to keep the pressure on Al-Qaeda and to guard against the future emergence of other nihilistic groups. This should mainly be an intelligence and police activity, backed up by special operations forces and on rare occasions, conventional forces. Once again, the United States will need to control its expectations and consider the dilemmas that arise. Being on the offensive all the time in failed or poorly governed states is an expensive way to fight terror. And it may produce unintended political consequences—creating new recruits for the adversary. Though we cannot show that U.S. offensive military action inevitably produces more terrorists and more terrorism, there is good reason to suspect that a high and martial profile helps to generate antipathy to the United States, which may create a more supportive environment for the more violent and determined enemies.

Nuclear proliferation will be an enduring problem for all advanced countries. Nuclear weapons have proven to be very valuable tools for nation-states trying to enhance their security against the risk of invasion. Dreams of the abolition of nuclear weapons are unlikely to overcome their powerful strategic utility. The United States must reconcile itself to the multilateral management of proliferation, rather than its prevention. At best proliferation can be slowed. This is advantageous. But the key to U.S. security in a nuclear armed world is a potent secure retaliatory capability backed by an intelligence and warning system that can properly attribute responsibility for any attack on the United States. The risk of nuclear weapons falling into the hands of violent nonstate actors can be limited, in the first instance through deterrence of attempts to transfer these weapons from states to such actors. The risk that weapons could simply be stolen or lost can be addressed through the sharing of best practices. The hardest case is the potential for theft, especially in the case of domestic instability in nuclear weapons states. The United States and other nuclear states must maintain contingency plans for such events, but we must also acknowledge that we cannot ensure against every eventuality. This is a fact of life in the nuclear age. The alternative, "preventive war" against potential new nuclear powers, is unlikely to be a sustainable answer.

[133]

No grand strategy promises the assurance of 100 percent security. It is easy to forget that the United States had no answer to the massive strategic nuclear forces of the Soviet Union other than deterrence. The United States could not successfully destroy all Soviet nuclear forces in a first strike and had essentially no defenses to degrade incoming Soviet missiles. Similarly, the United States lives every day with the possibility that domestic or foreign violent non-state actors will find resources within the borders of the United States with which to harm Americans. Properly employed, the U.S. military and intelligence services can prevent a wide range of threats, deter others, and reduce others to a low level. In this chapter I have sketched out the political ingredients of a Restraint Strategy. In the next chapter I develop the appropriate military strategy and force structure to support this grand strategy.

[3]

Command of the Commons

THE MILITARY STRATEGY, FORCE STRUCTURE, AND FORCE POSTURE OF RESTRAINT

This chapter develops a military strategy that supports the Grand Strategy of Restraint. It also outlines the military capabilities required. The Grand Strategy of Restraint is best served by a "maritime" military strategy. A maritime military strategy focuses on the development of disproportionate U.S. influence over global communications—the movement of goods and information. The United States presently enjoys substantial military influence over communications, which I have called "command of the commons."[1] In the past, communications strategies emphasized the sea, and hence past writers on maritime strategy provide the inspiration for the recommended military strategy. The United States presently enjoys command of the sea, but also command of the air over much of the globe, and command of space. I review these terms and defend my assessment in greater detail below. The important point is that the United States presently enjoys highly privileged access to these media and can under a range of circumstances significantly limit the access of others. The Grand Strategy of Restraint aims to preserve U.S. influence in Eurasia and to address new security threats that lie outside the realm of traditional geopolitical analysis, and to do so at the least political, military, and economic costs. A maritime strategy well serves these purposes militarily.

This military strategy and associated force structure are self-consciously resource constrained. My goal is to develop a military strategy and force structure that does not require more than 2.5 percent of GDP to support it. Why 2.5 percent? First, I have argued that there are a limited number of interests that truly matter to U.S. security, fewer interests than the current U.S. military effort is trying to achieve. Hence if Restraint is the grand strategy, the United States can surely spend less on the military than it does presently or intends to spend over the next decade.[2] Second, picking a ceiling imposes discipline on one's choices; it forces hard thinking about the real utility of any particular element of military power. It also creates pressures for efficiency throughout the force. Third, this goal responds to present concerns about the long-term fiscal health of the United States. Some cuts to spending plans for the next decade have already been imposed in order to contribute to bringing U.S. revenues and spending into an ultimate balance. It is likely that more cuts will be necessary. The United States is a prosperous country, it could afford to spend a much higher share of national wealth on the military, if it had to do so, and a healthy economy would make it easier to increase spending if that day ever comes.

"COMMAND OF THE COMMONS"

The U.S. military currently possesses command of the global commons: command of the sea, command of space, and command of the air. The "commons," in the case of the sea and space, are areas that belong to no one state and provide access to much of the globe.[3] Airspace does technically belong to the countries below it, but there are few countries that can deny their airspace above fifteen thousand feet to U.S. warplanes, although this is changing. Rich countries can purchase very effective air defense systems of a kind that we have not yet seen in combat. Command of the commons is analogous to command of the sea, or in Paul Kennedy's words, it is analogous to "naval mastery."[4] Command does not mean that other states cannot use the commons in peacetime. Nor does it mean that others cannot acquire military assets that can move through or even exploit them when unhindered by the United States. Command means that the United States gets vastly more military use out of the sea, space, and air than do others, that the United States can credibly threaten to deny their use to others, and that others would lose a military contest for the commons if they attempted to deny them to the United States. Having lost such a contest they could not mount another effort for a very long time, and the United States would preserve, restore, and consolidate its hold after such a fight. The insights of maritime and naval strategists can provide guidance for how command of the commons can be leveraged for future U.S. military strategy.

THE INSIGHTS OF MARITIME STRATEGY

Maritime strategists are interested in more than sea battles.[5] They are interested in how operations and capabilities at sea can influence events

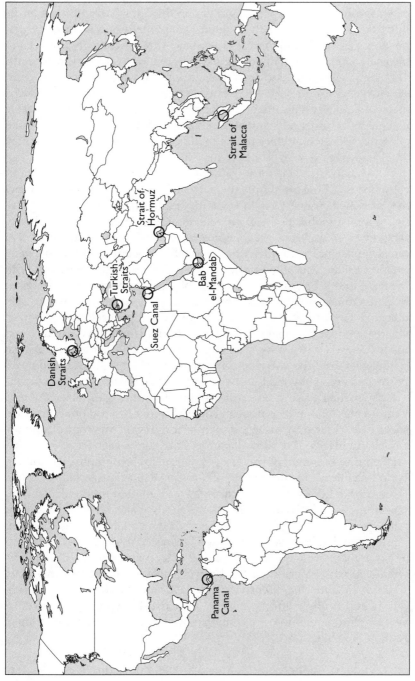

MAP 2 Major chokepoints

ashore by dominating the most significant channels of global communications. Most of world politics occurs on the Eurasian land mass, or its littorals, and aside from the United States, the world's consequential powers are to be found there. These powers are now deeply involved in international trade and depend greatly on that trade for their prosperity. Though some of this trade can move overland, water remains the least expensive way to move large quantities of finished goods, fuel, and raw materials. Energy imports in particular originate in politically unstable parts of the world, and if any of these powers were ever tempted to reach out with their own military power to protect their sources of supply, they would have to do so over the oceans.

World maps showing various "chokepoints" are a staple of geopolitical analysis.[6] These are simply the most obvious manifestation of the fact that maritime strategy depends greatly on the shape of things, the configuration of global political and economic power, overlaid on the arrangement of land and ocean. Sometimes this produces outcomes that remain constant for very long time periods. For example, by virtue of its location Britain was able to defend its empire and its home islands with the same forces. Britain's very position blocked the access of its continental peers to the wider world. And these peers also needed to fear each other on land, further limiting their ability to generate naval power, whereas Britain, an island, faced no such problem.[7] Thus Britain could easily focus on naval power, defend itself, and hold her empire against challengers until the late nineteenth century, when industrial and naval powers emerged beyond Europe, first the United States and then Japan.

Japan in the Pacific faced a different problem during the Second World War. A combination of European colonial weakness, a moment of local superiority created by the legacy of interwar naval arms control, and the strategic initiative did allow Japan to stake out a vast oceanic empire. That empire was still, however, "penned in" by geography. During the period of maximum British, French, and U.S. weakness, following the Pearl Harbor attack, Japanese carriers were able to raid the British Empire in the Indian Ocean. This was their only major foray beyond their initial winnings in the South China Sea. The map tells us why. The configuration of land and sea constrained Japan's access to the open oceans.[8] The island empire required a great deal of ship-borne trade to exploit its winnings, which permitted the United States to mount the only truly victorious submarine offensive of the last century. This problem is enduring and strongly affects China's future maritime prospects as well; it is, if anything even more boxed in than was Japan, in part because Japan is part of the box.

The geographic position of the United States is well suited to a maritime strategy. Though North America does not naturally block other

[138]

great powers from access to the open oceans, neither is there any geographical feature proximate to the United States that blocks U.S. access to either the Pacific or the Atlantic. The Panama Canal, though no longer under direct U.S. control, permits the United States to move naval power easily from one coast to the other. It can concentrate its navy when needed. Because the United States faces no great power neighbors, it is free to focus its military investments on an oceangoing navy and its supporting assets, and free to orient its army, however large or small, entirely on preparation for expeditionary operations. Only one other great power can access both the Pacific and Atlantic—Russia, and its Pacific reach is limited by the comparative underdevelopment and thin population of its eastern parts. Russia and continental Europe face chokepoints on the way to the open sea. India will ultimately be very strong in the Indian Ocean but would face obstacles breaking out, and China famously faces the "first and second island chains" obstructing its access to the open oceans.[9] Japan, presently the third most potent economy in the world, and likely to remain in the top five for years to come, dominates much of the second Island chain, so neutralizing that barrier would be a difficult problem for China. Japan itself faces no obstacle to her eastern access to the Pacific other than the United States.

Command of the open oceans only creates potential. Historically, sea power has lent strategic or tactical support to campaigns on land. The First and Second World wars were settled by land campaigns supported by sea and air power. The nuclear revolution, however, has fundamentally altered great power security relations. It is difficult to conceive of decisive land campaigns by one nuclear power against another. The essence of the nuclear revolution is that countries that possess secure retaliatory forces probably cannot be conquered; the risks to the attacker of attempting to do so are too great. The Cold War is our only case study of a great power competition among nuclear powers. Despite confronting one another across the world with massive nonnuclear forces, the two superpowers avoided direct combat. The risk of nuclear escalation seems to have created downward pressure against escalatory moves. So long as great powers possess nuclear weapons, their natural competition will likely be managed with great care. To the extent that force is used, one can expect proxy wars, attempts to coerce or conquer lesser nonnuclear states, shows of force, and in the event of direct military conflict, efforts to keep the combat limited in means, space, or duration. (The latter, for reasons discussed earlier, will not be easy.) Naval forces, supported by air and space assets, are good choices for this kind of conflict. Moreover, it seems that the principal powers are now essentially "bourgeois" states. They are all in it for the money, not for the spread of universal truths by the sword. This too exerts some downward pressure on escalation although nationalism could still be the source of serious clashes. One suspects therefore that we are in an age of limited rather than total war and that conflict will be linked with commerce. Command of the media by which most commerce occurs will be a powerful means of taking the profit out of war for one's adversaries.

The Strategic Dividends of Command of the Commons

Command of the commons, like command of the sea, contributes efficiently and directly to a balance-of-power strategy on the Eurasian land mass. Command of the commons allows the United States to build its own strength, weaken adversaries, and concentrate combat power to assist allies, or strike adversaries ashore.

In the first instance, coupled with the favorable U.S. geographic position, and with nuclear weapons, command buys the United States time to build up its own capabilities.[10] Although the United States no longer enjoys the huge superiority in productive capacity relative to all challengers that proved so decisive in the Second World War, it is still an enormously capable economy with significant reserves that can be mobilized when pressed. Command also allows the United States to import needed resources for such a mobilization from many parts of the globe and deny those parts to its adversaries. To the extent that other states are threatened, all can cooperate in improving their military capabilities. Because neither the United States nor any other advanced industrial power has launched a true mobilization since World War II, people forget how quickly new military power can be generated. Most of the combatants in that war were able to move from a peacetime economy to a very high degree of military production in roughly thirty months. Command of the commons enables a more efficient and more complete mobilization of resources.[11]

Command also allows the United States to bring together the extant military capabilities of other powers. Though U.S. allies currently devote too little to their military efforts, many have contributed something to the military operations of the last twenty years. None of these operations have opposed truly great powers, so enemy attacks on lines of communication have not been an issue. Nevertheless, unopposed use of the sea and even of the air has been a quiet but important fact of these operations. More important, command has allowed the United States to bring vast numbers of forces from other parts of the world to these contingencies. Command of the commons has permitted the United States to wage war on short notice even where it has had little permanent military presence. This was true of the 1991 Persian Gulf War, the 2001 war in Afghanistan, and the 2003 war with Iraq. The United States put a credible offensive capability into the Persian Gulf to counter Iraq's invasion of Kuwait by the end of November 1990, four months after the Iraqi invasion of Kuwait. The United States waited until January to start the war so that it could bring in even more force. The United States was at war with the Taliban regime in Afghanistan roughly a month after the terrorist attacks on New York and Washington, D.C., on September 11, 2001.

Command of the commons permits the isolation of the adversary from sources of political and military support, further increasing the U.S. margin of superiority and further allowing the passage of time to work in favor of the United States This is especially useful against adversaries who themselves depend on exports and imports. Allies of the United States do have large numbers of good, small-to-medium naval surface combatants, especially useful for maintaining a blockade.[12] (These ships performed surveillance missions in the worldwide war on terror as well.)[13] They played important roles in the isolation of Iraq, which was under economic embargo from 1990. This embargo itself was a consequence of a pre–Desert Storm U.S. diplomacy that worked assiduously to marshal international support to contain Iraq, after that country had clearly marked itself as an aggressor. Although between 1990 and 2003 Iraq illegally exported some oil and illegally imported some weapons and military technology, its military suffered greatly in those years. It essentially failed to modernize in any significant way and was prevented from recovering its ability to invade its neighbors. The erosion of Iraq's conventional combat power contributed to U.S. confidence as it considered an invasion of Iraq in the autumn of 2002. Once the Third Persian Gulf War began in March 2003, it rapidly became clear that Iraqi conventional weapons had on the whole not improved since 1991. Over the previous decade, the U.S. Navy and allied navies quietly helped to starve Iraq's army and air force. Had they not done so, U.S. casualties in March 2003 would surely have been higher. Presently the United States and its allies are putting a great deal of economic pressure on Iran to induce it to restrain its nuclear enrichment program. On the whole, trade and investment is being suppressed at the source, as corporations and countries are threatened with denial of access to United States and other markets if they continue to trade with Iran. That said, U.S. ability to monitor the trade through national intelligence means, and in extremis through naval surveillance and search, are powerful backstops to these agreements.

Under present conditions, command of the commons permits the United States to threaten economic costs to states heavily involved in international trade and investment. This is not a magic bullet. As the early twentieth-century British maritime strategy theorist Julian Corbett observed, "Unaided, naval pressure can only work by a process of exhaustion. Its effects must always be slow, and so galling both to our own commercial community and to neutrals that the tendency is always to accept terms of peace that are far from conclusive."[14] Given that we live in the nuclear age, most conflicts are likely to end "inconclusively." States dependent on imports of energy resources and raw materials would have to learn to do without these resources. Under extreme conditions, large continental powers have found ways to do without such imports: civilians tighten their belts, society recycles, inventors devise substitutes, and entrepreneurs smuggle at high prices. But a great degree of political mobilization and political control is required. Under the right circumstances a developed state can and will do this, but it seems unlikely that they will do it for minor matters. Though modern states do not have colonies abroad, in many cases they or their nationals have substantial investments. These they would also lose in a long confrontation. Costs of this kind probably cannot "win" a victory in a major dispute. But the threat may deter limited aggression, increase the odds that the initiator may suffer a net loss in a large conflict, or help bring a conflict to a negotiated conclusion.

Command of the commons also provides the United States with more useful military potential directly to affect developments ashore than any other offshore power has ever had. This should not be overstated, but it should not be dismissed either. When nineteenth-century Britain had command of the sea, its timely power projection capability ended at the maximum range of the Royal Navy's shipboard guns. The Royal Navy could deliver an army many places on the globe, but the army's journey inland was usually difficult and slow, and without such a journey, Britain's ability to influence events was limited. As the nineteenth century unfolded, the industrialization of the continental powers, improvements in land transportation, and the development of coastal warfare technologies like the torpedo and mine, reduced the strategic leverage provided by command of the sea.[15]

The United States enjoys the same command of the sea that Britain enjoyed, and it can also move large and heavy forces around the globe and prevent others from doing so. But the U.S. military is now better able directly to influence events inland than was Britain. Command of space allows the United States to see (and hear) across the surface of the world's land masses—to gather vast amounts of information on what is going on there. At least on the matter of medium-to-large-scale military developments, the United States can locate and identify military targets with considerable fidelity and communicate this information to offensive forces in a timely fashion.

Airpower, ashore and afloat, can reach targets deep inland, and with modern precision-guided weaponry, can often hit and destroy those targets. United States forces can even more easily do great damage to a state's transportation and communications networks, and economic infrastructure. Command of the sea allows the United States to take full advantage of a customary quality of sea power, the ability to concentrate force. Given scarce resources, concentration may not always be able to produce sufficient power to overwhelm a local defense, especially one mounted by a moderately wealthy state; it nevertheless offers the opportunity.

Though amphibious operations against a hostile shore are difficult projects, which modern technology is making more difficult, the United States is the only country in the world that can presently even contemplate such actions. Due to the prior operations of U.S. air forces, when U.S. ground forces venture inland, they do so against a weakened adversary, and they have decent intelligence, good maps, and remarkable knowledge of their own position from moment to moment. They can also call on a great reserve of responsive, accurate, and often deadly air-delivered firepower in reserve, which permits the ground forces considerable freedom of action. This capability depends greatly on the identity of the adversary. Wealthy and technologically advanced states probably can already build or acquire, and effectively operate modern ground-based air defense systems to defend against U.S. air attacks, and potentially deter such attacks if they can demonstrate sufficient effectiveness.[16]

Command of the commons also assists the United States as it endeavors to address current security issues, in particular the problem posed by the terror campaign organized and/or inspired by Al-Qaeda and the problem of nuclear weapons proliferation.[17] Disproportionate military influence over the global means of communications permits the United States to interfere with Al-Qaeda's ability to organize and plot internationally, and to maintain global pressure on the organization, including the occasional raid. It also permits the United States to aid its allies in this confrontation. Just as important is what it allows the United States not to do. Contrary to the past practices of the war on terrorism, the United States need not put large forces ashore in other countries. The United States can maintain much of its military power just over the horizon, or even farther away, and still engage militarily in regions that it judges to be important. This helps reduce the propensity of U.S. troop presence to irritate nationalist or religious sensibilities. Finally, Command of the commons provides the United States the ancillary capability to assist others in natural disasters. It appears that U.S. assistance in these extreme cases does help improve attitudes toward this country.

Command of the commons helps with the free riding and reckless driving problems outlined in the previous chapter. Prudence does require the United States to maintain significant military forces and an ability to intervene abroad if necessary. At the same time, however, we have seen how the United States has "overinsured" during the last decades. Though Americans spend a good deal of time worrying whether its friends find U.S. security promises credible, the problem is the obverse. United States friends clearly trust the United States too much; the evidence is that many do little to protect themselves, and some behave adventurously, apparently sure that the United States will catch them if they fall. The worldwide U.S. military presence helps encourage this kind of behavior. It would be better if U.S. allies were a bit more concerned about whether the United States would show up. Command of the commons allows the United States to show up, but it also provides the United States with freedom of action. Fewer U.S. troops based abroad will give pause to U.S. allies and friends. If they want help from the United States they will have to earn it. The risk that a reduced U.S. forward presence may "embolden" potential challengers is unavoidable in this strategy. Capable, but presently underactive, allies of the United States will need to do more for themselves if this is a genuine concern. They have the resources. The United States, as I have argued earlier, is sufficiently secure inherently that this risk is tolerable, given the other benefits that flow from reduced forward presence.

Command of the commons permits the United States to strengthen itself at leisure for operations abroad, concert and reinforce the actions of allies if they are available, weaken enemies through embargo and blockade, and erode the adversary's capabilities through direct attack. It also allows the United States to interdict the movements of terrorists and technology smugglers, and to mount offensive raids ashore when needed. It provides the United States with freedom of action to energize its allies to be more responsible for their own security. That the United States has the capabilities to ensure command of the commons, and that others understand them, is an important diplomatic asset. As Clausewitz observed, "Possible engagements are to be regarded as real ones because of their consequences."[18]

FORCE STRUCTURE

The United States maintains an array of military forces to support its national military strategy and its grand strategy. This includes air, space, sea, land, nuclear, and intelligence capabilities, distributed across five services—the army, navy, air force, marine corps, and coast guard. The shift to a Grand Strategy of Restraint permits significant cuts in U.S. nonnuclear capabilities but also requires a rebalancing of future U.S. military efforts in favor of naval, air, and space capabilities.

[144]

Qualitative Superiority

The specific weapons and platforms needed to secure and exploit command of the commons are expensive, as are the people to make them work. Command of the commons leverages years of U.S. investment in producing a military force of the highest quality. These capabilities depend on a huge scientific and industrial base for their design and production. In 2010 the U.S. Department of Defense allocated nearly as much money on military research and development as Germany and France together budgeted for their entire military effort.[19] The military exploitation of information technology, a field where the U.S. military excels, is a key element. The systems needed to command the commons require significant skills in systems integration and the management of large-scale industrial projects, where the U.S. defense industry excels. The design of new weapons and the development of new tactics both depend on decades of expensively accumulated tactical and technological experience embodied in the institutional memory of public and private military research and development organizations.[20] Finally, the military personnel needed to run these systems are among the most highly skilled and highly trained in the world. The barriers to entry to a state seeking the military capabilities to command the commons are very high.

Ground Forces

The mission of U.S. ground forces changes significantly in the Grand Strategy of Restraint. This permits sizeable cuts. The counterinsurgency operations of the last decade were largely misdirected and ought not be repeated. These types of operation provide part of the rationale for a significant share of U.S. army and marine units, and to a lesser extent air force units. Other rationales for U.S. ground forces include stationing them abroad to provide evidence of U.S. commitment or to offer diffuse reassurance. In some cases, such as Europe, this is simply unnecessary. In others, such as East Asia, these missions are overdone. In all cases, the surplus of U.S. forces abroad or at home energizes free riding. At the same time, the traditional strategic missions for which the United States maintained these kinds of forces—balance of power strategies in key regions—have become less pressing. A Grand Strategy of Restraint thus would reduce the forces dedicated to these purposes.

The United States does need a sizing principle for its ground forces. It is difficult to imagine a particularly compelling rationale, but the United States does want ground forces that are large enough to retain a base on which to build in the event that the international situation should change. And it should want a ground force that allows it to affect strategic developments ashore in the short term, should the strategic situation change more quickly than expected. A reasonable sizing principle would be that the United States should maintain an active force that permits it to alter the local military balance firmly in favor of its friends in a range of contingencies that could matter. The standard should be the ability to "defend," not to attack.

The ability to alter the local balance in favor of our friends is difficult to calculate, but recent experience suggests that U.S. ground and tactical air forces are very capable at destroying mobile ground forces, at least those of less advanced armies. In Operation Desert Shield in 1990, two army heavy (armored) divisions, an airborne division, air mobile (helicopter) division, a marine brigade, and a British armored brigade were sent to secure Saudi Arabia from the risk that Iraqi forces would go beyond their original conquest of Kuwait. At that time Iraq had roughly a dozen armored divisions in reasonably good shape, and many more infantry units. The Iraqis did attempt an offensive into Saudi Arabia with a pair of heavy divisions in 1990, one or both of which were annihilated by U.S. air power.[21] Out of an abundance of caution, the United States did bring in significant reinforcements—three more heavy divisions—in order to take back Kuwait. In 2003, the United States was more confident. Two heavily armed mobile divisions—a U.S. Army armored division and a task-organized U.S. Marine division—conquered Iraq in 2003. A somewhat smaller British armored division secured the United States flank and rear. Though the opposition was weak, it was not nonexistent. Iraq had perhaps a half dozen Republican Guard divisions at nearly full strength, and another seventeen regular army divisions at half strength or less. Iraq was a large country. Lines of supply were long and insecure. The U.S. forces were operating on the offense. Nevertheless Iraqi armored units were consistently outclassed and destroyed.

The U.S. Army

An active army of six divisions, with perhaps twenty "maneuver" brigades should be adequate for the missions that they would perform. An army of this size could easily implement the robust defense of Desert Shield, the counteroffensive of Desert Storm, or the full-fledged invasion of Iraqi Freedom. It would also be very close in size to the force level that the U.S. Army kept in Europe for much of the Cold War, to assist wealthy allies if they had to fend off the nineteen heavily armored divisions of the Group of Soviet Forces Germany, the like of which exist nowhere in the world today. In the new force structure, three U.S. divisions would be armored, one airborne, one air mobile, and one "light mechanized" (made up of wheeled armored vehicles such as the "stryker"). Each division would have three or four brigades. The diversity of units would permit a great deal of operational and tactical flexibility. All of these units would be based in the United States.

Many active U.S. Army units would be demobilized. The army built up to some forty-two maneuver brigades, commanded by ten division headquarters for the wars in Iraq and Afghanistan. Thus the elimination of four divisions should remove at least 120,000 personnel directly from the army active force structure.[22] Moreover, as the army loses perhaps an eighth of its personnel every year as they leave the service, another 15,000 persons would fall out of the training base. Some trainers would also leave the force, and some infrastructure would be closed. I estimate therefore that the army would diminish by roughly 140,000 soldiers relative to its current size, perhaps a few more. This would leave a U.S. Army of roughly 400,000 soldiers. By contrast, present Pentagon plans call for a reduction of roughly 70,000 troops to 490,000 soldiers.[23]

The U.S. Marine Corps

The marines *are* an important enabling element of the new strategy but the corps could nevertheless be reduced. Given that there will be fewer U.S. military personnel deployed abroad, the theoretical possibility of a future requirement to seize a base will reemerge. The marine corps should be refocused on the amphibious assault mission that it adopted in the 1930s and so heroically perfected in the Second World War. This mission should not be confused with direct assault on heavily defended enemy shores, which modern technology is making prohibitively costly.[24] Rather the marines must either go where the adversary is not very strong, which is possible when fighting lesser powers, or win races with a great power adversary trying to seize the same poorly defended areas, usually in a third country.[25] Another mission for the marines would be reinforcement by sea of an ally already under attack. The possibility that the struggle with terror will continue in one form or another for many years also argues for the retention of a sizeable ability to raid ashore, which is inherent to the marine corps' amphibious capability. The size of the marine corps today, however, seems to be more driven by the need for lengthy deployments for open-ended counterinsurgency campaigns than it does for amphibious assaults, small or large.[26] The navy has seldom possessed sufficient specialized amphibious assault shipping to employ all marine combat troops, and this shortfall is destined to worsen in coming years. At best the navy can presently lift one marine division. At 200,000, the marine corps is quite large relative to its Cold War average size and has grown considerably for the wars in Iraq and Afghanistan.

Presuming an end to current counterinsurgency campaigns, and a refocusing of the marine corps on amphibious assault, the corps should be cut by roughly a third, or sixty-five thousand. By contrast, present Pentagon planning calls for a cut of only twenty thousand.[27] Moreover, though this proposition will meet with resistance, a big part of this cut should come from the marine force structure, not merely its people. The corps presently has three divisions, supported by three air wings; this force structure was written into Public Law 416, in 1952, so cutting actual structure, rather than personnel would necessitate a bruising political fight. The definition of a division/wing combination is not written into law, so a less efficient means of cutting forces would simply be to shrink the size of all three active division/wing combinations. One of these division/wing combinations, the one based in Okinawa and other parts of Japan, is understrength even given the growth in marine personnel. Given that the Restraint Strategy calls for the removal of some forces from Japan, this formation is an ideal candidate for elimination. It is rendered even more ideal by the great political controversy caused in Okinawa by the marines' presence. Two marine division/wing teams would remain, one on the Atlantic coast and one on the Pacific coast, with forward elements at Guam. Shipping could be concentrated in either ocean as needed to support a division-sized assault. Following such as assault, shipping could be reconcentrated for a second operation, if necessary.[28] In peacetime the marine corps usually maintains several reinforced battalions afloat aboard amphibious assault shipping (Marine Expeditionary Units, or MEUs). This practice should continue to the extent that the fleet of amphibious ships permits, probably two MEUs.[29]

U.S. Air Force

The U.S. Air Force, like the navy, carries a good deal of the burden of the military strategy associated with Restraint, but the air force would not be entirely free of cuts. Though the air force does not like to admit it, much of its fighter and airlift force structure is driven by the number of army divisions it would need to support. There is no simple way to determine an appropriate number of air force units to eliminate, nor the particular type. Marine corps practice can provide a clue, however. The marines argue that they need their own air units because to get ashore, their units need to be lean. Once ashore, they rely on fire support from elsewhere, which only marine aviation can supply, according to them. This argument is not bulletproof, but we can look at the types and numbers of aircraft the marines deploy relative to their ground forces for clues as to possible air force reductions, discounting somewhat for the marines' relatively heavy reliance on air power and adjusting for the role that the air force would play in the Strategy of Restraint. The marines maintain roughly nineteen active fighter squadrons to support three active divisions. This suggests a ratio of six squadrons per division. Marine fighter squadrons are typically a dozen aircraft each for a total of 72 aircraft per division. Each wing seems to have its own small tanker squadron as well, a dozen KC130s. Estimating roughly therefore, the removal of four U.S. Army divisions should permit reductions of as many as 84 combat and support aircraft per division. United States Air Force squadrons tend to be a bit larger than marine squadrons, but the elimination of three air force squadrons, roughly 54 aircraft, per army division is reasonable, for a total of 216 aircraft. The total of a dozen squadrons should imply reductions of perhaps 30,000 air force personnel overall.[30] More air force personnel might be eliminated if the strategic airlift forces were assessed. With fewer contingencies, and fewer forces, it is plausible that these forces too could be reduced.

Perhaps the most contested element of U.S. command of the commons is command of the air. The problem is not air-to-air combat, but rather the challenge posed by modern ground-based air defenses. The air force, navy, and marine advantage in air-to-air combat seems nearly overwhelming, notwithstanding the fact that other countries, including Russia build good aircraft.[31] China is working on its own advanced designs, which could be operational by the end of the decade. Individual planes, however, do not simply duel with their counterparts in single combat. Advantages in training, command, control, and intelligence, and air-to-air weaponry all play a role in U.S. superiority. Though a "troubled" aircraft, acquired in only small numbers due to its very high cost, the F22 is the most capable air-to-air combat aircraft in anyone's inventory today, when it is working. The F35, an aircraft in development, but also troubled, will likely be a very capable, if quite expensive, aircraft once it enters the inventory. The quality of in-service U.S. aircraft relative to that of other states is not the main problem for U.S. air superiority.

The challenge to command of the air comes from ground-based air defenses, including surface-to-air missiles, radars, and command and control systems of advanced design. Since the Vietnam War, the U.S. military has had to contend with the costs that these systems can impose on offensive operations. The United States, and other militaries such as that of Israel, have developed systems and doctrine for the Suppression of Enemy Air Defenses—termed SEAD.[32] Russia presently builds the best air defense weapons, aside from those built in the West, and China will become increasingly capable of building such systems. Some modern systems have been sold, and others will likely be sold, to second-tier powers. The late Cold War Soviet designs, and their follow-on systems, the so-called double digit SAMS, can offer real resistance to the U.S. military.[33] Fortunately, these systems are expensive, and Russian manufacturers prefer those who can pay cash. China has purchased a significant

[149]

number from Russia, and other countries will likely follow.[34] China, as noted above, also has a capable indigenous system, the HQ9. It is difficult to discern whether these acquisitions have already made U.S. air strikes against China prohibitively costly, but they surely have increased the costs and risks to a level that the United States has encountered nowhere else since the end of the Cold War.[35] United States SEAD capabilities may have a difficult time keeping up with this threat, much less staying ahead of it, though the United States has not stood still.[36] The Pentagon will need to work the SEAD problem assiduously, and it may nevertheless prove the case that the airspace of great powers will simply become too well defended to attack with aircraft.

U.S. Navy

The navy bears most of the weight in supporting a Grand Strategy of Restraint and is the key service for achieving and exploiting command of the commons. The U.S. Navy thus has defensive and offensive missions. Its defensive mission is to prevent others from inhibiting the free movement of goods, and if necessary military materiel, across the globe. Its offensive missions are to prevent others from moving their military materiel and goods across the globe, and to serve as a source of highly mobile, easy to concentrate firepower, to affect combat ashore.

The principal threat to commerce and global strategic mobility would be a middle or great power with a sizeable submarine force. That force would need to have many long-range vessels with considerable endurance and would need an intelligence and command and control apparatus to support it. Presently, there is no country that can mount a significant campaign of this kind in the open oceans. Russia maintains some of the assets that could mount such a campaign but would need to work very hard to bring them up to the necessary standard of readiness. China is building a submarine force, but presently that force includes many older vessels of limited quality and range. These two countries *could* presently mount local campaigns to disrupt trade or military reinforcements in the narrow seas that abut them. If they pay attention to these capabilities their ability to impose high costs on challengers in these regions will grow. Ultimately, China may be able to mount a broader open ocean sea denial campaign, but the challenges to them are daunting given China's maritime geography, unless Japan, Russia, and the United States simply choose not to compete, which is unlikely.

The United States must retain the ability to thwart open ocean submarine offensives. This requires two costly efforts. The United States needs an ability to sustain antisubmarine operations far forward in any geographical chokepoint that hinders an adversary's access to the open oceans. This means that the United States must maintain a strong fleet of advanced nuclear attack submarines. The United States must also maintain an ability to protect the remainder of its surface-based naval power, as well as its trade. This means antisubmarine (and antiair) warfare capabilities—multipurpose destroyers, long range antisubmarine warfare aircraft, sensors, and command and control.

The Nuclear Attack Submarine Force

Nuclear-powered attack submarines (SSNs) have several missions. They often accompany carrier task forces or amphibious task forces: at various times analysts have assumed a ratio of one or two SSNs per task force, depending on the expected adversary submarine threat.[37] Presumably their main purpose is to help defend the task group from enemy submarines. Nuclear-powered attack submarines have key intelligence gathering functions in peace and in war, but these are highly classified, and we cannot know how many the country actually requires for this purpose.[38] Nuclear-powered attack submarines and nuclear powered guided missile submarines SSGNs (Ohio class ballistic missile submarines converted into cruise missile launch platforms) also seem to have the mission of providing ready, though limited land attack cruise missile support in a variety of regions. One can imagine that this supports counterterror or counterproliferation purposes. Nuclear attack submarines can be used to sink surface vessels, but this does not presently seem to be a major mission.

For much of the Cold War, SSNs were a primary U.S. antisubmarine warfare asset, to be employed well forward. As enemy submarines become quieter, this mission will grow more difficult, but for now it still seems important.[39] As in the Cold War, the SSN force in wartime has the primary mission of hunting and killing adversary attack submarines, and more controversially adversary nuclear ballistic missile submarines. Because the ocean is wide, and submarines are elusive targets, antisubmarine forces like to catch their adversaries in "chokepoints" where there is a better probability of finding and killing a transiting adversary submarine. The most forward "chokepoint" is an adversary's submarine base, and only the SSN is stealthy enough to survive in such waters. Some reported SSN missions go together: forward intelligence gathering efforts in part have the purpose of keeping an eye on the status of other nations' submarines and collecting information on their signatures. In the event of a wartime mobilization and surge, they have the mission of providing warning. They may preemptively attack these enemy submarines as they try to depart their bases, or they may try to trail them to permit later attack.

TABLE 8. U.S. nuclear attack submarines, proposed force structure

Cooperation with (eight) carrier battle groups	8
Cooperation with amphibious assault groups[1]	4
Patrol of the Luzon Straits and the Ryuku Islands[2] *(18×2)*[3]	36
Total[4]	48

[1]Large amphibious assault ships of the Wasp and/or America class, which normally carry a mix of helicopters, VSTOL fighter aircraft, and marines, could be repurposed for standard naval missions. If so, then the navy would likely task an SSN to assist. In the event of a large-scale wartime amphibious assault the navy would be very concerned about vulnerability to submarine attack and would thus mount a major effort to protect amphibious assault ships, which could argue for SSNs in support to help ward off enemy submarine attacks. To allow for these options I assume that the amphibious force generates a requirement for four SSNs.

[2]I have simply measured the distance from Luzon to Japan, (seven hundred miles less Taiwan) and assumed a forty-mile patrol zone per SSN based on the publicly estimated (twenty-four to thirty-one mile) range of a Mk 48 torpedo, yielding a requirement for eighteen SSNs. To do this assessment properly we would need to know a great deal more about likely enemy submarines, the acoustical properties of these waters, and the quality of U.S. intelligence. Most of this information is classified. Moreover, many SSNs might be pushed forward into China's home waters. For a detailed assessment, see Owen R. Cote Jr., "Assessing the Undersea Balance between the U.S. and China," February 2011, SSP Working Paper WP11-1, http://web.mit.edu/ssp/publications/working_papers/Under sea%20Balance%20WP11-1.pdf.

[3]SSNs cannot remain on station forever. For ease of calculation I assume that under wartime conditions these boats will be on operations roughly half the time. Ronald O'Rourke, long-time naval analyst at the Congressional Research Service, suggests that at some point following a decision to surge, the navy can increase the share of its SSNs at sea to roughly 75 percent. I have calculated this percentage from figures offered in *Navy Virginia (SSN-774) Class Attack Submarine Procurement: Background and Issues for Congress*, Congressional Research Service, July 30, 2010, 7. During the Cold War, the SSBN force achieved a high sustained operational tempo, with perhaps 50 percent of the force regularly at sea, though SSBNs typically had two crews and SSNs only have one. Eric Labs, *Increasing the Mission Capability of the Attack Submarine Force* (Washington DC: Congressional Budget Office, March 2002), 16–17.

[4]The total is nearly identical to the size of the present SSN force—fifty-four boats. The navy has asserted an ultimate requirement for ten forward deployed SSNs in peacetime, and thirty-five in wartime. It aims for a total force of forty-eight boats. See Ron O'Rourke, *Navy Virginia (SSN-774) Class Attack Submarine Procurement: Background and Issues for Congress*, Congressional Research Service, July 30, 2010, 6–8.3.

Because military power is expensive, one should size U.S. military forces on the basis of wartime requirements. Unfortunately this means assuming a contingency, which inevitably means naming an adversary for planning purposes. Presently, and in the medium-term future, this means China, not because war is inevitable or even likely, but because it is the power that is developing the capabilities that could ultimately prove troublesome. I make them the adversary in this calculation out of respect, not fear or enmity. Given limited information on U.S. SSN operations, I offer the above estimate.

The Nuclear Powered Aircraft Carrier Force

In the Restraint Strategy, the size of the navy's carrier forces, like other U.S. forces, should be governed by potential wartime requirements, but the range of potential missions and contingencies makes this a difficult proposition. Nuclear powered aircraft carriers and their associated escorts have long been the principal elements of the U.S. Navy's surface forces. Given their complexity, and the associated cost of their combat aircraft, they contribute greatly to the overall size of the navy's budget. Though carrier task forces are useful for many things, their most important use historically has been for strike warfare at sea and against land targets. To operate successfully, they must also defend themselves, which permits them to contribute, if necessary, to air or missile defense ashore in some contingencies. In the open oceans there are no surface navies in the world today that can challenge the U.S. Navy. For that to occur the most plausible medium and long-term challenger, China, or perhaps a resurgent Russia, would have to invest vast sums of money over many years. It is worth noting that the Soviet Union barely achieved a capability to challenge the U.S. Navy in the open oceans after years of Cold War competition. Because the Grand Strategy of Restraint largely dispenses with forward presence ashore, U.S. carrier aviation could be called on to help defend an ally in trouble. Depending on the situation, this could mean providing a reserve of defensive or counteroffensive firepower.

There has been no systematic public justification for the size of the U.S. carrier force since the Clinton administration's "Bottom Up Review" in 1993. The Clinton Pentagon viewed the experience of Operation Desert Storm as a reasonable metric for force sizing; six carriers were deployed to that theater. The study concluded that four to five carriers would be sufficient to support a single conflict.[40] The Clinton Pentagon settled on a force of eleven carriers and ten air wings, having concluded that this total would not only support the ability to wage two nearly simultaneous major theater wars, but would allow more than two carriers to be forward deployed on a regular basis. Operation Iraqi Freedom (2003) saw five carriers in the campaign, and their aircraft played a more significant role than they did in 1990. Carriers mounted perhaps half of the combat sorties. Carrier aviation evolved into a more potent weapon than it once was due to improvements in the aircraft themselves, which have made them more reliable, and more capable of night operations and the delivery of precision-guided munitions.[41] The navy now also keeps large stocks of such munitions; in Desert Storm the navy had very few.

The initial phase of the air war in Operation Desert Storm in 1991 can provide a demanding principle for estimating a reasonable size for the

[153]

future carrier fleet. In the first few days U.S. strikes destroyed or suppressed Iraq's air defenses and won "air supremacy." At the outset of the crisis that precipitated the war, Iraq had a large air force, and an intact integrated air defense system, including radars; command, control and communications systems; a large, diverse, and somewhat modern inventory of air defense missiles; and very large numbers of antiaircraft guns. Many key assets, including tactical aircraft and command and control centers, were protected in steel reinforced concrete bunkers that could only be destroyed by direct hits from heavy armor piercing bombs. Although the U.S. military came to understand the integrated air defense system, and vanquished it with minimal losses, taking it down was a very big job. The requirements of that SEAD operation help to support the estimate of four carriers as a reasonable offensive force. It is generally agreed that the United States established air superiority over Iraq in the first several days of the war. Though the first day of the war saw perhaps 1,200 discrete strikes against discrete targets, perhaps 500 of those strikes assisted the establishment of air and sea control.[42] In some cases one aircraft armed with precision-guided munitions, then a relatively scarce resource, made more than one strike per sortie. Over the next several days the number of strikes diminished, as did the number directed at air and sea control.

Four carriers should provide sufficient destructive potential to prosecute the air superiority phase of a contingency as large as Desert Storm. A nuclear powered aircraft carrier can, during a four-day surge, generate nearly two hundred strike sorties per day, each carrying two thousand-pound precision guided bombs, giving a four-carrier force the potential to attack sixteen hundred targets per day.[43] Precision weaponry thus makes it possible for four carriers and their associated air wings to attack a target set, and accomplish a mission, that in Desert Storm took many more aircraft—naval, marine, and air force. That said, fewer attacking aircraft makes life easier for the air defense, so several additional tactics would be necessary.[44] Electronic warfare would be employed to deceive and degrade air defense radars and command and control systems. It would be reasonable to add large numbers of cruise missiles to the initial attacks, which would do further damage to critical targets and help saturate air defenses.[45] The destroyers and cruisers that customarily defend carrier task forces, as well as one or more Ohio class cruise missile submarines could accommodate several hundred land attack cruise missiles.[46] As unmanned air vehicles are perfected for combat against active air defenses, they too can assist in this mission. If carrier air operations of this magnitude can degrade the defense sufficiently, then long-range aircraft from the U.S. Air Force, such as the B2, supported by tankers, could follow up with larger numbers of heavier precision-guided munitions.[47]

[154]

Moreover, in a range of plausible scenarios, the United States could have allies that might provide land bases close enough to the objective to be useful. United States land based fighter aircraft could also play a role under those circumstances.

For several reasons, the United States could need more than four carriers. If the United States is to be able to assemble a task force of four carriers on short notice, then it will need additional vessels to compensate for any in extended overhaul, or carriers early in their training cycles.[48] This speaks to a need for perhaps six carriers with associated air wings, and a seventh in long overhaul. This would also permit the forward deployment on a regular basis of a single task force for diplomatic purposes if this is judged necessary. Because the Grand Strategy of Restraint relies so heavily on the navy, however, it is reasonable to consider an even larger force. We should remember that war at sea can be incredibly lethal when practiced by those who understand it: four of the seven carriers that the United States had at the outset of the Second World War were destroyed by the end of 1942.[49] Leaders and the public should be under no illusions when they decide for war against a distant major power: there will be high costs. The United States should maintain a cushion against the worst. It is also reasonable to maintain a capability to do more than one operation, though not necessarily a major offensive against a well-prepared enemy in its own country, or in conquered terrain that it has had time to reinforce. Whenever there is a possibility of serious opposition, two is probably the minimum number of carriers one ought to deploy.[50] These additional carriers could also reinforce a major offensive, if this were necessary. In sum, a force of seven to nine carriers seems reasonable to support the Grand Strategy of Restraint; I favor the higher figure.[51] Today's carrier fleet consists of eleven nuclear-powered aircraft carriers, and ten active air wings. Thus, there is some scope for cuts in the navy's force structure in the Restraint Strategy.[52]

One caveat is in order. There may come a time when the U.S. Navy cannot safely operate carrier task forces close enough to some adversaries to be effective in offensive operations.[53] It is probably already true that the U.S. Navy would prefer not to operate carrier groups within several hundred miles of the Chinese coast in the event of a conflict. Admiral Horatio Nelson famously observed that "a ship is a fool to fight a fort."[54] Economically capable nation-states should be able to assemble quite respectable littoral defenses—"forts" that may become too difficult to fight. These forts will consist not only of modern air defenses, as discussed above, but antiship cruise missiles fired from shore batteries, surface craft, or aircraft, as well as submarines able to deliver both antiship cruise missiles and powerful torpedoes. On balance I expect carriers to have an increasingly difficult time mounting sustained air attacks against the homelands of major powers. I do expect them to remain useful for raids against major powers and for more sustained operations against small and middle powers. They could also serve as a mobile reserve to support or defend land bases under sustained attack and as tools to prevent other states from mounting amphibious attacks against allies and neutrals.

Space

The United States spends vast amounts on reconnaissance, navigation, and communications satellites, which provide a standing infrastructure to conduct military operations around the globe. General Bruce Carlson, formerly director of the National Reconnaissance Office observes, "We fight wars based on the fact that we have domination in space, that we're able to use that high ground to whatever degree we choose or not choose to use it."[55] According to the Union of Concerned Scientists, the United States presently has 436 operational satellites in orbit, of which 115 are military, 193 commercial, 118 other government, and 10 civil.[56] The Rumsfeld Pentagon in the George W. Bush administration set itself the mission of "space control . . . to ensure the freedom of action in space for the United States and its allies and, when directed to deny such freedom of action to adversaries."[57]

The Obama administration approaches space with equal energy but somewhat less bold rhetoric. "The National Security Space Strategy" draws upon all elements of national power and requires active U.S. leadership in space. The United States will pursue a set of interrelated strategic approaches to meet our national security space objectives:

- Promote responsible, peaceful, and safe use of space;
- Provide improved U.S. space capabilities;
- Partner with responsible nations, international organizations, and commercial firms;
- Prevent and deter aggression against space infrastructure that supports U.S. national security; and
- Prepare to defeat attacks and to operate in a degraded environment."[58]

Other states can and do exploit space for military and civilian purposes. Though there is concern that some commercial satellites have military utility for reconnaissance and communications, many of those that do are in the hands of U.S. companies, or U.S. allies, and full exploitation of their capabilities by U.S. adversaries can be disrupted.[59] The

NAVSTAR/GPS constellation of satellites, designed and operated by the U.S. military, but now widely exploited commercially, permits highly precise navigation and weapons guidance anywhere in the world.[60] Full exploitation of GPS by other military and civilian users is permitted electronically by the United States, but this permission is revocable.[61] GPS has, however, proven so useful for military, governance, and commercial purposes that other states have decided to deploy their own navigation satellites. Though it has suffered from reliability and durability problems, Russia has nearly completed its GLONASS system, which had atrophied early in the post–Cold War period. China is following with its fast-expanding Beidou system, while Europe is building its Galileo system.[62]

United States dependence on satellites for its ability to project conventional military power does make the satellites an attractive target for future U.S. adversaries.[63] But all satellites are not equally vulnerable; low-earth-orbit (LOE) satellites are more vulnerable to more types of attack than are high-earth-orbit satellites.[64] China has had one successful test of a direct ascent antisatellite weapon against one of its own satellites in low earth orbit.[65] Jamming communications links between satellites and ground stations is the simplest form of harassment. Optical Reconnaissance satellites could be "blinded" by attacks from ground based lasers. Some fear more exotic attacks—for example, space mines or the use of a so-called microsatellites as long-duration orbital interceptors.[66] The U.S. military does have some insurance against the loss of satellite reconnaissance capabilities; it can substitute in part its fleet of reconnaissance aircraft and unmanned aerial vehicles. A challenge by another country could do some damage to U.S. satellite capabilities and complicate military operations for some time. Many of the tricks that a weaker competitor might use against the United States would probably not be useable more than once. The United States would then need to put a new generation of more resilient satellites in orbit. One estimate suggests that the exploitation of almost every known method to enhance satellite survivability would roughly double the unit cost.[67] The present stress on resilience in stated U.S. space policy suggests that the United States may already be "hardening" its space capabilities.

The United States also has its own offensive potential. Though the United States has not publically committed itself to the pursuit of kinetic antisatellite weaponry, the U.S. ballistic missile defense system has some antisatellite capability against targets in low earth orbit. In 2008 the United States employed an Aegis cruiser to destroy an errant satellite in what many believe to have been a proof of principle that the United States has an antisatellite capability.[68] The United States had a number of antisatellite research and development programs under way for many years, so presumably it understands the technical issues very well.[69] Conventional U.S. military capabilities for precision attack, even without its full panoply of space assets, are not trivial. It is likely that an opponent's ground stations and bases for attacking U.S. satellites would come under sustained attack. The United States also maintains the ability to jam communications satellites.[70] The most plausible outcome of a conflict that included space assets is that the United States would, after a period of difficulty, find substitutes for some assets and reconstitute others. The fight would probably leave the adversary in worse shape than the United States, and it seems likely that should the United States "win" the conflict, constraining an adversary's access to space would be one of the subjects of any war termination negotiations.

The Pentagon has been hinting for some time that it would like to put weapons into space both for antisatellite attacks and for attacks on terrestrial targets. Many independent space policy analysts oppose this because the United States gets more out of space than any other state, and thus the U.S. benefits from the fact that other states capable of space activities have eschewed putting weapons in space. Ultimately the United States has more to lose than to gain from such a competition.[71] These analysts acknowledge that U.S. space assets are an attractive target, but they argue that "hardening" satellites, ground stations, and the links between them, makes more sense than starting an expensive arms competition in space. An ability quickly to reconstitute some space capabilities should also be maintained, as should alternative reconnaissance means— aircraft and drones. The United States should also maintain some counteroffensive capabilities for purposes of deterrence and defense, including antisatellite weapon research and development programs.

GLOBAL FORCE POSTURE

Force posture is the term for how U.S. military forces are arrayed around the world. This includes numbers and types of major combat units and associated military personnel, and the array of bases that house or support them.

Troop Deployment

As of December 31, 2012, the Pentagon reported 173,000 active duty troops regularly stationed abroad. The Pentagon reported 140,000 troops deployed to Afghanistan or the Persian Gulf, some from overseas stations, but most from the continental United States.[72] These troops staff units from all the services. Under a Grand Strategy of Restraint most of

[158]

these units would be withdrawn from their present bases over a period of years. Many of these units, as well as units elsewhere, would be demobilized because they are superfluous to a Grand Strategy of Restraint.

- Roughly 140,000 troops, mainly army and marine, were deployed in or close to Afghanistan. President Obama plans to conclude the direct combat mission for U.S. force in Afghanistan by the end of 2014, but some forces are planned to remain in support. Under a Grand Strategy of Restraint most of these forces would be removed. The U.S. strategy in Afghanistan would change to what would essentially be an Al-Qaeda overwatch, containment, and harassment mission based in the center and north of the country and aligned with those factions seriously willing to combat the Taliban and Al-Qaeda. This mission ought not to require many personnel. Perhaps 40,000 people are in the Persian Gulf Region, with many based in Kuwait. This number ought to be pared, but even given limited purposes in the region, some forces would remain.

- Roughly 70,000 troops were stationed in Europe. Ultimately, nearly all U.S. military personnel should be withdrawn from Europe.

- Perhaps 80,000 troops were stationed in Asia, mainly in Japan, including Okinawa, and also in the Republic of Korea. (For reasons not explained, the Pentagon has not recently been willing to share exact figures on troop levels in Korea, so I estimate their share from other sources.) Many, but not all of these forces should be disengaged, though as discussed earlier, this disengagement would need to be slower and less complete than in Europe because the political situation is more sensitive. Ground forces would leave first, including the army units in Korea, and the marine corps units in Okinawa. Air and naval forces would be reduced slowly, as discussed in the preceding chapter. That said, the United States would need to set clear objectives and work toward them in a sustained way.

Bases

The United States should reduce significantly its overseas base structure and reorganize much of what it keeps. The United States grew accustomed to having many large fixed bases overseas during the Cold War; some 598 major "sites," in foreign countries, remain.[73] During the George W. Bush administration the Pentagon conducted the "Global Force Posture Review" with an eye to reducing the overseas base structure and the presence of U.S. troops.[74] Though the review itself is classified, it was a comprehensive exercise, and the authors did convince

[159]

themselves that the United States could get by with fewer permanent bases and still sustain the expansive grand strategy of the Bush administration. The review divided the U.S. base structure abroad into three classes of facilities: main operating bases (MOBs), forward operating sites (FOS), and cooperative security locations (CSL). Main operating bases are elaborate facilities with infrastructure to support the permanent stationing of U.S. forces, often accompanied by their family members. Forward operating sites are "expandable facilities," overseen by small numbers of U.S. troops, which may include prepositioned equipment. Cooperative security locations are useful locations to which the U.S. military has access depending on circumstances, but which normally have no regular U.S. military presence.[75] One purpose of the review was to reduce the number of bases in the first class to the minimum number needed to fulfill U.S. strategic purposes (which were then quite expansive). The review proposed reductions that would bring home 60,000–70,000 military personnel and nearly 100,000 family members, and which would amount to a net reduction of 35 percent of overseas facilities. Many of these reductions have occurred: at the time of the review (2004) the Pentagon claimed 850 sites overseas and announced a target of 550 sites by the end of ten years.[76] A recent unclassified analysis by the RAND Corporation provides a flavor of how an analysis of this kind is conducted but concludes unsurprisingly that to implement its present strategy, the United States must sustain a massive presence abroad. Nevertheless, the authors also imply that "much of the remaining Army presence in Europe; much of the Air Force presence in the UK and some of its forces in Central Europe; the level of rotational presence in the Middle East; and Army, Air Force, and, to a lesser degree, marine corps presence in Japan" could be eliminated without much damage to actual U.S. combat capability.[77]

Under a Grand Strategy of Restraint, the United States would shed more of its forces stationed overseas and their bases. Some 265 of the 500 sites overseas are associated with the U.S. Army; the Grand Strategy of Restraint would demobilize most U.S. Army troops based abroad, so those bases would ultimately close. Most remaining bases in Europe would also be closed with the transformation of NATO into a political alliance, but the United States might wish to negotiate the transformation of some important MOBs into FOSs and CSLs to support ongoing counterterror and counterproliferation activities, and to provide an infrastructure for the return of U.S. forces in extremis. Such arrangements would likely prove attractive to some allies, as they would wish to preserve the possibility of future U.S. assistance. Similarly, the United States could review its various prepositioning arrangements, in which equipment is stockpiled overseas ashore or afloat to permit combat units

[160]

quickly to reach a theater of action by air, and "marry up' with their equipment, or draw necessary supplies and munitions.[78] In some cases it would be prudent to increase prepositioning; in others it would make sense to move prepositioned materiel from sites ashore to ships.

Given the maritime nature of the military strategy proposed here, there are a few obvious locations that will continue to be of great utility to the United States. Examples include the Azores, Diego Garcia, and the island of Guam (a U.S. Trust Territory). Some bases in the Mediterranean do provide support to the U.S. Navy, and it is reasonable to try to preserve some of these in one form or another. Though the United States does not have any MOBs in Australia, there are major and minor DOD sites that add up to twenty thousand acres, and the DOD does have a very well-developed set of security relationships with that country consistent with the long-standing ANZUS treaty, which should be maintained. The United States seems to have an arrangement with Singapore that could be termed a CSL; the government of Singapore has constructed a pier capable of handling U.S. nuclear aircraft carriers, which often visit. This relationship is quite useful. Though bases in Japan dedicated to the army and the marines should be closed under the Strategy of Restraint, the bases dedicated to air and naval assets should remain for some time. Kadena Air Force Base in Okinawa is a very useful facility and could be made more useful if known techniques to "harden" airfields against preemption were fully implemented. Over time, as Japan takes on a greater share of responsibility for its own defense, many bases could be converted into FOSs, and CSLs.

Exercises

United States forces are constantly involved in training efforts and exercises with the military forces of other countries.[79] Some of this serves the purpose of improving interoperability with forces that may find themselves next to the United States in a shared military operation. Other training efforts and exercises aim to improve the capabilities of local forces, so that the United States need not do so much.[80] Still other exercises aim simply to cement political relationships, supplementing the activity of the State Department.[81] And still others aim to send messages of deterrence to possible adversaries. In the abstract, these are all worthy purposes. In practice, many of these exercises serve purposes that are less important to Restraint Strategy than they are to present U.S. grand strategy.[82] This exercise program should be pared, though it is difficult to generate a precise program to do so because the public and even the official data on these exercises are so poor. A recent report by the RAND Corporation notes that "DoD's primary tool for collecting security cooperation data is the Theater Security Cooperation Management Information System. Not all security cooperation events are captured in this database, while those that are may reflect only a portion of the associated forces and costs. Comparisons between COCOMs are especially problematic, as each COCOM has its own approach to managing its data."[83] It is difficult to believe that the Pentagon is fully capable of assessing the utility of its exercise program to its present strategy.[84]

AFFORDABLE AND EFFECTIVE

A Restraint Strategy is best supported by a maritime military strategy, a strategy that relies on U.S. command of the commons—naval, air, and space superiority. This military strategy focuses U.S. military power on key interests and threats: the maintenance of an ability to intervene in Eurasia if necessary, counterterror, and counterproliferation.

The preservation of command of the commons is itself a demanding project. The United States must credibly demonstrate that it retains the capability to reengage on the Eurasian land mass in a timely fashion and to organize coalitions against expansionist states, if these expedients prove necessary. The United States must also be able to retaliate quickly and effectively against direct attacks on the United States. The United States will need surveillance and interdiction capabilities that permit the harassment of global terrorist networks, interference with any illegal trade in nuclear technology, and overwatch of the legal trade in nuclear technology. I have outlined the air, naval, and space capabilities that the United States needs to accomplish these missions. The navy looms particularly large in the Restraint Strategy: costly aircraft carriers, their associated aircraft, and nuclear attack submarines are central elements. Over time the aircraft carrier may recede in importance, to be replaced or supplemented by another ship design, probably a submarine-based system analogous to the present Ohio class SSGN. The air force will need to focus on fewer aircraft, with longer range.

I have argued in this chapter that U.S. military capabilities should be sized for the military actions that could be necessary to protect these interests and respond to imminent threats. Large U.S. ground forces play a diminished role in the Restraint Grand Strategy and would be cut substantially. Restraint eschews intervention into the internal politics of other states, and thus the ground forces that support large counterinsurgency campaigns are unnecessary. Restraint aims to energize other advanced industrial states into improving their own capabilities to defend themselves, so the garrisons of ground forces, whose peacetime purpose seems to be mainly diplomatic, and whose wartime missions seem easily carried by the nations where they have been based, can return home and furl their colors.

A maritime strategy helps to avoid the problems of recent years. A maritime strategy is responsive to the volatility of identity politics in an era of rapid social, economic, and political change. It reduces U.S. military presence abroad in a way that lowers the U.S. political profile, and thus diminishes inchoate but still dangerous local political antipathies to the United States. At the same time, reductions of forces abroad should energize some U.S. allies to do more to defend themselves and cautions others to do fewer of the things that they do that are inimical to U.S. interests.

Restraint will save a great deal of money. Personnel levels fall by roughly 20 percent, and force structure measured as an average of reductions in army brigades, fighter squadrons, carrier task groups, and marine division/wings falls by roughly 30 percent. Recent history suggests that with such large force structure reductions, the total Department of Defense Budget could fall in rough proportion, which means that spending could decrease by perhaps 20 percent in real terms from present levels.[85] If the cuts were accomplished over five years, this could soon take the DOD's share of GDP down to 2.5 percent. Presuming that the economy continues to grow, defense managers could then seek modest real increases in defense spending to sustain the new force structure without increasing the burden on the economy. The money saved by Restraint can either assist in long-term deficit reduction or be diverted to other national needs.

Conclusion

A Sustained Debate

The Grand Strategy of Restraint was first conceptualized in the mid-1990s, the early years of the post–Cold War world. This was the "unipolar moment" when the United States was indeed the most capable state in international politics by a wide margin. Restraint advocates saw the momentum building for an activist U.S. foreign and security policy and argued that such a policy was unnecessary and unprofitable. It was, however, possible. The policy was driven forward by overwhelming American power. There was simply nothing to stop the United States. But this was not the only cause. Liberalism was victorious in the Cold War, so the United States, along with its democratic allies, succumbed to a kind of triumphalism. Democracy and free markets would be the order of the day, and U.S. power would protect and nurture this long expected evolution. George Herbert Walker Bush coined the phrase "new world order," which sounds incongruous coming from a Cold War realist and spymaster.

Activist policies were supported by a wide coalition of interests. The United States had built a huge organizational infrastructure for the Cold War in its foreign and intelligence services, the military, defense industry, and a network of think tanks. All of these institutions had a way of looking at the world, and they agreed with Secretary of State Madeleine Albright that the United States was the "indispensable nation." These institutions also needed new projects in order to thrive. A combination of great power, luck, and at least at the outset, prudent diplomacy, permitted the United States several relatively inexpensive early successes—the first Gulf War, the enlargement of NATO, and the interventions in Bosnia and in Kosovo. The Restraint "critique" did not get much traction, though advisors to George W. Bush such as Dr. Condoleezza Rice, later secretary of state, suggested at his election that U.S. grand strategy could

[164]

be a bit more focused on great powers, and a bit more humble, than in the Clinton years. The terrorist attack on September 11, 2001, changed this; the second Bush administration embraced Liberal Hegemony.

The last decade has not been kind to Liberal Hegemony. Though the United States remains the strongest power in the world, the margin is shrinking. China's capabilities are growing; soon its economic output may outstrip that of the United States. Other states, particularly India, may briskly pursue China. Meanwhile, the financial crisis of 2008 and concomitant recession have slowed U.S. growth and reduced U.S. global influence. The Global War on Terror has been costly and undisciplined. Though Osama Bin Laden is dead, Al-Qaeda, in some form, survives. The two demanding counterinsurgencies that the United States took on to reform the politics of Iraq and Afghanistan have produced mixed results at best.

Many analysts believe that the unipolar moment is over, or soon will be. The basic distribution of global capabilities is changing, as the National Intelligence Council's *Global Trends 2025: A Transformed World* famously predicted, and as its more recent effort *Global Trends 2030: Alternative Worlds* reiterates. We may soon confront a new bipolar competition with China, or we may face a new multipolar world, in which several nation-states or confederations of great capability stand together at the top of the global pecking order, each warily eyeing the other and simultaneously calculating one another's potential utility as allies. Whichever future we encounter, Liberal Hegemony is a poor answer. It depends too much on a U.S. power advantage that is disappearing. And it did not work very well even when the United States had such an advantage. Unfortunately, this strategy is deeply rooted in the U.S. national security community. Liberal Hegemony serves the interests of many institutions, and it matches the worldview of the U.S. establishment, and even the broader public. The continued pursuit of this policy without the real power to match it, however, will likely prove not merely costly and counterproductive, as it has been in the recent past, but disastrous.

In this book I have explained why Liberal Hegemony has not worked particularly well. The strategy has precipitated some balancing by other nation-states and will likely precipitate more as the relative power advantage enjoyed by the United States wanes, and others feel more capable of tilting against the United States. The strategy has made the United States the center of political attention in a world undergoing rapid social, political, and economic change. The United States is sufficiently strong and omnipresent to be blamed by the losers but not strong enough to do much affirmatively to alleviate the stresses and strains that rapid development often causes. The strategy underrates the enduring power of nationalism and the inclination of self-aware peoples to resist

[165]

direction by outsiders. And the strategy overlooks the extent to which the capacity for organized violence has diffused, rendering even relatively small counterinsurgency efforts hugely expensive. Finally, the strategy leads directly to the issuance of blank security checks to U.S. allies. Some cash the check for increased welfare spending in their own societies, as do the European allies and Japan; they cheap ride. Others cash the check to pay for their own extravagant security adventures; clients as different at Afghanistan and Israel drive recklessly. For all these reasons, Liberal Hegemony has proven an expensive and counterproductive grand strategy.

I have outlined an alternative grand strategy, military strategy, and accompanying force structure. Restraint sketches a more limited set of political objectives abroad and more limited means to achieve them. The objectives are best supported by a more focused military strategy and force structure—a maritime strategy underpinned by a strong navy, a smaller but more agile marine corps, and a long armed air force. A global network of access agreements and carefully chosen but largely unmanned base infrastructure would facilitate the movement of these forces. This would provide a sound defense against current threats, an insurance policy against sudden changes in international politics, and a firm foundation on which to construct additional military power if that ever proves necessary. The force structure to support this strategy provides the ability to police the legal and harass the illegal trade in nuclear materials. It allows the United States to interdict the movements of nonstate actors, and to organize disruptive raids against them should they find havens in ungoverned or undergoverned spaces. Finally, should major security threats emerge, command of the sea would permit the United States to organize coalitions, assemble military power from disparate contributors, and even facilitate the mobilization of allied economies for war, while complicating the efforts of adversaries to do the same. The termination of U.S. wars and the paring of U.S. force structure should make it possible to sustain this military strategy for the long term for 2.5 percent of GDP or less, barring a major increase in global tensions. This would save a great deal of money, which the country could use to address other pressing problems.

Politically, the United States must do less. It must focus on the most important dangers to its security. The greatest danger to U.S. sovereignty is a hegemon on the Eurasian land mass. This danger is low now, but the United States must always be prepared to counter it should it reemerge. If such a challenge does reemerge, however, the United States ought not manage it like it did the Cold War, shouldering the bulk of the burden, because the U.S. relative power position is unlikely to be as favorable. The United States will need real allies, not the security dependencies it has now. Moreover, it would be foolish to reenact the riskiest aspect of the Cold War, the effort to extend nuclear deterrent guarantees to nonnuclear countries threatened by a great power. Paradoxically, to have capable allies later, preparations must start now. The only way to prepare them is to renegotiate and reduce the current level of U.S. commitment.

The greatest short-term dangers to the United States are to be found in the diffusion of the ability to produce weapons of mass destruction, especially nuclear weapons, and the possibility such weapons could fall into the hands of nonstate actors of a type that cannot be deterred from using them. These twin problems are difficult to address, and perfect insurance is unavailable. Nevertheless a strong nuclear retaliatory force can deter nation-states from attacking the United States or from giving nuclear weapons away. A sustained and measured policy to retard the spread of nuclear weapons technology, and to encourage new nuclear states to adopt best practices to secure their materials, can buy a great deal of security at modest cost. Finally, sustained attention from U.S. intelligence agencies, and sustained cooperation with the intelligence agencies of like-minded states, all of whom have a very strong collective interest in not being victims of nuclear terrorism, should permit the suppression of nihilistic groups and help deny them access to nuclear weapons.

The United States will need to give up some objectives. The coercive reform and political reorganization of other countries has proven expensive and "success" has proven elusive. The often asserted connection of these projects to the elimination of groups such as Al-Qaeda is tenuous. If the United States forgoes the objective of coercive reform, it can forgo many of the ground forces retained for this purpose. This is where the biggest savings are to be found. The United States will also need to give up or reduce its military guardianship of rich countries that are well able to defend themselves. The relationship with Europe must be transformed entirely. The relationship with Asian allies, especially Japan, must be reformed significantly. Japan can make a much bigger contribution to its own defense. Giving up these objectives means that some nuclear proliferation would be tolerated. Preventive nonproliferation wars that depend for their ultimate success on deep changes in the politics and government of target states will often prove to be more costly than they are worth. And trying to keep Germany, or Japan, or the Republic of Korea from getting nuclear weapons if they ever feel truly threatened will implicate the United States in extended deterrence commitments that in the past have had an unfortunate property. They have pushed the United States to pursue conventional and nuclear capabilities that are ultimately destabilizing.

[167]

The Liberal Hegemony Critique

Criticism of the Grand Strategy of Restraint focuses on two categories—opportunities forgone and costs and risks incurred. Liberal Hegemonists are most concerned about opportunities forgone. Realists, whose ideas are closer to my own, concern themselves with costs and risks. I briefly review these critiques and suggest why I find them less than compelling.

At bottom, supporters of Liberal Hegemony believe that international politics can be reformed if only the United States is willing to take advantage of the "unipolar moment." They accept that international politics may have been deeply conflictual in the past, but *not* mainly for the reason adduced by realists. Realists argue that the absence of a sovereign order-keeper, a world government, simply forces nation-states to look out for themselves. "Liberal Hegemonists" believe instead that the most important problems causing conflict in international politics arise from the nature of states and the nature of economics.

First, imperfect states, which means nondemocracies, fight each other and fight democracies. Democracies fight imperfect states because they must but do not fight other democracies. Imperfect states fight for any number of reasons, but the most important is that they are unconstrained by the rational desire of individual citizens for peace, which cannot be expressed in their undemocratic domestic politics. Imperfect states also have no way to arrive at predictable and reliable understandings with each other, because the absence of internal political constraints means that defection from international agreements is easy. Democracies seldom fight democracies because they can build trust and because they know that one another's citizens will reject war if they can.

Second, prior to the evolution of capitalism, wealth could be expropriated through conflict more easily than it could be generated by domestic economies. With the evolution and diffusion of capitalism, states have other ways to grow wealthy besides robbery. Indeed free market capitalism and international trade are more efficient than conflict. Moreover, trade among capitalist states builds "interdependence," which may also create additional barriers to conflict, as profitable relationships would be torn asunder by war.

Finally, many supporters of Liberal Hegemony also believe that this is the moment to rid the world of the threat of nuclear weapons. They understand that nuclear weapons are terrifically attractive to states that have security problems. In the short term, the suppression of proliferation requires a mixture of security guarantees for states that could adopt nuclear weapons out of fear, and coercion of states who might be adopting them out of greed. In the medium and long term, if a world of liberal market democracies can be constructed, states will feel less need for nuclear weapons, and U.S. hegemony will make all liberal states feel more secure in any case. A comprehensive arms control agreement among liberal democracies would eliminate nuclear weapons that are ready to fire at short notice, lock any latent capabilities that remain well out of easy reach, and surround these remnants with reliable verification mechanisms.

Advocates of Liberal Hegemony understand that the world is still imperfect, and full of imperfect states. Many old-fashioned sources of conflict remain, and they wish to use the U.S. power advantage to suppress as much conflict as they can, in the belief that a prolonged period of peace, and the workings of globalization and economic and political development, will ultimately transform states and the relations among them. The United States should help to expand the community of capitalist democracies and protect trade, investment, and other communications among them. The United States should defend these same states from aggression by nondemocracies. The United States should intervene in the internal affairs of nondemocratic, imperfectly capitalist states to set them on the right path, or help internal political movements that seem to want to move in this progressive direction. And the United States should do everything it can to prevent states that do not have nuclear weapons from getting them. If the United States can use its power advantage to secure all of these objectives, then ultimately the U.S. security burden will be reduced.

To believe that the United States must incur the high costs of Liberal Hegemony reviewed in chapter 1, one would need to believe not only that these arguments are true, but that the United States has sufficient power to bring about these changes, and to do so without significantly weakening ourselves. Advocates of Restraint are skeptical of these arguments. First, we doubt that the internal political and economic makeup of states is such a reliable bulwark against conflict. Though democracies have seldom fought each other, their domestic and foreign behavior seems sufficiently erratic that we doubt that even a world in which all the great and middle powers were democratic would be so peaceful and so stable. Second, we doubt that this world is reliably in sight or can be brought about by U.S. power. Peoples must find their own way to democracy, and the practice of democracy is inevitably tailored to the history of each people. Even if it were true that perfect democracies seldom fight each other, real democracies are likely to remain imperfect. Third, market capitalism is not a reliable brake on overseas expansion. Some resources abroad, or the paths to them, will always prove tempting. The U.S. obsession with the oil producers of the Persian

Gulf is perhaps the best example. Fourth, economic interdependence is not a reliable bulwark against conflict. On the eve of the First World War, the major industrial powers traded intensively with one another; this did not prove a bulwark against war. Finally, advocates of Restraint are skeptical about the practicability or the wisdom of a world of no nuclear weapons. Too many states see themselves as having security problems that cannot be addressed in any other way. Pakistan, Israel, and Russia are notable examples. These states will not give up their nuclear weapons, and if they do not, neither will anyone else. Moreover, the advantages of nuclear weapons ought not to be lightly cast aside. Ambitious states have a very difficult time generating persuasive schemes to conquer others armed with nuclear weapons; this is a cause of peace.

The Realist Critique

Restraint is a fundamentally Realist grand strategy, but Realists do not agree on everything. Though Realists agree that international politics is a competitive environment, they disagree on how competitive it might be, both generally, and in specific eras. Advocates of Selective Engagement are also Realists, and they see the need for a much more active role for the United States. Indeed, the policies they recommend are nearly indistinguishable from those associated with Liberal Hegemony. They reason from both general tendencies in international politics and from history. The argument is simple. The United States was drawn into the Second World War, the greatest war in history, despite a general inclination to insulate itself from power politics. Nazi Germany and Imperial Japan were not deterred because they did not face imminent, decisively superior power. Neighboring states paid a very high price for these wars, and the United States paid a much lower, but still meaningful price. Once these hegemonic bids were underway, the United States discovered or rediscovered its interests in preventing continental hegemony and was forced to wage expensive wars to roll back German and Japanese gains. The argument therefore is that if the United States does have an interest in preventing a Eurasian hegemon, it is cheaper and safer simply to admit it, get on to Eurasia at both ends, and stay there. And, peace has a value all its own, which the United States should defend for both narrow and altruistic reasons.

This is a strong argument, but not decisive. The key fact of the historical record in Europe is that there were viable candidates for hegemony, in the First and Second World wars, and in the late 1940s. There is no viable candidate for hegemony in Europe today, and none is on the horizon. Hence there is no need for the United States to guard against it on

[170]

the western end of Eurasia. Moreover, as argued in chapter 3, key powers in Europe possess nuclear deterrents. This is perhaps cold comfort to nonnuclear Germany, but the presence of three nuclear weapons states ensures that no state can achieve hegemony.

Asia is a more difficult case for Restraint. China may reach a point where it has sufficient power to bid for hegemony. Its options are limited, however. It too would face nuclear adversaries in Russia and India. There are nonnuclear states in range, and China may find it expedient to attempt to coerce these neighbors, but many of these neighbors are island nations, and thus they can only truly be conquered with successful amphibious assaults, among the most difficult of military operations. As I argued in chapter 2, the United States should retain a presence in Asia to ensure against such boldness. It is even more important for the United States to do what it can to energize and strengthen local balancing coalitions. Should a major confrontation emerge, which I do not rule out, the United States will need allies who are ready to defend themselves. China does not yet possess much real offensive capability; it can punish and harass, but not crush or conquer. So now is the time both to restore our own economic health and habituate our regional clients to making strong efforts in their own defense.

An alternative critique could be leveled by "offensive realists." They believe that international politics is highly competitive. If China continues to grow, they see a serious challenge as all but inevitable. For some the remedy is to contain China now. The United States should begin to organize a defensive coalition, even if some local actors are not quite ready for it. Though left unstated, confronting China now could provide an opportunity for preventive action—to stall China's growth, or involve it in a limited but losing war, which might humiliate and collapse the regime. I doubt that the gains of such preventive action would outweigh the costs and risks. More traditional preventive war is seldom discussed, probably due to the high nuclear risks that such a war would incur.

Offensive realists are right to alert us to China's medium- and long-term power potential, and the possibility that it could prove greedy and ambitious. That said, I am wary of rushing into a containment strategy. Realists like to quote the nineteenth-century German statesman Otto von Bismarck, who said preventive war is like committing suicide for fear of death. Preventive "cold war" also has that quality. China must confront many challenges before its power will be sufficient to support a bid of hegemony. Most states in Asia are wary of China, and we have seen that even occasional heavy handed slipups precipitate "balancing" by China's neighbors, even if that consists mainly of efforts to elicit greater U.S. attention. China's power and geography have a powerful tendency to make them seem a security problem for others. United States diplomacy should aim to ensure that China appears as the source of disharmony. The regional powers will not thank the United States for a regional Cold War, much less a hot war, if it does not appear absolutely necessary.

A final concern, often unspoken, is shared by many in the foreign policy community. This is the fear that even strong states proximate to rising powers, will either flagrantly appease the aggressor or even bandwagon with it to glean a share of the spoils. Realists observe that sovereign nation-states exist for a reason; the polities that inhabit them have over a long period of history worked to achieve and sustain their independence. Realists predict that the absence of a world government incentivizes nation-states to do things to protect themselves against predation; states are expected to build their internal capabilities and seek alliances when threatened. They will not give away much to bullies, because that can make the bully too strong to fight later. And they will not often bandwagon with an expansionist in the hopes of sharing the spoils, unless they are both greedy and perceive that their own power is sufficient to secure these spoils at a later date from their equally greedy partner. If a bandwagoner is that strong, then it will soon fall out with its partner, because each will fear that the other will gain more, and ultimately emerge as too powerful to oppose. Balancing is the general record in international politics. If it were not, modern history's aspiring hegemons would have succeeded; Europeans would all speak French, or German, or Russian.

Small states are suspected of being particularly susceptible to the temptation of appeasement. Realists observe that small states have the fewest assets with which to balance, so opposing the very strong can seem not only dangerous, but futile. Though logical, history suggests that even small states balance. They value their sovereignty as much as big ones do and will sacrifice to maintain that sovereignty if they think they have a chance of success. Had Czechoslovakia had any hope at all of British and French assistance in 1938, it would have fought rather than capitulate at Munich. Finland fought Russia in 1939, with little expectation of assistance. Neutral Sweden, though isolated from the possibility of allied assistance, built a huge military to deter German aggression, and remained independent throughout the Second World War.

Finally, some fear that democracies are natural appeasers because their publics reasonably fear war, and their leaders fear going to war without overwhelming public support, which is difficult to mobilize. Only the United States and Israel are believed to have escaped this illness. Though the historical debate about the late 1930s continues, Britain and France did endeavor to balance Germany. They slowly glued together a military alliance, and they improved both their extant military capabilities and their ability to mobilize. They did not, however, balance effectively or sufficiently. Germany's apparent superiority to the sum of their power potential encouraged them to try every effort to avoid war, as did the fresh memories of the recent bloodletting in the trenches of the First World War. Though many condemn Britain and France on ethical grounds for their behavior at Munich, it is their strategic blunder that matters more. Normal diplomacy often involves compromises that one or the other observer will polemically condemn as appeasement. Appeasement at Munich was not compromise, but the award to a clearly avaricious state of power assets that could only improve its future prospects as an aggressor. Munich is the rare historical example of this kind of self-destructive behavior, which is why it is the cautionary analogy that is usually invoked in discussions of appeasement.

The Strategy of Restraint, as I have discussed it above, is mindful of the potential for things to go wrong in Eurasia. The purpose of a large, globally capable military, which aims to retain command of the commons, is to preserve the ability of status quo powers to cooperate effectively with one another, and with the United States, should that prove necessary.

The United States is still the most capable power in the world by a significant margin. United States grand strategy is in the hands of a hugely self-confident, globally ambitious, and persistently self-replicating national security elite. A consensus on an assertive foreign and security policy spans the Republican and Democratic parties. The U.S. military and intelligence effort is lushly endowed. Though the U.S. Congress can be stingy with foreign development assistance, U.S. policymakers seem to have the economic resources they need to dole out, when they need it. Domestic and international politics across the world is constantly active. Political violence is common on television and computer screens of the American people. The U.S. presence across the world has been such a stable feature, for such a long time, that danger anywhere can seem like a threat. The allies have finely honed the diplomatic skills and techniques that help them induce the United States to continue to protect them. They dole out just enough contributions to the common defense to dampen U.S. ire, and then quietly cut their contributions again until the next time the United States gets energized about burden sharing. When U.S. policymakers consider reductions in the presence of U.S. forces, local actors hint at imminent disasters: factions in their countries will rush to appease local aggressors, turn viciously on local rivals, wildly underspend on defense, or simply decline for one reason or another to ally with one another. The U.S. foreign policy community eagerly consumes such arguments and takes them at face value, rather than the product of skilled and long practiced buck-passing diplomacy. The Liberal Hegemony project will not be easily abandoned.

[173]

Nevertheless some potential causes of change are evident. There is a diffusion of power in the world. The gap between the United States and others will narrow; military capability is spreading; the cost of U.S. interventions is going up. Though seldom discussed, the people in the U.S. military are exhausted from more than a decade of constant warfare and increasingly dubious about the projects they are asked to undertake. The U.S. economy will take time to recover from the effects of the financial crisis that began in 2007 and to improve the fiscal condition of the U.S. government, both of which may limit the resources available for national security policy.

The Grand Strategy of Restraint is responsive to these powerful facts. There are three possible paths to adjustment:

- The least likely is that politicians will read arguments offered by advocates of Restraint, have a eureka moment, and decide to transform our grand strategy. There is little to suggest that this moment is imminent.

- A second path to reform would arise from crisis. Had the collapse of Lehman Brothers, and the ensuing contraction of global liquidity in 2008 been permitted to run its course, the United States and much of the world would probably have entered a great depression. It is hard to believe that the United States would have continued lavish spending on security projects far from home under those circumstances. I would rather not have reform come this way, but it could.

- The final path to reform is typical of modern pluralist democracies, change would be incremental. If Liberal Hegemony is to be replaced, this seems the most likely path. Slowly but surely the big facts outlined above would begin to make themselves felt in U.S. choices. Economic scarcity may yet break the privileged hold that lavish military spending now has on both parties: advocates of an expansive grand strategy, fiscal restraint, and social spending may *all* find themselves in open conflict with one another. Defense budgets will be cut, costly wars will be brought to an indeterminate and unsatisfying close, new wars may be avoided, military forces will slowly be withdrawn from positions abroad. Writing in the spring of 2013, when the first year of cuts imposed by the "bipartisan" Budget Control Act has resulted in the sequestration of some defense expenditures in a manner observers agree to be entirely irrational, it seems this open conflict is upon us. The incremental process will likely continue to prove inefficient. Allies can continue to console themselves with the knowledge that the United States still seems to be present, even if the intensity of the commitment appears to wane, so their progress toward true independence will be slow, and perhaps nonexistent. Failure to admit what we are doing will ensure that U.S. resources will not be focused on the main capabilities that support the most crucial interests of the United States, but will be spread like peanut butter. Ambiguity may permit the advocates of Liberal Hegemony to promote policies that involve the United States in more half-baked and costly misadventures.

The major obstacles to Liberal Hegemony that I have advanced in this book will likely prove enduring, and indeed will probably intensify. Against this backdrop, advocates of Restraint can and must continue to refine and press their critique. If true disaster strikes, the United States will profit from having a clear alternative waiting in the wings. If instead Liberal Hegemony suffers the death of a thousand cuts, then in this disputatious political environment advocates of Restraint can bring a bit more direction, order, and efficiency to the necessary change.

Notes

INTRODUCTION

1. Marc Trachtenberg, "A 'Wasting Asset': American Strategy and the Shifting Nuclear Balance, 1949–1954," *International Security* 13, no. 3 (winter 1988–89): 32–44, http://www.jstor.org/stable/2538735.

2. See Hillary Rodham Clinton, "Security and Opportunity for the Twenty-First Century," *Foreign Affairs* 86, no. 6 (November/December 2007): 3–16; John McCain, "An Enduring Peace Built on Freedom," *Foreign Affairs* 86, no. 6 (November/December 2007): 19–34; Barack Obama, "Renewing American Leadership," *Foreign Affairs* 86, no. 4 (July/August 2007): 2–16. Also noting the overlapping positions on Iran is David Rieff, "But Who's Against the Next War?" *New York Times*, March 25, 2007. Foreign policy did not play a major role in President Obama's reelection campaign.

3. G. John Ikenberry, *Liberal Leviathan: The Origins, Crisis, and Transformation of the American World Order* (Princeton: Princeton University Press, 2011), especially 2, 169–93. Christopher Layne, *The Peace of Illusions: American Grand Strategy from 1940 to the Present* (Ithaca: Cornell University Press, 2006) makes a similar argument, terms the U.S. grand strategy "hegemony" but develops a much more critical perspective. See especially figure 1, p. 31. Stephen M. Walt, *Taming American Power: The Global Response to U.S. Primacy* (New York: Norton, 2005), 13, 40–41, 246–47, argues that the U.S. position in the world is one of Primacy—"it enjoys an asymmetry of power unseen since the emergence of the modern state system," but that its grand strategy has aimed to preserve and deepen this asymmetry. Primacy is both a condition, and a strategy. Ikenberry argues that Liberal Hegemony has been good for the world and for the United States; Layne argues it has probably not been good for the world and is sure that it has been harmful to the United States; Walt argues that Primacy has a good and a bad side for both the world and the United States and that sagacious U.S. policy could tip the balance in favor of the good, but that it probably won't.

4. Michael C. Desch, "America's Liberal Illiberalism: The Ideological Origins of Overreaction in U.S. Foreign Policy," *International Security* 32, no. 3 (winter 2007/2008): 7–43, reviews the intellectual history in the United States of the notion that the U.S. liberal political system can only be truly safe in a world of similar states. He argues that both the Clinton and subsequent Bush administration shared this view, but that the "unipolar" moment made the carrying of these ideas abroad with power possible and seductive after the fall of the Soviet Union. In periods when the

[177]

United States has not had such an advantage in relative power, it has instead been content to expand democracy through example.

5. Barry R. Posen and Andrew L. Ross, "Competing Visions of U.S. Grand Strategy," *International Security* 21, no. 3 (winter 1996/97): 5–53, summarizes the initial phase of the post–Cold War U.S. grand strategy debate and lays out the four key strategies.

6. Ibid., 23–30; for the core works, see Ashton B. Carter, William J. Perry, and John D. Steinbruner, *A New Concept of Cooperative Security*, Occasional Paper (Washington, DC: Brookings Institution, 1992); Janne E. Nolan, ed., *Global Engagement: Cooperation and Security in the 21st Century* (Washington, DC: Brookings Institution, 1994); Paul B. Stares and John D. Steinbruner, "Cooperative Security and the New Europe," in *The New Germany and the New Europe*, ed. Paul B. Stares (Washington, D.C.: Brookings Institution, 1992), 218–48. For a shorter exposition see Randall Forsberg, "Creating a Cooperative Security System," in *After the Cold War: A Debate on Cooperative Security*, Institute for Defense and Disarmament Studies Reprint, first published in *Boston Review* 17, no. 6 (Nov./Dec. 1992).

7. "Proliferation of destructive technology casts a shadow over future U.S. security in a way that cannot be directly addressed through superior force or readiness. Serious economic and environmental problems point to an inescapable interdependence of US interests with the interests of other nations." Carter, Perry, and Steinbruner, *A New Concept of Cooperative Security*, 4.

8. Madeleine K. Albright, "Realism and Idealism in American Foreign Policy Today," *U.S. Department of State Dispatch* 5, no. 26 (June 27, 1994), 434–37, offered an explicit and comprehensive statement of these views, which she developed in her commencement address at Harvard University's Kennedy School of Government on June 8, 1994.

9. Commission on America and the New World, *Changing Our Ways: America and the New World* (Washington, DC: Carnegie Endowment for International Peace, 1992), suffers from vagueness but seems to recommend a Cooperative Security Strategy, while maintaining a U.S. capability for unilateral action. See 73–75 for a discussion of nuclear proliferation.

10. Charles A. Kupchan and Clifford A. Kupchan, "Concerts, Collective Security, and the Future of Europe," *International Security* 16, no. 1 (summer 1991), 149–50. See also Richard Ullman, *Securing Europe* (Princeton: Princeton University Press, 1991), 76: "Only democratic polities would have the openness that is the precondition of confidence. Only democracies share a commitment both domestically and internationally to the rule of law and to the peaceful settlement of disputes." The argument is largely about the feasibility of establishing an elaborate collective security regime in Europe.

11. Posen and Ross, "Competing Visions," 32–42.

12. Charles Krauthammer, "The Unipolar Moment," *Foreign Affairs* 70, no. 1 (1990/91): 23–33. "Excerpts from Pentagon's Plan: 'Prevent the Emergence of a New Rival,'" *New York Times*, March 8, 1992, 14. For reportage, see Patrick E. Tyler, "U.S. Strategy Plan Calls for Insuring No Rivals Develop," *New York Times*, March 8, 1992, 1, 14; and Barton Gellman, "The U.S. Aims to Remain First among Equals," *Washington Post*, March 16–22, 1992, 19.

13. "Excerpts," 14.

14. Krauthammer, "Unipolar Moment," 31–32. "The post-Cold War era is thus perhaps better called the era of weapons of mass destruction. The proliferation of

weapons of mass destruction and their means of delivery will constitute the greatest single threat to world security for the rest of our lives. That is what makes a new international order not an imperial dream or a Wilsonian fantasy but a matter of the sheerest prudence."

15. William Kristol and Robert Kagan, "Toward a Neo-Reaganite Foreign Policy," *Foreign Affairs* 75, no. 4 (July/August 1996): 18–32; Joshua Muravchik, *The Imperative of American Leadership: A Challenge to Neo-Isolationism* (Washington, DC: The AEI Press, 1996). See also Krauthammer, "Unipolar Moment."

16. Stanley A. Renshon, *National Security in the Obama Administration: Reassessing the Bush Doctrine* (New York: Routledge, 2010), 31. This book is mistitled; it is largely about the Bush administration's national security policy.

17. Krauthammer, "Unipolar Moment," 25–26; see also Krauthammer, "The Unipolar Moment Revisited," *The National Interest* (winter 2002/03), 11–13, for a typically critical after action review of the multilateralism of the Clinton administration.

18. Posen and Ross, "Competing Visions," 44.

19. Ryan C. Hendrickson, *The Clinton Wars: The Constitution, Congress, and War Powers* (Nashville: Vanderbilt University Press, 2002).

20. John H. Moxley and Cindy Williams (co-chairs), *Manpower and Personnel Needs for a Transformed Naval Force* (Washington, DC: The National Academies Press, 2008): 20–21, lists these new benefits and their "history of adoption." For a discussion of increases in retiree benefits, see Cindy Williams, "Making the Cuts, Keeping the Benefits," *New York Times*, 11 January 2005.

21. President William Jefferson Clinton, *A National Security Strategy for a Global Age, Preface* (White House, December 2000), 3, available at http://www.au.af.mil/au/awc/awcgate/nss/nss_dec2000.pdf

22. "Our ability to respond to the full spectrum of threats requires that we have the best-trained, best-equipped, most effective armed forces in the world. Our strategy requires that we have highly capable ground, air, naval, special operations, and space forces supported by a range of enabling capabilities including strategic mobility and Command, Control, Communications, Computers, Intelligence, Surveillance, and Reconnaissance (C41SR). Maintaining our superior forces requires developing superior technology, and exploiting it to the fullest extent. . . . Access to sufficient fleets of aircraft, ships, vehicles, and trains, as well as bases, ports, pre-positioned equipment, and other infrastructure will of course be an imperative if we are to deploy and sustain U.S. and multinational forces in regions of interest to us." Ibid., 26.

23. G. John Ikenberry and Anne-Marie Slaughter, *Forging A World of Liberty under Law*, the Princeton Project on National Security, September 27, 2006 (Woodrow Wilson School of Public and International Affairs, Princeton University), 6.

24. Ibid., 29–30.

25. Condoleezza Rice, "Promoting the National Interest," *Foreign Affairs* 79, no. 1 (2000): 45–62; Renshon, *National Security in the Obama Administration*, 31–32.

26. Rice, "Promoting," 51–54, implies but does not clearly state that humanitarian military intervention is generally a bad idea. For more pointed remarks by Dr. Rice, see Michael R. Gordon, "Bush Would Stop U.S. Peacekeeping in Balkan Fights," *New York Times*, October 21, 2000, 1. "We don't need to have the 82nd Airborne escorting kids to kindergarten."

27. George W. Bush, *The National Security Strategy of the United States of America*, The White House, September 2002, 5.

28. Krauthammer, "Unipolar . . . Revisited," 15.

29. Bush, *National Security Strategy of the United States*, September 2002; *National Security Strategy of the United States*, March 2006; Renshon, *National Security in the Obama Administration*, 34–35, 53–54, notes that the emphasis on democracy began as early as 2002 but agrees that the spread of democracy assumed much more importance in the 2006 version of the Bush strategy.

30. Secretary of State Condoleezza Rice, "Transformational Diplomacy: Shaping US Diplomatic Posture in the 21st Century," Speech at Georgetown University's School of Foreign Service, Jan 18, 2006, available at http://www.cfr.org/publication/9637/transformational_diplomacy.html; see also Sebastian Mallaby, "Rice's Blind Spot," *Washington Post*, January 23, 2006, 15, which notes Rice's conversion in her 2006 speeches on "transformational diplomacy."

31. U.S. Department of Defense, *Quadrennial Defense Review Report* (Washington, DC: Department of Defense, February 2010), 9–10 [hereafter *QDR*, 2010].

32. As the 2002 *National Security Strategy* offered: "The United States will not use force in all cases to preempt emerging threats, nor should nations use preemption as a pretext for aggression. Yet in an age where the enemies of civilization openly and actively seek the world's most destructive technologies, the United States cannot remain idle while dangers gather"; Bush, *National Security Strategy*, 2002, 15. Though the document uses the term *preemption*, it uses it incorrectly. Preemption means striking first when one has good reason to suspect that attack by the other side is imminent. Preventive war, or prevention, mean striking now because one fears that a competitor may choose to attack later, usually because the other is improving his capabilities, or because one's own capabilities seem to be deteriorating. The logic is "war now is better than war later." For a brief history of the ubiquity of preventive war thinking in the United States. see John Lewis Gaddis, *Surprise, Security, and the American Experience* (Cambridge: Harvard University Press, 2004), 16–22.

33. On the matter of attacking Iraq, Secretary of State Albright averred in 1998, "But if we have to use force, it is because we are America; we are the indispensable nation. We stand tall and we see further than other countries into the future, and we see the danger here to all of us"; Madeleine K. Albright, interview by Matt Lauer, *The Today Show*, NBC, February 19, 1998.

34. Ikenberry and Slaughter, *Liberty under Law*, 31–32.

35. "Further, the Department must prepare to contain WMD threats emanating from fragile states and ungoverned spaces. Success in this area will hinge on the ability to prevent and respond to global WMD crises, such as situations in which responsible state control of nuclear, chemical, or biological materials is not guaranteed. Faced with such emergencies, the Department will require the ability to locate and secure WMD and WMD-related components, as well as interdict them on land, on sea, or in the air;" *QDR*, 2010, 35.

36. "I have said that when it comes to preventing Iran from obtaining a nuclear weapon, I will take no options off the table, and I mean what I say. (Applause.) That includes all elements of American power: A political effort aimed at isolating Iran; a diplomatic effort to sustain our coalition and ensure that the Iranian program is monitored; an economic effort that imposes crippling sanctions; and, yes, a military effort to be prepared for any contingency. (Applause.) . . . Iran's leaders should understand that I do not have a policy of containment; I have a policy to prevent Iran

from obtaining a nuclear weapon. (Applause.) And as I have made clear time and again during the course of my presidency, I will not hesitate to use force when it is necessary to defend the United States and its interests. (Applause.)" The White House, Office of the Press Secretary, "Remarks by the President at AIPAC Policy Conference," March 04, 2012, Washington Convention Center, Washington, DC, available at http://www.whitehouse.gov/the-press-office/2012/03/04/remarks-president-aipac-policy-conference-0.

37. U.S. Department of Defense, Washington Headquarters Services Directorate for Information Operations and Reports, *Active Duty Military Personnel Strengths by Regional Area and by Country*, December 31, 2000, 1–5, available at http://siadapp.dmdc.osd.mil/personnel/M05/hst1200.pdf.;

38. U.S. Department of Defense "Total Military Personnel and Dependent End Strength by Service, Regional Area, and Country, As of December 31, 2012," available at http://siadapp.dmdc.osd.mil/personnel/MILITARY/miltop.htm.

39. Clinton, *Strategy for a Global Age*, 6, 9, 12, 13, 53, 55, 62, 74, extols the virtues of presence generally, and specifically in Asia, Bosnia, Kosovo, the Persian Gulf, and at sea.

40. U.S. Department of Defense, *Strengthening U.S. Global Defense Posture: Report to Congress*, September 2004, 2, 9–13 (hereafter *Defense Posture*).

41. Ibid., 11. These individuals were associated mainly with the two U.S. heavy (armored/mechanized) divisions still stationed in Europe.

42. Charles Kupchan and Peter L. Trubowitz, "The Illusion of Internationalism's Revival," *International Security* 35, no. 1 (summer 2010): 99–100, 102–9, ably rebut their critics and summarize their research, which persuasively suggests a partisan split on attitudes to international institutions on the basis of both congressional votes and public opinion.

43. United States citizens are broadly supportive of the UN, but skeptical on specifics. "Americans have in recent years shown significant dissatisfaction with the UN's performance in fulfilling its mission. This mixture of strong support for the UN in principle and dissatisfaction with its actual performance seems to contribute to surprisingly erratic overall evaluations of the UN as an institution." "U.S. Opinion on International Institutions," *Public Opinion on Global Issues*, March 16, 2012, 1, available at http://www.cfr.org/public_opinion.

44. Walter Russell Mead, "The Tea Party and American Foreign Policy: What Populism Means for Globalism," *Foreign Affairs, 90:2* (March/April 2011):35.

45. Danielle Pletka, "Think Again: The Republican Party," *Foreign Policy,* January 2, 2013. http://www.foreignpolicy.com/articles/2013/01/02/think_again_the_republican_party.

46. Renshon, *National Security in the Obama Administration*, 50–53, coins a new term for the Bush administration's ideas for both reformed and new institutions, a "New Internationalism."

47. For purposes of assessing relative power, I rely on GDP measured at exchange rates, rather than at purchasing power parity. The latter provides a better comparison of GDP for purposes of assessing living standards. The former, however, offers a better comparison of where economies stand in terms of their ability to generate modern military power, with its high technological component. Making this argument is Albert Keidel, "China's Economic Rise—A Technical Note (Draft)," Carnegie Endowment for International Peace, July 9, 2008, 6–7, available at http://www.carnegieendowment.org/files/Technical_Note.pdf.

48. National Intelligence Council, *Global Trends 2030: Alternative Worlds*, NIC 2012–001, Washington D.C. (December 2012), 15–16, available at http://www.dni.gov/nic/globaltrends.

49. Ibid.

50. Albert Keidel, "China's Economic Rise—Fact and Fiction," Carnegie Endowment for International Peace, Policy Brief 61, July 2008, Table 2, "U.S. and China GDP Growth Potential, Twenty-First Century," 6, available at http://www.carnegieendowment.org/files/pb61_keidel_final.pdf, suggests that on the basis of reasonable assumptions, China's GDP could be almost twice that of the United States by 2050, as measured by exchange rates. Slightly less alarming from a geostrategic viewpoint is John Hawksworth and Danny Chan, *The World in 2050, The BRICs and Beyond: Prospects, Challenges and Opportunities*, "Appendix B, "Additional Projections for GDP at Market Exchange Rates," Price Waterhouse Coopers, January 2013, 23, available at http://www.pwc.com/gx/en/world-2050/the-brics-and-beyond-prospects-challenges-and-opportunities.jhtml, which estimates that China's GDP at market exchange rates could equal that of the United States by 2030 and exceed it by 27 percent by 2050. A more refined perspective on the Chinese economy also yields evidence of China's competitiveness. The value of the output of the manufacturing sector of China's economy surpassed that of the United States in 2011. United Nations, National Accounts Main Aggregates Database, "GDP/breakdown at current prices in US Dollars (all countries)," available at http://unstats.un.org/unsd/snaama/dnlList.asp.

51. Hawksworth and Chan, *The World in 2050, BRICs*, 23.

52. "The Soviet Economy on average grew faster than the US economy from the mid-1960s to the mid-1970s, raising Soviet GNP from 49 to 57 percent of US GNP. After 1975, however, the US economy grew faster, and Soviet GNP fell to 52 percent of the US level in 1984." U.S. Central Intelligence Agency, *A Comparison of the US and Soviet Economies: Evaluating the Performance of the Soviet System*, A Reference Aid, Office of Soviet Analysis, Directorate of Intelligence, October 1985, Confidential, Released as Sanitized 1999, v. Even this estimate was probably too high.

53. The fiscal crisis in the eurozone in 2011 reduced somewhat the willingness of central bankers to hold euro denominated assets as reserves, but so far as one can tell the effects have been surprisingly small. An IMF survey showed that euro-denominated central bank reserves fell from 26.7 percent in mid-2011 to 25 percent at the end of the year. The dollar portion rose from 60.5 percent to 62.1 percent. See Claire Jones, "Central Bankers Snub Euro Assets," *Financial Times*, April 17, 2012.

54. Archival research by Galen Jackson suggests that Woodrow Wilson did not enter the first World War for immediate balance of power concerns, though such concerns had been raised previously by his advisors. He and his advisors did not fear at that moment that the allies were on the verge of collapse. Once in the war, however, they found the allied situation much more dire than they had previously understood, and accepted the need for much greater exertions than they had expected, to forestall German victory. See Jackson, "The Offshore Balancing Thesis Reconsidered: Realism, the Balance of Power in Europe, and America's Decision for War in 1917," *Security Studies* 21, no. 3 (July–Sept. 2012): 455–89, esp. 475–76, 480–82; see also Ross A. Kennedy's review of the article in H-Diplo, ISSD, January 23, 2013, available at http://www.h-net.org/-diplo/ISSF/PDF/ISSF-AR18.pdf, who, while agreeing with Jackson's main finding, notes that Wilson had been fearful of the consequences of German victory from the outset of the War.

55. Kenneth Waltz, *Theory of International Politics* (New York: McGraw-Hill, 1979), is the father of "structural realism." Hans J. Morgenthau, *Politics among Nations: The Struggle for Power and Peace*, 2nd ed., revised and enlarged (New York: Alfred Knopf, 1956), first published in 1948, introduced American scholars, students and policymakers to the "classical" realist tradition in the study of international politics, and offered guidance for U.S. conduct in the Cold War. Though there were progenitors in U.S. academia, Morgenthau is the best known of the first-generation realists. In my judgment, only the second edition of the work captures the author's full analytic intent. Morgenthau and Waltz are in agreement about how international politics works, but Waltz attributes regularities mainly to the absence of a sovereign, whereas Morgenthau vacillates between that and human nature as the tap root of power-seeking behavior.

56. John J. Mearsheimer, *The Tragedy of Great Power Politics* (New York: W. W. Norton, 2001), is the foremost proponent of offensive realism, arguing that states will generally try to amass almost all the power they think they can get, with the caveat that they will lose interest when they bump up against geographical barriers that create very, very strong advantages to the defense, particularly oceans.

57. Stephen M. Walt, *The Origins of Alliances* (Ithaca: Cornell University Press, 1987): 17–26, develops a realist theory of alliance formation that adds evidence of malign intentions to the great capability of an actor to explain alliance making.

58. Carl Von Clausewitz, *On War*, ed. and trans. Michael Howard and Peter Paret (Princeton: Princeton University Press, 1976, 1984), 373–76, writing between 1816 and 1827, advanced the argument that the strategic defense has the advantage, in part due to the general propensity to ally against expansionists. "The sum total of relations between states thus serves to maintain the stability of the whole rather to promote change; at least, that tendency will generally be present. . . . This we suggest, is how the idea of the balance of power should be interpreted; and this kind of balance is bound to emerge spontaneously whenever a number of civilized countries are in multilateral relations."

59. Mearsheimer, *Tragedy*, 138–67, succinctly categorizes and reviews the limited range of strategies available to states in an anarchic world.

60. Robert Jervis, *The Meaning of the Nuclear Revolution, Statecraft and the Prospect of Armageddon* (Ithaca: Cornell University Press, 1989), 1–45.

61. Roger D. Petersen, *Understanding Ethnic Violence: Fear, Hatred, and Resentment in Twentieth-Century Eastern Europe* (Cambridge: Cambridge University Press, 2002), 40–53, 254–59, takes ethnic identity as a given and examines the conditions under which it most often leads to violence among groups. He finds that groups easily can come to resent other groups "above" them in a status hierarchy in the larger society, and that this triggers powerful emotions that often lead to violence.

62. Ernst Haas, "What Is Nationalism and Why Should We Study It?" *International Organization* 40, no. 3 (summer 1986): 709; Karl W. Deutsch, *Nationalism and Social Communication: An Inquiry into the Foundations of Nationality*, 2nd ed. (Cambridge, MA: MIT Press, 1966), 86–105; Ernest Gellner, *Nations and Nationalism* (Ithaca: Cornell University Press, 1983), 35–38, 139–43; Jerry Z. Muller, "Us and Them: The Enduring Power of Ethnic Nationalism," *Foreign Affairs* 87, no. 2 (Mar.–Apr., 2008): 18–35.

63. Benedict Anderson, *Imagined Communities, Reflections on the Origin and Spread of Nationalism* (London: Verso, 1991), 1–7.

64. Stephen Van Evera, "Hypotheses on Nationalism and War," *International Security* 18, no. 4 (spring 1994): 5–39, reviews the then extant literature on nationalism and deduced from it hypotheses on the relationship between nationalism and conflict. He observed, however, that as of the time of publication, "the impact of nationalism on the risk of war has barely been explored." Since then, as a consequence of the many civil wars that followed the collapse of the Soviet Union, scholars have attacked this problem.

65. Barry R. Posen, "Nationalism, the Mass Army, and Military Power," *International Security* 18, no. 2 (fall 1993): 80–124.

66. Von Clausewitz, *On War*, 605–610.

1. The Perils of Liberal Hegemony

1. These are direct budgetary costs. Stephen Daggett, *Costs of Major U.S. Wars*, RS22926, Congressional Research Service, June 29, 2010. Inclusion of future costs for health care for veterans and interest on the debt incurred to finance the war could drive total budgetary costs of the Iraq war alone much higher. Joseph E. Stiglitz and Linda J. Bilmes, *The Three Trillion Dollar War* (New York: W. W. Norton, 2008). See also Cindy Williams, Précis Interview, MIT Center for International Studies, spring 2013, 2, who notes that total war spending has continued to rise to nearly $1.4 trillion. Nonwar defense spending also increased by 50 percent after 2001, to a total of nearly $1.4 trillion. By 2013 the United States had spent nearly $2.8 trillion dollars more on defense than previously planned, amounting to nearly a quarter of the national debt held by the public.

2. Stephen Daggett and Nina M. Serafino, *Costs of Major U.S. Wars and Recent U.S. Overseas Military Operations*, RS21013, Congressional Research Service, October 3, 2001, 4. I have estimated a conversion of their total to 2011 dollars.

3. "Operation Iraqi Freedom (OIF) U.S. Casualty Status," June 6, 2013, available at http://www.defense.gov/news/#BRIEFINGS.

4. Ibid.

5. Hannah Fischer, "U.S. Military Casualty Statistics: Operation New Dawn, Operation Iraqi Freedom, and Operation Enduring Freedom," Congressional Research Service, February 5, 2013, RS22452, is the source of PTSD and TBI figures.

6. A conservative estimate, sustained over the course of the war and reliant on press reports, puts just over 100,000 Iraqi civilians killed between 2003 and 2012, most at the hands of other Iraqis. See the estimates of the Iraq Body Count project, available at http://www.iraqbodycount.org. We cannot know whether similar levels of internal violence would have occurred in the absence of U.S. intervention. Aside from wars, some estimate that Saddam's regime killed 200,000 Iraqis. John F. Burns, "How Many People Has Hussein Killed?" *New York Times*, January 26, 2003, available at http://www.nytimes.com/2003/01/26/weekinreview/the-world-how-many-people-has-hussein-killed.html.

7. Pay and benefits, which are already fully competitive with the private sector, nevertheless tend to rise much faster than the rate of inflation. Though the DOD has tried to bring these costs under control, Congress has not cooperated. See Cindy L. Williams, "Making Defense Affordable," The Hamilton Project, February 2013, 15–18.

8. Carl Conetta, *An Undisciplined Defense, Understanding the $2 Trillion Surge in US Defense Spending* (Cambridge, MA: Project on Defense Alternatives, January 18, 2010), 44, figure B-1.

9. NATO, "Financial and Economic Data Relating to NATO Defence," press release, February 19, 2009, 6, table 3, available at http://www.nato.int/cps/en/natolive/news_85966.htm?mode=pressrelease.

10. NATO, "Financial and Economic Data Relating to NATO Defence," press release, April 13, 2012, 6, table 3, available at http://www.nato.int/cps/en/natolive/news_85966.htm?mode=pressrelease.

11. Stephen G. Brooks and William C. Wohlforth, *World out of Balance* (Princeton, NJ: Princeton University Press, 2008), 45–48, essentially expect no balancing for a very long time, because the U.S. lead is so great, in so many areas, that no state or coalition can plausibly match it, so they will not even try. They present a great deal of compelling evidence demonstrating the present U.S. lead. They go on to argue that this lead will indeed cow others into accepting U.S. hegemony.

12. Reviewing these influences on both the extent and the limits of counter-U.S. balancing is Stephen M. Walt, "Alliances in a Multipolar World," in *International Relations Theory and the Consequences of Unipolarity*, ed. G. John Ikenberry, Michael Mastanduno, and William C. Wohlforth (Cambridge: Cambridge University Press, 2011), 111–12, 115–23.

13. Robert Pape, "Soft Balancing against the United States," *International Security* 30, no. 1 (summer 2005): 7–44; T. V. Paul, "Soft Balancing in the Age of U.S. Primacy," *International Security* 30, no. 1 (summer 2005): 46–71.

14. Martha Finnemore, "Legitimacy, Hypocrisy, and the Social Structure of Unipolarity: Why Being a Unipole Isn't All It's Cracked Up to Be," *World Politics* 61, no. 1 (January 2009): 58–85.

15. Dane Liselotte Odgaard, "China's Premature Rise to Great Power," April 2007, MIT Center for International Studies, Audit of the Conventional Wisdom.

16. Stephen G. Brooks and William C. Wohlforth, "Hard Times for Soft Balancing," *International Security* 30, no. 1 (summer 2005): 72–108; and Keir Lieber, "Waiting for Balancing: Why the World Is Not Pushing Back," *International Security* 30, no. 1 (summer 2005): 109–39, argue that soft balancing is not a very useful concept, and that even if it were, there is no soft balancing happening. The argument that soft balancing is not particularly decisive is reasonable. The argument that neither soft nor hard balancing is occurring seems myopic. The authors stare balancing in the face, and as Robert Art notes, they simply redefine it out of existence by calling it normal diplomacy; Robert J. Art, "Correspondence, Striking the Balance," *International Security* 30, no. 3 (winter 2005–6): 177–85.

17. Office of the Secretary of Defense, *Military Power of the People's Republic of China 2009*, Annual Report to Congress, U.S. Department of Defense, March 2009, 29 (hereafter *Military Power of the PRC*, 2009); see also Elizabeth Wishnick, *Russia, China, and the United States in Central Asia: Prospects for Great Power Competition and Cooperation in the Shadow of the Georgian Crisis*, U.S. Army War College, Strategic Studies Institute, February 2009: 18–32, available at http://www.StrategicStudiesInstitute.army.mil/.

18. *Military Power of the PRC*, 2009, 37; observing that arms sales slowed after a 2003 dispute over Chinese copying of Russian designs but seem poised to accelerate, see

Kor Kian Beng, "China, Russia Growing Closer Despite Distrust; Warming Ties Help Boost Defence Cooperation and Drive Arms Sales," *Straits Times* (Singapore), April 2, 2013.

19. Chikako Ueki, *The Rise of "China Threat" Arguments* (Ph.D. diss., Massachusetts Institute of Technology, 2006).

20. The complex negotiations ending the Soviet presence in East Germany are detailed in Mary Elise Sarotte, "Perpetuating U.S. Preeminence," *International Security* 35, no. 1 (summer 2010): 110–37. Sarotte also shows that these assurances were disingenuous, and that the United States and other NATO members were already thinking about membership for East European states. Gorbachev and subsequent Russian leaders felt betrayed that the informal assurances were subsequently ignored: 133,137. See also Daniel Deudney and G. John Ikenberry, "The Unravelling of the Cold War Settlement," *Survival* 51, no. 6 (December 2009): 39–62.

21. Barry R. Posen, "European Union Security and Defense Policy: Response to Unipolarity?" *Security Studies* 15, no. 2 (2006): 166–73, 178–82, 183–84. See also Art, "Striking the Balance," 177–85.

22. "Time to Decide: America's Nuclear Deal with India," *Economist*, August 30, 2008; John Lee, "Bush Legacy: Better US-India Relations," *Straits Times* (Singapore), October 8, 2009; Lara Marlowe, "US Seeks 'Defining Partnership' with India," *Irish Times*, November 25, 2009.

23. *Military Power of the PRC*, 2009, 4.

24. See GlobalSecurity.org, "Iran Defense Industry," February 2009, available at http://www.globalsecurity.org/military/world/iran/industry.htm; Alon Ben-David, "Iran Launches New Surface-to-Air Missile Production," *Jane's Intelligence Weekly*, February 13, 2006; Robin Hughes, "Iran and Syria Advance SIGINT Co-Operation," *Jane's Defence Weekly*, July 19, 2006.

25. See the excellent study by Andrew Exum, *Hizballah at War, A Military Assessment*, Policy Focus No. 63 (Washington, DC: Washington Institute for Near East Policy, December 2006), 7, 11.

26. For an accessible review and critique see Amitai Etzioni, "Who Authorized Preparations for War with China?" *Yale Journal of International Affairs* (summer 2013): 37–51; see also Raoul Heinrichs, "America's Dangerous Battle Plan" *The Diplomat*, August 17, 2011, http://thediplomat.com/2011/08/17/america%E2%80%99s-dangerous-battle-plan/?all=true.

27. Daryl G. Press, *Calculating Credibility: How Leaders Assess Military Threats* (Ithaca: Cornell University Press, 2005), 1–7, 10–20.

28. In a 2008 Public Agenda poll, "85% said that only taking military action with the backing of allies is 'very important' (51%) or 'somewhat important' (34%)." A German Marshall Fund poll in 2005 found that 53 percent of respondents said that "NATO approval makes military action legitimate." Council on Foreign Relations, "U.S. Opinion on General Principles of World Order," *Public Opinion on Global Issues*, December 16, 2011, chapter 9, available at http://www.cfr.org/public_opinion; The Chicago Council on Global Affairs has been polling U.S. public attitudes for many years and notes in its most recent poll, "As in the past, without a clear specification that the intervention would be multilateral, majorities of Americans oppose most possible uses of U.S. troops cited in the survey, including if China invaded Taiwan . . . and if North Korea invaded South Korea." The Chicago Council on Global Affairs, *Global Views 2010—Constrained Internationalism: Adapting to New Realities, Results*

of a 2010 National Survey of American Public Opinion, 55 available at http://www. thechicagocouncil.org/files/Studies_Publications/POS/POS2010/Global_ Views_2010.aspx.

29. The notable exception to this rule is Operation Desert Storm, the ejection of Iraq from Kuwait in 1991. The United States actually made money on that war with total funding requirements coming to $47.5 billion against allied cash and in-kind contributions of $48.3 billion; see General Accounting Office, *Operation Desert Shield/Storm: Costs and Funding Requirements,* Report to the Chairman, Committee on the Armed Services, House of Representatives, September 1991, 1–2.

30. Timothy W. Crawford and Alan J. Kuperman, "Debating the Hazards of Intervention," and Kuperman, "Suicidal Rebellions and the Moral Hazard of Humanitarian Intervention," in *Gambling on Humanitarian Intervention, Moral Hazard, Rebellion and Civil War,* ed. Crawford and Kuperman (New York: Routledge, 2006),1–25, offer a theoretical foundation for this behavior.

31. U.S. Department of Defense, *2004 Statistical Compendium on Allied Contributions to the Common Defense,* available at http://www.defense.gov/pubs/allied_con trib2004/allied2004.pdf.

32. The National Defense Authorization Act for FY 2004 calls for such a report and asks that it be submitted in unclassified form. I have searched for this report and have not found it. See *National Defense Authorization Act for Fiscal Year 2004,* Public Law 108–136, 108th Cong., 1st. sess. (November 24, 2003), Sec. 1231.

33. NATO, *The Alliance's Strategic Concept* (Washington, DC: North Atlantic Council), April 24, 1999, para. 20, available at http://www.nato.int/cps/en/natolive/ official_texts_27433.htm.

34. NATO Update, "NATO Response Force declared fully operational," November 30, 2006, http://www.nato.int/docu/update/2006/11-november/e1129c.htm.

35. NATO, *Defence Transformation: Transforming Allied Forces for Current and Future Operations,* Briefing, April 2008, available at http://www.nato.int/ebookshop/ briefing/defence_transformation/html_en/dtc01.htm, 5–6. As noted in the document, NATO members "directed that a new graduated force option should be developed, with the agreed NRF concept as an interim solution, as long as operational requirements remain so high." Available at http://www.nato.int/nato_static/as sets/pdf/pdf_publications/20120116_defence_transformation2008-e.pdf. See also the statement of General Knud Bartels, chairman of NATO's Military Committee, "Revitalizing the NATO Response Force will be crucial to this endeavour . . . I believe the NATO Response Force is the perfect platform to develop and refine common doctrines and bring transformation forward." "NATO Chiefs of Defence Bring Transformation to the Forefront," 16 Jan. 2013—17 Jan. 2013, available at http:// www.nato.int/cps/en/natolive/news_94089.htm. One infers from the need for "revitalization" that not much progress was made from 2008 to 2013.

36. Eric Schmitt, "NATO Sees Flaws in Air Campaign against Qaddafi," *New York Times,* April 14, 2012; Thom Shanker and Eric Schmitt, "Libya Role Revealed NATO Deficiencies; Region in Revolt," *International Herald Tribune,* October 22, 2011.

37. Ellen Williams, "Out of Area and Very Much in Business? NATO, the U.S., and the Post-9/11 International Security Environment," *Comparative Strategy* 27, no. 1 (January/February 2008): 68–71, 73–75.

38. For details of the operation see NATO, "International Security and Assistance Force [ISAF] Afghanistan," available at http://www.isaf.nato.int/.

39. A diagram of this complicated structure can be found in US DOD, *Report on Progress toward Security and Stability in Afghanistan*, November 2010: 13, available at http://www.defense.gov/pubs/November_1230_Report_FINAL.pdf.

40. To quote one NATO official, "Later on the Americans realized that the immediate bureaucratic complications of working through the alliance would have been far outweighed by the political benefits of having the Europeans involved in the global war on terror up front as partners." Quote from Williams, "Out of Area," 70.

41. Jeremy Shapiro and Nick Witney, *Toward a Post-American Europe: A Power Audit of EU-US Relations* (London: European Council on Foreign Relations, October 2009), 53.

42. Vincent Morelli and Paul Belkin, *NATO in Afghanistan: A Test of the Transatlantic Alliance*, RL33627, Congressional Research Service, December 3, 2009, 18–21.

43. Editorial, "NATO and Afghanistan," *International Herald Tribune*, December 15, 2009. Germany agreed to add five hundred soldiers to the forty-five hundred it had in Afghanistan, though the United States and other allies asked for two thousand; see Gerrit Wiesmann and Ben Hall, "Berlin Set to Bolster Afghan Mission," *Financial Times*, January 26, 2010. Canada and the Netherlands had already announced their intention to withdraw their contingents. Morelli and Belkin, *NATO in Afghanistan*, 35.

44. USDOD, "The Security and Defense Agenda (Future of NATO)," *As Delivered by Secretary of Defense Robert M. Gates, Brussels, Belgium, Friday, June 10, 2011*, available at http://www.defense.gov/speeches/speech.aspx?speechid=1581.

45. U.S. secretary of defense Robert Gates has argued "that NATO needs more cargo aircraft and more helicopters of all types—and yet we still don't have these capabilities. And their absence is directly impacting operations in Afghanistan. Similarly, NATO requires more aerial refueling tankers and intelligence, surveillance, and reconnaissance platforms for immediate use on the battlefield," Remarks Delivered at the NATO Strategic Concept Seminar (Future of NATO), National Defense University, Washington, D.C., Tuesday, February 23, 2010, http://www.defense.gov/speeches/speech.aspx?speechid=1423. See also Morelli and Belkin, *NATO in Afghanistan*, 34.

46. Morelli and Belkin, *NATO in Afghanistan*, 10–12.; Andre de Nesnera, "European Governments Restrict Their NATO Forces in Afghanistan," Voice of America, March 5, 2010, available at http://www1.voanews.com/english/news/europe/European-Governments-Restrict-Their-NATO-Forces-In-Afghanistan-86627212.html. The caveats issue and stories covering it were very prominent through 2008. Fewer stories have appeared recently, but it is not clear that this reflects an easing of the problem or an admission that not much can be done to solve it.

47. The UK's participation in operations appears to be affecting the readiness of the remainder of its military for exactly this reason. Tom Coghlan, "UK Military Creaking under Strain of Iraq and Afghanistan, Report Says," *London Times*, February 10, 2010.

48. Secretary Gates highlighted "national caveats that tied the hands of allied commanders in sometimes infuriating ways, the inability of many allies to meet agreed upon commitments and, in some cases, wildly disparate contributions from different member states." USDOD, "The Security and Defense Agenda (Future of NATO)."

49. Hillary Rodham Clinton, "The U.S.-Japan Security Consultative Committee Marking the 50th Anniversary of the Signing of The U.S.-Japan Treaty of Mutual

[188]

Cooperation and Security," U.S. Department of State, Washington, DC, January 19, 2010, available at http://www.state.gov/secretary/rm/2010/01/135312.htm.

50. Michael Finnegan, *Managing Unmet Expectations in the U.S.-Japan Alliance*. NBR Special Report #17, National Bureau of Asian Research, November 2009, 13–15, 19–20.

51. George Packard, "The United States-Japan Security Treaty at 50," *Foreign Affairs* 89, no. 2 (March/April 2010): 92–103.

52. Most discussions of the U.S.-Japan Security Treaty include a brief history. See Packard, "United-States Japan Security Treaty at 50," 93–96; Finnegan, *Managing Unmet Expectations*, 6–9.

53. Jennifer M. Lind, "Pacifism or Passing the Buck?: Testing Theories of Japanese Security Policy," *International Security* 29, no. 1 (summer 2004): 94–101, offers a systematic review of Japan's extensive military capabilities, and some of its limitations.

54. The percentage decline is based on figures from Japan Ministry of Defense, *Defense of Japan 2009*, trans. Erklaren Inc. (Tokyo: Erklaren, 2009), 164; and *Defense Programs and Budget of Japan, Overview of FY 2013 Budget*, 37, available at http://www.mod.go.jp/e/d_budget/pdf/250516.pdf; These figures include roughly $1.7 billion a year to help defray the local costs of maintaining U.S. forces in Japan.

55. Finnegan observes, "A decade after the drafting of the 1997 Defense Guidelines, Japan still lacks key capabilities in areas where it has 'primary responsibility' per the guidelines, such as antisubmarine warfare and air defense;" see Finnegan, *Managing Unmet Expectations*, 15.

56. The National Institute for Defense Studies, Japan, *East Asian Strategic Review 2012* (Tokyo: Japan Times, 2012), 251–56.

57. Defense Manpower Data Center, "Active Duty Military Personnel by Service by Region/Country," (as of June 30, 2013), https://www.dmdc.osd.mil/appj/dwp/reports.do?category=reports&subCat=milActDutReg; Office of the Deputy Under Secretary of Defense (Installation and Environment), "DOD Base Structure Report FY 2013 Baseline," 85–87, lists sixty-seven U.S. military sites in Japan, but I judge a dozen to be large enough to be called a base. http://www.acq.osd.mil/ie/.

58. For a vague review of the state of progress and future goals, see US Department of State, "Toward a Deeper and Broader U.S.-Japan Alliance: Building on 50 Years of Partnership, Joint Statement of the U.S.-Japan Security Consultative Committee," Media Note, Office of the Spokesperson, Washington, DC, June 21, 2011, available at http://www.state.gov/r/pa/prs/ps/2011/06/166597.htm. The communique offers a lengthy list of cooperative activities yet to be done that one would have thought would have been done already. For example, "The Ministers decided to expand joint training and exercises, study further joint and shared use of facilities, and promote cooperation, such as expanding information sharing and joint intelligence, surveillance, and reconnaissance (ISR) activities, in order to deter and respond proactively, rapidly and seamlessly to various situations in the region."

59. Richard L. Armitage and Joseph S. Nye, "The U.S.-Japan Alliance: Anchoring Stability in Asia," a report of the CSIS Japan chair, CSIS (August 2012), 11–12.

60. Condoleeza Rice, Robert M. Gates, Taro Aso, and Fumio Kyuma, "Joint Statement of the U.S.-Japan Security Consultative Committee Alliance Transformation: Advancing United States-Japan Security and Defense Cooperation," May 1, 2007, available at http://www.usfj.mil/Documents/JointStatementoftheSecurityConsultativeCommittee.pdf; David Arase, "Japan, The Active State? Security Policy after 9/11,"*Asian Survey* 47, no. 4 (July/August 2007): 581–82.

61. Though Japan possesses military forces, the Japanese government and polity still seem unwilling to admit that they might use them, and use them in cooperation with the United States, even in self-defense. The constitution is formally to blame, but this is a deeper political issue. Finnegan, *Managing Unmet Expectations,* 13–16; see also Japan, Ministry of Defense, *Defense of Japan 2011,* part III, chapter 1, "Operations of Self-Defense Forces for Defense of Japan and Responses to Diverse Situations," especially section IV, "Efforts towards High Readiness for Armed Attack Situations," 214, suggesting that some effort is being made to improve responsiveness, including more exercises with the U.S. Available at http://www.mod.go.jp/e/publ/w_paper/pdf/2011/29Part3_Chapter1_Sec1.pdf.

62. "The Ministers welcomed the establishment of a bilateral extended deterrence dialogue on a regular basis as a consultative mechanism to determine the most effective ways to enhance regional stability, including that provided by nuclear capabilities, in the near-term and long-term." "Joint Statement of the U.S.-Japan Security Consultative Committee," June 21, 2011.

63. Armitage and Nye, "U.S.-Japan Alliance," 14.

64. An extra layer of irony is added by the fact that Japanese policymakers also believe that the United States is doing too little to avert nuclear proliferation. The Western arms control community believes that it is hard to advance the cause of nuclear nonproliferation if the United States is at the same time stressing nuclear war fighting for extended deterrence in its declaratory policy and in its force structure. Finnegan, *Managing Unmet Expectations,* 18.

65. Aaron David Miller, *The Much Too Promised Land: America's Elusive Search for Arab-Israeli Peace* (New York: Bantam, 2008), 367. See also Dana H. Allin and Steven Simon, "The Moral Psychology of US Support for Israel," *Survival* 45, no. 3 (autumn 2003): 139–40. Though Osama Bin Laden's grandiose, hateful, and murderous project for global jihad stemmed from many sources and is inexcusable, the Israeli-Palestinian dispute does seem to have played a role in his youthful radicalization. Lawrence Wright, *The Looming Tower: Al-Qaeda and the Road to 9/11* (New York: Alfred Knopf, 2006), 75–76, 131, 150.

66. "In this complex threat environment, Israel's dependence on U.S. security guarantees, strategic cooperation, and regional influence—already substantial for decades—may increase. . . . If that is the case, one probable result is that most international actors will hold the United States responsible to a greater degree for Israel's actions." Jim Zanotti, *Israel: Background and U.S. Relations,* Congressional Research Service 7-5700, RL33476, February 29, 2012, available at http://www.dtic.mil/cgi-bin/GetTRDoc?AD=ADA560390.

67. Natasha Mozgaveya, "Petraeus to Ashkenazi: I Never Said Israel Policy Endangers U.S.," *Haaretz,* March 25, 2010, available at www.haaretz.com/hasen/spages/1159165.html. The article discusses a controversy that arose from remarks that General David Petraeus, then U.S. commander in the region, had made to the effect that the Arab-Israeli conflict was not helpful to U.S. efforts in the Middle East. Secretary Gates then publicly echoed these concerns.

68. As of 2010, there were some 500,000 Israelis living in the territory seized during the 1967 war: "approximately 311,100 Israeli settlers live in the West Bank (2010); approximately 186,929 Israeli settlers live in East Jerusalem (2010)." See U.S. Central Intelligence Agency, "The West Bank," entry in, *The World Factbook, 2012,* available at https://www.cia.gov/library/publications/the-world-factbook/geos/we.html.

69. The George W. Bush administration's effort to craft a "road map" to guide the establishment of a Palestinian state alongside Israel garnered the support of the European Union, Russia, and the United Nations; see U.S. Department of State, *A Performance Based Roadmap to a Permanent Two-State Solution to the Israeli-Palestinian Conflict,* Washington, DC, April 30, 2003, http://www.mfa.gov.il/mfa/foreignpolicy/peace/guide/pages/a%20performance-based%20roadmap%20to%20a%20permanent%20two-sta. aspx, available at The UN Security Council supported a two-state solution to the Israeli-Palestinian Conflict; see United Nations, *Resolution 1397* (2002), Adopted by the Security Council at its 4489th Meeting, March 12, 2002, available at http://unispal.un.org/unispal.nsf/0/4721362DD7BA3DEA85256B7B00536C7F. See also the UN Press Release, "Security Council Demands Immediate Cessation of all Violence in Middle East; Affirms Vision of Two States, Israel And Palestine," March 12, 2002, available at http://unispal.un.org/unispal.nsf/22f431edb91c6f548525678a0051be1d/4d583669 5dec698785256b7b00506b30?OpenDocument. Shortly after the passage of UNSC 1397, the Arab League, led by Crown Prince (currently King) Abdullah of Saudi Arabia, also endorsed a variant of the two-state solution in the Arab Peace Plan of 2002; see Council of the League of Arab States, *Arab Peace Plan of 2002,* Beirut, Lebanon, March 28, 2002, http://news.bbc.co.uk/2/hi/middle_east/1844214.stm. The Arab League reaffirmed the two-state solution during a 2007 summit in Riyadh; BBCNews.com, "Arab Leaders Relaunch Peace Plan," March 28, 2007, http://news. bbc.co.uk/2/hi/6501573.stm.

70. For a comprehensive account of the emergence of the two-state solution and obstacles to its realization, see Asher Susser, *Israel, Jordan, and Palestine: The Two-State Imperative* (Waltham, MA: Brandeis University Press, 2012).

71. As Allin and Simon observe, "Americans have neglected some important problems and have been prisoner to some dangerous illusions. The most dangerous of these illusions was the implicit assumption that the new facts on the ground created by a relentless Israeli policy of establishing settlements in the occupied territories was either irrelevant to a negotiated peace, or might even constitute a useful bargaining chip"; Allin and Simon, "Moral Psychology," 136. The article overall places a great deal of responsibility for the failure of negotiations on the Palestinians; see also Susser, *The Two-State Imperative,* 43, 165–67.

72. On the necessity of creating legitimacy for any future settlement to work, see Walter Russell Meade, "Change They Can Believe In: To Make Israel Safe, Give Palestinians Their Due," *Foreign Affairs* 88, no. 1 (January/February 2009): 59–76. Meade does not emphasize a capital in East Jerusalem as the key problem. Instead he argues that the "right of return" is the most important issue; the United States needs to recognize the legitimacy of this claim while at the same time organizing and contributing generously to an international effort to compensate the Palestinians for relinquishing it.

73. Efraim Inbar employed this term for the announcement. He blamed the Americans for the ensuing controversy. The paper lucidly and economically presents the views of the Israeli center-right on the matter of settlements and the relationship with the United States. See Efraim Inbar, "Netanyahu Can Say 'No,'" Begin-Sadat Center for Strategic Studies, Perspectives Papers on Current Events, no. 103, March 25, 2010, available at http://www.biu.ac.il/SOC/besa/perspectives103.html.

74. Quoted in John Goshko, "Baker Scathing on Israeli Settlement Expansion as Biggest Obstacle to Peace in Middle East," *Guardian* (London), May 23, 1991. Baker continued, "This does violate United States policy. It is the first thing that Arabs—Arab governments—the first thing that Palestinians in the territories—whose situation is

really quite desperate—the first thing they raise when we talk to them. I don't think there is any greater obstacle to peace than settlement activity that continues not only unabated but at an advanced pace." Testimony of U.S. Secretary of State James Baker," Foreign Operations Subcommittee of the House Appropriations Committee, Fiscal Year '92 Appropriations, May 22, 1991 (Washington, DC: Federal Information Systems Corporation, Federal News Service, 1991).

75. Herb Keinon and Tovah Lazaroof, "Tenders for Ma'aleh Adumim Trigger Protest from Peace Now, but Not U.S." *Jerusalem Post,* January 16, 2007; Griff Witte, "Israel Planning to Build Hundreds of New Homes," *Washington Post,* April 1, 2008; Herb Keinon, "Israeli Sources: Rice's Criticism of J'lem Building Plan Ruffles Few Feathers," *Jerusalem Post,* June 16, 2008.

76. Hilary Leila Krieger, "As Bush Flies in Crisis Looms Over Settlements: Secretary Rice Tells 'Post' US Is Completely Opposed to Har Homa," *Jerusalem Post,* January 9, 2008.

77. Thomas L. Friedman, "Driving Drunk in Jerusalem," *New York Times,* March 13, 2010.

78. Jeremy M. Sharp, *U.S. Foreign Aid to Israel,* RL 33222, Congressional Research Service, December 4, 2009, i.

79. Ibid., 21–24.

80. Ibid., 3.

81. International Institute for Strategic Studies (hereafter IISS), *The Military Balance 2009* (London: Routledge, 2009), 249–51. Israel has the most capable military in the region and one of the most capable military organizations in the world. Much of the credit for this achievement goes to Israeli society, which produces excellent soldiers and airmen. Much of the credit also goes to the United States, which provided Israel with some of the finest weaponry in the world. Since 2008 there is even U.S. legislation committing the United States to maintain Israel's "qualitative military edge." Sharp, *Foreign Aid to Israel,* 1–2.

82. On reconciliation, see U.S. Department of Defense (hereafter DOD), *Measuring Stability and Security in Iraq: Report to Congress,* March 2007: 1–3, available at http://www.defense.gov/pubs/pdfs/9010_March_2007_Final_Signed.pdf.

83. Marc Lynch, "Bush's Finest Moment on Iraq Was the Status of Forces Agreement, Not the Surge," (Blog Post) January 18, 2009, available at http://lynch.foreignpolicy.com/posts/2009/01/18/sofa_not_the_surge; Tony Karon, "Iraq's Government, Not Obama, Called Time on the U.S. Troop Presence," *TIME/CNN* Blog Post, October 21, 2011, http://world.time.com/2011/10/21/iraq-not-obama-called-time-on-the-u-s-troop-presence.

84. U.S. Department of Defense (hereafter DOD), *Measuring Stability and Security in Iraq: Report to Congress,* June 2010: x, available at http://www.defense.gov/pubs/pdfs/June_9204_Sec_Def_signed_20_Aug_2010.pdf; the language is almost the same in the report written six months earlier, see U.S. Department of Defense (hereafter DOD), *Measuring Stability and Security in Iraq: Report to Congress,* December 2009 viii, available at http://www.defense.gov/pubs/pdfs/Master_9204_29Jan10_FINAL_SIGNED.pdf.

85. A notably pessimistic assessment is found in "Iraq Report: Political Fragmentation and Corruption Stymie Economic Growth and Political Progress," a Minority Staff Trip Report to the Committee on Foreign Relations United States Senate, One

Hundred Twelfth Congress, Second Session, April 30, 2012, 1–5, available at http://www.gpo.gov/fdsys/.

86. Mohammed Abbas and Muhanad Mohammed, "Former Iraq PM: Poll Ban Risks Civil War," *Reuters*, February 8, 2010, available at http://www.reuters.com/article/idUSTRE6173KS20100208.

87. Leila Fadel, "In Iraq, Candidates Seek an Edge with Post-Election Maneuvers," *Washington Post*, March 30, 2010, available at http://www.washingtonpost.com/wp-dyn/content/article/2010/03/29/AR2010032901358.html.

88. Gareth Stansfield and Liam Anderson, "Kurds in Iraq: The Struggle between Baghdad and Erbil," *Middle East Policy* 16, no. 1 (spring 2009): 134.

89. On the fighting in Khanaqin, see ibid., 136. For a full account of the dispute between the Iraqi central government and the Kurdish regional government, see International Crisis Group, "Iraq and the Kurds: Confronting Withdrawal Fears," Middle East Report No. 103, March 28, 2011, available at http://www.crisisgroup.org/~/media/Files/Middle%20East%20North%20Africa/Iraq%20Syria%20Lebanon/Iraq/103%20Iraq%20and%20the%20Kurds%20--%20Confronting%20Withdrawal%20Fears.pdf; see also International Crisis Group, "Déjà Vu All Over Again? Iraq's Escalating Political Crisis," Middle East Report No. 126, July 30, 2012: 3, 7–10, available at http://www.crisisgroup.org/~/media/Files/Middle%20East%20North%20Africa/Iraq%20Syria%20Lebanon/Iraq/126-deja-vu-all-over-again-iraqs-escalating-political-crisis.pdf.

90. For a candid U.S. government appraisal of the situation in Iraq, see U.S. Department of State, Bureau of Democracy, "Human Rights, and Labor, Country Reports on Human Rights Practices for 2011," *Iraq*: 1–2, available at http://www.state.gov/documents/organization/186638.pdf.

91. The complexity and contentiousness of this debate is illustrated in Stephen Biddle, Jeffrey A. Friedman, and Jacob N. Shapiro, "Testing the Surge: Why Did Violence Decline in Iraq in 2007?" *International Security* 37, no. 1 (summer 2012): 7–40; and the subsequent exchange with five of their critics, John Hagan, Joshua Kaiser, and Anna Hanson; and Jon R. Lindsay and Austin G. Long, "Correspondence: Assessing the Synergy Thesis in Iraq," *International Security* 37, no. 4 (spring 2013): 173–98.

92. On the failure to pass a "hydrocarbons law," DOD, *Measuring Stability and Security in Iraq: Report to Congress*, June 2010: 2, 6.

93. International Crisis Group, "Déjà vu," i–ii.

94. "Iraq Death Toll 'Tops 1,000' in July, Highest in Years," BBC, August 1, 2013, available at http://www.bbc.co.uk/news/world-middle-east-23531834.

95. Barry R. Posen, "Nationalism, the Mass Army, and Military Power," *International Security* 18, no. 2 (autumn 1993): 80–124.

96. Modern scholarship ranks the emergence and organization of local nationalism as only one of three causes of the postwar retreat of empire. Developments within the metropoles are given equal or greater causal weight. The Cold War, and the opposition of both the Soviet Union and the United States to empire, also gets some credit. Integrated with these macrocauses is an understanding that these empires typically could only rule efficiently when they could co-opt local elites; these arrangements unraveled for any number of local reasons, but the macrolevel causes seemed to work against their survival. John Springhall, *Decolonization since 1945*

(Houndsmills, UK: Palgrave, 2001), 1–17, 203–19; R. F. Holland, *European Decolonization 1918–1981: An Introductory Survey* (New York: St. Martin's, 1985), 2–33, 191.

97. Lotta Harbom and Peter Wallensteen, "Armed Conflicts 1946–2008," *Journal of Peace Research* 46, no. 4 (July 2009): 579, figure 1. There were twenty-two armed conflicts against colonial empires, which these analysts dub "extrasystemic conflicts," between 1946 and 1975, when the last European colonial empire, Portugal, gave up in Angola and Mozambique. These authors rely on Nils Petter Gleditsch et al., UCDP/PRIO Armed Conflict Dataset Version 4, available at http://www.prio.no/CSCW/Datasets/Armed-Conflict/UCDP-PRIO/, 2009. See also Uppsala Conflict Data Program and Centre for the Study of Civil Wars, International Peace Research Institute, Oslo (PRIO), *UCDP/PRIO Armed Conflict Dataset Codebook*, Version 4, 2010, available at www.ucdp.uu.se, and Nils Peter Gleditsch et al., "Armed Conflict 1946–2001: A New Dataset," *Journal of Peace Research* 39, no. 5 (September 2002): 615–37.

98. Jeffrey Record and W. Andrew Terrill, *Iraq and Vietnam: Differences, Similarities, and Insights* (Carlisle, PA: U.S. Army Strategic Studies Institute, May 2004), 13–14.

99. Ronald H. Spector, *After Tet: The Bloodiest Year in Vietnam* (New York: Random House), 71–91, esp. 84–91.

100. Harbom and Wallensteen, "Armed Conflicts 1946–2008," 579, figure 1.

101. An agreed single database characterizing the causes of violent conflicts does not exist. R. William Ayres, "A World Flying Apart? Violent Nationalist Conflict and the End of the Cold War," *Journal of Peace Research* 37, no. 1 (January 2000): 105–17, does attempt an enumeration of nationalist conflicts from the end of World War II to 1996 and finds 77 such conflicts, some of them quite small. He excludes rebellions against empires from his data set and assumes that civil wars between groups contending for control of the state apparatus in a given territory are by definition not nationalist. He characterizes 38 of the 108 conflicts in the 1989–97 time slice from Harbom and Wallensteen, "Armed Conflicts," as nationalist, some 35 percent. Andrew Wimmer, Lars-Erik Cederman, and Brian Min, "Ethnic Politics and Armed Conflict: A Configuration Analysis of a New Global Data Set," *American Sociological Review* 74, no. 2 (April 2009): 324–27, assess that ethnic politics—disputes about the distribution of internal power and wealth among ethnic groups—was at the root of 110 of the 215 internal conflicts that occurred between 1946 and 2005 (327). I judge from these data that between a third and a half of internal violent conflicts since the end of the Second World War have been about nationalism or ethnicity.

102. Jonathan Kirshner, "Globalization, Power, and Prospect," in *Globalization and National Security*, ed. Jonathan Kirshner (New York: Routledge, 2006), 321–38.

103. Michael Mousseau, "Market Civilization and Its Clash with Terror," *International Security* 27, no. 3 (winter 2002–3): 2–29, makes a similar argument, though he emphasizes mainly the connection between capitalism and liberal democracy, and the emergence of a kind of danger zone once capitalism begins to emerge, but before liberal democratic institutions can be built. See especially 9–19.

104. The urban population of the world is expected to increase by roughly 50 percent, or 1.6 billion people over the next two decades, with most of the growth in the developing world. Many of these people will be poor, and young. Young people aged fifteen to twenty-four commit the largest number of violent acts. The revival of religion, including radical Islam, has been associated with the recent wave of urbanization. See UN Population Fund, *State of World Population 2007: Unleashing the Potential of Urban Growth* (United Nations Population Fund, 2007), 6, 26–27.

105. Audrey Kurth Cronin, "Behind the Curve: Globalization and International Terrorism," *International Security* 27, no. 3 (winter 2002/2003): 38, 45, 51–58, argues for a causal relationship between globalization and the most recent wave of jihadi terrorism.

106. Alexander Cooley, *Base Politics: Democratic Change and the U.S. Military Overseas* (Ithaca: Cornell University Press, 2008); Kent E. Calder, *Embattled Garrisons, Comparative Base Politics and American Globalism* (Princeton, NJ: Princeton University Press, 2007).

107. Mature democracies that have considered the U.S. presence and approved it through their own legitimate processes usually do not have very strong negative public reactions to the bases. Strongly affected localities can prove resistant, such as in Okinawa, but they can also turn out to be supporters due to the resources that bases bring. Autocracies usually do not worry too much about public reaction. They offer the United States access in exchange for resources that they believe improve their domestic and international power position. Calder, *Embattled*, 47,112–14; Cooley, *Base Politics*, 16–18.

108. As Katzenstein and Keohane, summarizing the findings of a collaborative study of anti-Americanism, observe, "But when they [local populations] fear U.S. actions that could damage the interests of their polity, sovereign-nationalists respond with intense anti-Americanism, such as one has seen in China, Serbia, or Iraq." Peter J. Katzenstein and Robert O. Keohane, "Varieties of Anti-Americanism: A Framework for Analysis," in *Anti-Americanisms in World Context*, ed. Katzenstein and Keohane (Ithaca: Cornell University Press), 35.

109. Giacomo Chiozza, "Disaggregating Anti-Americanisms: An Analysis of Individual Attitudes towards the United States," in Katzenstein and Keohane, *Anti-Americanisms*, 125–26.

110. Marc Lynch, "Anti-Americanisms in the Arab World," in Katzenstein and Keohane, *Anti-Americanisms,* 199–204, finds evidence of sustained anti-Americanism in the Arab media. Chiozza finds similar evidence from polling data; see Chiozza, "Disaggregating," in Katzenstein and Keohane, *Anti-Americanism*, 125–26.

111. Lynch, "Anti-Americanisms," 204–10, 223–24; Shahram Akbarzadeh and Kylie Baxter, "Anti-Americanism in the Middle East," in *Anti-Americanism: History, Causes, Themes*, ed. Brendan O'Connor (Oxford, UK: Greenwood, 2007), 3, 281–301, systematically reviews the particular U.S. policies that they believe contribute to anti-Americanism in the Middle East.

112. Alexander B. Downes and Jonathan Monten, "Forced to Be Free: Why Foreign-Imposed Regime Change Rarely Leads to Democratization," *International Security* 37, no. 4 (spring 2013): 90–131, esp. 90–94, 130–31. Sonja Grimm counts seventeen efforts to export democracy after military action since World War II. The three outstanding successes, the occupations of Germany, Austria, and Japan are not repeated. Combining, when possible, two widely used indexes of democratization, only five of the other fourteen cases since World War II are gauged as even partially successful, and two of those are marginal. Only four of these efforts involve clear ethno-nationalist conflicts: Bosnia, Kosovo, Iraq, and Afghanistan. And none of these can yet be viewed as stable democracies. See Grimm, "External Democratization after War: Success and Failure," *Democratization* 15, no. 3 (June 2008): 525–49, see especially 527–29, 534.

113. Patrice C. McMahon and Jon Western, "The Death of Dayton: How to Stop Bosnia from Falling Apart," *Foreign Affairs* 88, no. 5 (September/October 2009): 69–83.

In their early remarks, McMahon and Western note, "After 14 years of intense inter-national efforts to stabilize and rebuild Bosnia, the country now stands on the brink of collapse" (69). Likewise, Fabrice Randoux discusses the ineffectiveness of the lure of EU membership—"conditionality"—as an incentive to the parties to suspend their sectarian disputes; Fabrice Randoux, "EU's Power of Attraction in Question," *Europolitics*, January 15, 2010.

114. Steven Woehrel, "Bosnia and Herzegovina: Current Issues and U.S. Policy," Congressional Research Service, R40479, January 24, 2013: 4–5.

115. As McMahon and Western succinctly put it, "If the international community cannot fulfill its promises in Bosnia—given the country's location in the middle of Europe, the leverage that the EU and NATO possess there, and the massive amount of money invested thus far—the prospects for international state building elsewhere are extremely grim"; McMahon and Western, "Death of Dayton," 71. The authors judge the effort thus far as largely unsuccessful but somewhat contradictorily rec-ommend a new series of tougher international management initiatives that will somehow produce a success.

116. Kelly M. Greenhill, *Weapons of Mass Migration: Forced Displacement, Coercion, and Foreign Policy* (Ithaca: Cornell University Press, 2010), 1–37, argues persuasively that actors in these internal conflicts often intentionally drive refugees toward other countries for the purpose of discomfiting the recipient in order to gain coercive le-verage over outsiders whose intervention they are either trying to encourage or discourage. This is not the only reason why refugees are forced out of their countries, but it is common, and Liberal Hegemony seems to invite it.

117. A notable but unpersuasive effort to come up with clear rules is Robert Pape, "When Duty Calls: A Pragmatic Standard of Humanitarian Intervention," *International Security* 37, no. 1 (summer 2012): 41–80, esp. 52–61. Though the author strives mightily to develop not only a "pragmatic," but an entirely ethical standard, some of his criteria are so demanding that they probably rule out most actions. For ex-ample, the author properly reminds us that the state has moral duties to its own citizens and soldiers not to pay high costs to realize objectives for which neither "signed up." So he concludes that the interveners must determine ex ante that "the cost in lives . . . approaches the risks of complex peacetime and training operations and so is effectively near zero." This is a very hard thing to know in advance about a shooting match. As low as U.S. casualties were in the Kosovo War, they were prob-ably in excess of this standard. If this cannot be known, the author argues that the intervention is still ethical if the soldiers who do it volunteer individually for the specific mission. This is impractical because the effectiveness of most military units depends on their "team" qualities, and if some volunteer, and some do not, then the risks of significant casualties would rise. Moreover, as the author also points out, if anything goes wrong, then the same criteria would need to apply to rescue forces, which would be impractical because of the short timelines required when things do go wrong (55, 74).

118. Daggett and Serafino, *Costs of Major Wars*, 2.

119. U.S. Central Intelligence Agency, "Imports of Military Equipment and Materiel by North Vietnam in 1974," Interagency Intelligence Memorandum, January 10, 1975, 2, available at http://www.foia.cia.gov; U.S. Central Intelligence Agency, "Soviet Military Aid to North Vietnam," Memorandum S3838, October 13, 1971, 1, available at http://www.foia.cia.gov; Stockholm International Peace Research Insti-tute, *SIPRI Yearbook 1976: World Armaments and Disarmament* (Cambridge, MA: MIT Press, 1976), 161. I have added the estimated value of arms imports to the estimated

defense budget of North Vietnam and converted these to constant 2008 dollars for a total of $61 billion. I cannot estimate the dollar value of Chinese troops stationed in North Vietnam, nor of taxes levied by the National Liberal Front in South Vietnam. In Iraq the United States did not wage a costly air campaign against an air defense system designed by the Soviet Union. One would like to break out of the Vietnam war costs the communist investment in air defense, and the U.S. investment in air attack, to arrive at the balance of costs in the ground war in the south, but the data does not permit this.

120. John F. Burns and Kirk Semple, "U.S. Finds Insurgency Has Funds to Sustain Itself," *New York Times*, November 26, 2006. According to a classified report obtained by the *Times*, the insurgents were then raising $70–200 million a year within Iraq from illegal activities. Qusay Hussein reportedly smuggled a billion dollars in cash out of the country, which funded the war in its early phases. Assuming the highest internal income for five years, and adding it to Qusay's war chest, we get $2 billion. The insurgency had access to arms and weapons previously purchased by the Ba'ath regime, and I cannot estimate what those were worth.

121. Record and Terrill, *Iraq and Vietnam*, 11, 29.

122. Jim Michaels, "19,000 Insurgents Killed in Iraq Since '03," *USA Today*, September 26, 2007, available at http://usatoday30.usatoday.com/news/world/iraq/2007-09-26-insurgents_N.htm. This is the only time in the course of the war that the U.S. government released an estimate of total insurgent deaths. Assuming for analytic purposes that insurgents continued to be killed at a steady rate through the end of 2008, we can estimate roughly 25,000 deaths; 2009 was relatively a much less violent year.

123. For the last four and half years, an average of twelve people have died from a combination of bomb blasts and gunfire every day in Iraq. See Iraq Body Count "Database," available at http://www.iraqbodycount.org/database/.

124. For a recent, and quite comprehensive example of this kind of argument, see Stephen G. Brooks, G. John Ikenberry, and William C. Wohlforth, "Don't Come Home America: The Case against Retrenchment," *International Security* 37, no. 3 (winter 2012–13): 7–51. The authors call the strategy they support "deep engagement," but it is what I call "Liberal Hegemony," and what Ikenberry has called "Liberal Hegemony" in other work. The authors dismiss or ignore the costs outlined in this chapter and exaggerate the benefits discussed below.

125. Charles P. Kindleberger, *The World in Depression, 1929–1939* (Berkeley: University of California Press, 1973), 291–308.

126. For a cogent analysis of the evolution of the theory, see Duncan Snidal, "The Limits of Hegemonic Stability Theory," *International Organization* 39, no. 4 (autumn 1985): 580–90.

127. Edward Spezio, "British Hegemony and Major Power War, 1815–1939: An Empirical Test of Gilpin's Model of Hegemonic Governance," *International Studies Quarterly* 34, no. 2 (June 1990): 165–81, esp. 167–71.

128. Snidal, "Limits of Hegemonic Stability Theory," 586–87; G. John Ikenberry, *Liberal Leviathan* (Princeton: Princeton University Press, 2011), 1–32, 61–117. Robert O. Keohane "The Demand for International Regimes," *International Organization* 36, no. 2 (spring 1982): 325–55, argues that hegemony may be an important contributor to the formation of international regimes, sets of agreed principles, norms, rules, and decision making procedures in given issue areas, but that the regimes can make themselves so useful to the participants that they may survive the passing of the concentrated power that gave them birth.

129. Snidal. "Limits of Hegemonic Stability Theory," 582–84; Spezio, "British Hegemony."

130. Dan Drezner, "Military Primacy Doesn't Pay (Nearly as Much as You Think)," *International Security* 38, no. 1 (summer 2013): 52–79, systematically challenges the premise that the United States derives clear and important economic benefits from its high relative level of military investment.

131. OECD, "Share of International Trade in GDP," in *OECD Factbook 2013: Economic, Environmental and Social Statistics* (Paris: OECD, 2013), available at http://dx.doi.org/10.1787/factbook-2013-30-en.

132. U.S. Department of Commerce, U.S. Census Bureau, "Top Trading Partners—April 2013," available at http://www.census.gov/foreign-trade/statistics/high lights/topcurmon.html. Mexico, Canada, and China were the top three U.S. trading partners that month, with China at 13. percent. The top fifteen states accounted for 73 percent of U.S. trade.

133. Peter Liberman, "Trading with the Enemy: Security and Relative Economic Gains," *International Security* 21, no. 1 (1996): 147–75.

134. Livia Chitu, Barry Eichengreen, and Arnaud Mehl, "When Did the Dollar Overtake Sterling as the Leading International Currency? Evidence from the Bond Markets" (European Central Bank, 2012), 1–7.

135. Robert Work, Undersecretary of the Navy, "The Coming Golden Age of Seapower," Address to the Current Strategy Forum, Naval War College, June 12, 2012, slide 10. available at http://www.usnwc.edu/Events/CSF/2012/Videos.aspx.

136. Kenneth Waltz, *Theory of International Politics* (Reading, MA: Addison Wesley, 1979), 26–27; Hans J. Morgenthau, *Politics among Nations: The Struggle for Power and Peace,* 2nd ed., rev. and enlarged (New York: Alfred Knopf, 1956), 51.

137. For a similar dynamic, see John S. Galbraith, "The 'Turbulent Frontier' as a Factor in British Expansion," *Comparative Studies in Society and History* 2, no. 2 (January 1960): 150–68, available at http://www.jstor.org/stable/177813.

2. The Case for Restraint

1. Eugene Gholz, Daryl G. Press, and Harvey M. Sapolsky, "Come Home, America: The Strategy of Restraint in the Face of Temptation," *International Security* 21, no. 4 (spring 1997): 5–48, make the seminal argument for Restraint. Their main goal for U.S. strategy is to ensure the physical security of the United States. They observe that the United States is very powerful and favored by geography; there is a crude self-sustaining balance of power in Eurasia, also sustained by geography, and therefore little danger of a successful continental hegemon. Nuclear deterrence not only protects the United States—it protects the principal powers in Eurasia from each other and further reduces the odds of a successful continental hegemon. Only nuclear attacks truly endanger the United States, and these can be deterred. They also presciently noted the cheap and free riding that would attend open-ended U.S. guarantees, and the costs that the United States would bear if it tried to spread its values abroad through military action. See especially 8–17.

2. Barack Obama, *National Security Strategy of the United States of America* (Washington, DC: The White House, May 2010), 23.

3. Steven E. Miller and Scott D. Sagan, "Nuclear Power without Nuclear Proliferation?" *Daedalus* 138, no. 4 (fall 2009): 7–18. The authors observe that thirty states presently operate one or more nuclear power plants, and that fifty others have sought assistance from the IAEA to help them consider such plants (ibid., 7).

4. Thomas C. Schelling, "A World without Nuclear Weapons?" *Daedalus* 138, no. 4 (fall 2009): 124–29.

5. Owen Cote, *The Third Battle: Innovation in the U.S. Navy's Silent Cold War Struggle with Soviet Submarines, Phase III of the Third Battle: ASW and the Happy Time: 1960–1980*, "The Delta Threat," March 2000, available at http://www.dtic.mil/cgi-bin/GetTRDoc?AD=ADA421957.

6. J. Michael Legge, "Theater Nuclear Weapons and the NATO Strategy of Flexible Response," April 1983, RAND Corporation, R2964FF, 40–43, 84–88.

7. Barry R. Posen, *Inadvertent Escalation: Conventional War and Nuclear Risks* (Ithaca: Cornell University Press, 1991).

8. Gholz, Press, and Sapolsky, "Come Home," 34, make this point very strongly.

9. Some skeptics doubt that Iran would be deterred from nuclear attacks on its neighbors by the threat of U.S. nuclear retaliation, because they believe that a confused and supine United States would not retaliate, and they assume that coolly vicious sociopathic Iranian leaders would share their views. "Rather, most see the usual hemming and hawing about 'certainty,' 'provocations' and 'escalation' as the far more likely rhetoric should such an event occur. And if we in Washington see it that way, why would the Iranians think differently." This attributes to Iranian leaders a lack of concern for the survival of their own states and people that makes one wonder how they have managed to hold on to power for thirty years, indeed why they even bothered. See the op-ed by Danielle Pletka, "Why Iran Can't Be Contained," *Washington Post*, December 15, 2009.

10. Thomas Schelling makes the point nicely: "I don't think the ayatollahs or anyone else in Iran wants their own nation wiped off the map. They know that Israel has enough nuclear weapons and delivery systems to utterly destroy Iran in retaliation for any attack on Jerusalem or Tel Aviv. This would deter them. To hit Israel would be suicide." See Thomas C. Schelling, "Iranian Nuke Would Be Suicide Bomb," *NPQ: New Perspectives Quarterly* 23, no. 1 (winter 2006): 58–59.

11. Yossi Klein Halevi, "Clock's Ticking toward an Iranian Bomb; if the West Does Not Impose Real Sanctions, the Israeli Consensus Is for Preemptive Action," *Globe and Mail* (Canada), January 10, 2009, reviews the arguments of many Israeli policymakers for preemption. Included in the standard arguments is that "a lunatic regime in Tehran, driven by messianic theology and hatred of Zionism, might be tempted to launch a nuclear attack." The argument is reinforced by Tehran's flirtations with holocaust denial, including hosting a conference on the subject in 2006. Others expect Tehran to give nuclear weapons away to a "terrorist proxy." See also Roger Cohen, "Israel Cries Wolf," *New York Times*, April 8, 2009.

12. Israeli Prime Minister Benjamin Netanyahu reportedly believes that Iran is led by a "messianic apocalyptic cult" and that its possession of nuclear weapons would permit it to take very great risks in confrontations with Israel. Jeffrey Goldberg, "Israel's Fears, Amalek's Arsenal," *New York Times*, May 17, 2009; Jeffrey Goldberg, "Netanyahu to Obama: Stop Iran—Or I Will," *The Atlantic*, March 2009, available at http://www.theatlantic.com/magazine/archive/2009/03/netanyahu-to-obama-stop-iran-or-i-will/7390/.

13. Elihu D. Richter and Alex Barnea, "Tehran's Genocidal Incitement against Israel," *Middle East Quarterly* (summer 2009): 45–51, available at http://www.me forum.org/2167/iran-genocidal-incitement-israel, review a range of inflammatory Iranian statements about Israel, arguing that they amount to incitement to genocide and could literally be a crime under the genocide treaty. It takes more than a collection of quotations to sustain such a legal argument, but the record they review is nonetheless quite disturbing. Iranian president Mahmoud Ahmadinejad (2005–13) regularly ventured the opinion in one form or another that Israel should disappear from the Middle East, though seems not to have explicitly committed Iran to be the actual agent of such a disappearance.

14. "When combined with Iran's longstanding support for Palestinian Islamic Jihad and *Hezbollah* of Lebanon, two groups that have killed numerous Israelis, and Mr. Ahmadinejad's refusal to acknowledge the Holocaust, it is hard to argue that, from Israel's point of view, Mr. Ahmadinejad poses no threat. Still, it is true that he has never specifically threatened war against Israel." Ethan Bronner, "Just How Far Did They Go, Those Words against Israel," *New York Times*, June 11, 2006, available at http://www.nytimes.com/2006/06/11/weekinreview/11bronner.html?_r=1.

15. Andrew Grotto, "Is Iran a Martyr State?" *Brown Journal of World Affairs* 16, no. 1 (fall/winter 2009): 45–58. See especially pages 50–54, in which the author demonstrates that Mahdiism in general does not recommend that Shiites initiate extreme violence to bring about the Mahdi's return, and that there was no evidence that Admadinejad believes to the contrary.

16. Graham Fuller, in a concise description of Iran's decision to end the conflict, notes, "In basic terms, Khomeini faced a stark choice between pursuing an increasingly unattainable revolutionary victory over Iraq and the survival of the Islamic Revolution itself"; see Graham E. Fuller, "War and Revolution in Iran," *Current History* 88, no. 535 (February 1989): 81. See also Grotto, "Martyr State," 50.

17. Mark Fitzpatrick, "Assessing Iran's Nuclear Program," *Survival* 48, no. 3 (autumn 2006): 13.

18. One need not rely on religion to craft an argument that a state or its leaders will be difficult to deter. Prior to the 2003 war with Iraq, a long-time observer of Saddam Hussein argued not that he was irrational, rather, he attributed to Saddam "a number of pathologies that make deterring him unusually difficult. He is an inveterate gamble and risk-taker who regularly twists his calculations of the odds to suit his preferred course of action. He bases his calculations on assumptions that outsiders often find bizarre and has little understanding of the larger world. He also gets little advice and is fed intelligence that has been filtered to suit his predispositions." See Kenneth M. Pollack, "Next Stop Baghdad?" *Foreign Affairs* 81, no. 2 (March–April 2002): 36. For counterarguments see John J. Mearsheimer and Stephen M. Walt, "Can Saddam Be Contained? History Says Yes," Paper, Belfer Center for Science and International Affairs, Cambridge, MA, November 12, 2002, available at http://belfercenter. ksg.harvard.edu/publication/3114/can_saddam_be_contained_history_says_yes. html.

19. Bunn, *Securing the Bomb 2010*, 13–16, discusses Aum Shinrikyu and Al-Qaeda as the primary terrorist organizations with nuclear ambitions but also alludes to mixed evidence that some secessionist groups in the north Caucasus and one Pakistani group Lashkar y Taiba have shown some interest. Though conceding Al-Qaeda's interest in nuclear weapons, one close observer finds the evidence of any Al-Qaeda progress in getting them to be thin. "The assessment of al Qaeda's nuclear

capabilities is based on very little information." See Brian Michael Jenkins, "Have We Succumbed to Nuclear Terror?" *The Long Shadow of 9/11, America's Response to Terrorism*, ed. Brian M. Jenkins and John Paul Hodges (Santa Monica, CA: Rand Corporation, 2011), 87–100, 90.

20. Though conceding Al-Qaeda's interest in nuclear weapons, Brian Jenkins found little evidence of success. He argues that fear of the consequences, not facts, has caused a kind of reification of nuclear terrorism, in which a very low probability event has come to seem quite likely in policy discourse, so much so that a range of costly countermeasures are necessary. See Jenkins, "Have We Succumbed," 90, 97.

21. The United States determined quickly that the Bin Laden organization was responsible for the embassy bombings in Africa. Samuel Berger, U.S. national security adviser, stated that "we had very specific information about very specific threats with respect to very specific targets" which apparently included electronically intercepted communications pointing to a plan for a truck-bomb attack at an unknown location. See Carla Anne Robbins and Thomas E. Ricks, "Striking Back: American Forces Hit Alleged Terrorist Bases In Afghanistan, Sudan—Citing Embassy Bombings, Possible New Attacks, U.S. Targets Bin Laden—Support, Mostly, in Congress," *Wall Street Journal*, Aug. 21, 1998, A1. In the ten years since the September 11, 2001, attacks the United States built a very detailed account of how the crime was planned. See U.S. District Court Southern District of New York, "The Terrorist Attacks of September 11, 2001" (counts 1–9), Indictment (s14) 93 Cr. 180 (KTD), available at http://www.justice.gov/opa/documents/ksm-indictment.pdf. See also Keir A. Lieber and Daryl G. Press, "Why States Won't Give Nuclear Weapons to Terrorists," *International Security* 38, no. 1 (summer 2013), 80–104.

22. Iraq mounted a regional charm offensive towards its Arab neighbors, though failed to placate the United States. Howard Schneider, "Iraq Makes Push to Restore Diplomacy," *Washington Post*, February 6, A12, http://www.lexisnexis.com.libproxy.mit.edu/lnacui2api/api/version1/getDocCui?lni=4532-DY60-010F-94Y8&csi=8075&hl=t&hv=t&hnsd=f&hns=t&hgn=t&oc=00240&perma=true; Iran was also quite cooperative on Afghanistan. See James Dobbins, "Time to Deal with Iran," *Washington Post*, May 6, 2004. See report that senior clerics condemned the 9/11 attacks in Najmeh Bozorgmehr and Guy Dinmore, "Iran Changes Tack in Support of U.S. Terrorist Attack; Leading Conservative Ayatollah Condemns Slaughter of Innocent People," *Financial Times*, Sept. 15, 2001, 13.

23. Matthew Bunn, *Securing the Bomb 2010* (Cambridge, MA: President and Fellows of Harvard College, 2010), reviews thoroughly the state of worldwide security measures, offers a range of necessary reforms, and discusses the president's initiative.

24. For the panoply of programs, see International Atomic Energy Agency, "Nuclear Security Advisory Services," 2010, available at http://www-ns.iaea.org/security/advisory.htm.

25. Richard A. Meserve, "The Global Nuclear Safety Regime," *Daedalus* 138, no. 4 (fall 2009): 100–111, discusses the elaborate global nuclear safety regime, offers an array of proposals to strengthen safety, and suggests that materials security measures must be integrated with safety efforts. Matthew Bunn notes that the NPT does not "contain any provisions requiring states to secure nuclear materials from theft" and that cooperation with the IAEA Office of Nuclear Security is voluntary. He concludes, "Immediate action is needed around the world to improve security for nuclear weapons and the materials needed to make them, focusing on those sites and transport routes that pose the highest risks. The job is big and complex but finite and

doable"; see Matthew Bunn, "Reducing the Greatest Risks of Nuclear Theft and Terrorism," *Daedalus* 138, no. 4 (fall 2009): 119, 122.

26. Many analysts of nuclear proliferation either implicitly or explicitly share this perspective. Writing on Iran, Schelling offers, "We should assist the Iranians in making sure custody of their weapons is secure in any time of disruption. In the case of a riot in the streets, will the weapons be safe? Who might grab them in case of civil war?" Schelling, "Iranian Nuke Would Be Suicide Bomb," 58–59; Bunn, *Securing the Bomb*, 28–31, reviews what is known about security measures in Pakistan and what little is known about the extent of U.S.-Pakistani cooperation on nuclear security.

27. See for example the discussion of plans by U.S. special operations forces to secure Pakistan's nuclear weapons in Jeffrey Goldberg and Marc Ambinder, "Nuclear Negligence," *National Journal* (Nov. 5, 2011). available at http://www.nationaljour nal.com/magazine/the-pentagon-s-secret-plans-to-secure-pakistan-s-nuclear-arse nal-20111104.

28. Lawrence Wright, *Looming Tower: Al-Qaeda and the Road to 9/11* (New York: Alfred Knopf, 2006), 100–120.

29. John Rollins, *Al Qaeda and Affiliates: Historical Perspective, Global Presence, and Implications for U.S. Policy*, R41070, Congressional Research Service, February 5, 2010.

30. Barry R. Posen, "The Struggle against Terrorism: Grand Strategy, Strategy, and Tactics," *International Security* 26, no. 3 (winter 2001–2): 39–55. The quotation is from page 42.

31. "The death or capture of prominent al-Qa'ida figures since bin Ladin's death has shrunk the layer of top lieutenants directly under Zawahiri. These losses, combined with the long list of earlier losses since CT operations intensified in 2008, lead us to assess that core al-Qa'ida's ability to perform a variety of functions—including leadership and conducting external operations—has weakened significantly." James R. Clapper, director of National Intelligence, "Unclassified Statement for the Record on the Worldwide Threat Assessment of the U.S. Intelligence Community for the Senate Select Committee on Intelligence," January 31, 2012, 1–4, available at http://intelli gence.senate.gov/120131/clapper.pdf.

32. Clapper, "Worldwide Threat Assessment," 2, 4. Keeping a low profile in these countries seems a good way to avoid this pitfall, as he intimates later in his testimony, when he suggests that new terrorist recruits could be produced by "a galvanizing event or series of events perceived to reflect an anti-Islamic bias," or "U.S. or Western military involvement in another Muslim country."

33. As many have observed, the culture of the FBI is about making cases against criminals. The United States cannot afford to make cases against terrorists after the fact; plots need to be prevented. The FBI now has a dedicated "National Security Branch" for this purpose. See Gregory Treverton, "Intelligence Test," *Democracy*, no. 11 (winter 2009): 54–65, esp. 56–58.

34. Len Scott and Gerald R. Hughes, "Intelligence in the Twenty-First Century: Change and Continuity or Crisis and Transformation?" *Intelligence and National Security* 24, no. 1 (February 2009): 6–25, esp. 9–11. See also Adam D. M. Svendsen, "Connecting Intelligence and Theory: Intelligence Liaison and International Relations," *Intelligence and National Security* 24, no. 5 (October 2009): 700–729, esp. 700–708.

35. Posen, "The Struggle against Terrorism," 39–55.

36. Eric V. Larson, "Al Qaeda's Propaganda: A Shifting Battlefield," 71–85, in Jenkins and Hodges, *Long Shadow*, 74–78.

37. Summarizing the modest sustained improvement in views of the United States in Indonesia, with the absence of sustained improvement in Pakistan, "Disaster relief efforts . . . are more likely to have a significant effect on public attitudes in countries where there is at least a reservoir of goodwill toward the United States. In nations such as Pakistan, where countervailing issues and deeply held suspicions drive intense anti-Americanism, enhancing America's image through humanitarian aid may prove considerably more difficult." Richard Wike, "Does Humanitarian Aid Improve America's Image?" Pew Global Attitudes Project, March 6, 2012 available at http://www.pewglobal.org/2012/03/06/does-humanitarian-aid-improve-americas-image/.

38. Barry Eichengreen, "The Dollar Dilemma: The World's Top Currency Faces Competition," *Foreign Affairs* 88, no. 5 (September/October 2009): 53–68, argues that the U.S. dollar, though under pressure, will likely remain the world's reserve currency, but that the euro is becoming quite powerful not only in the European Union but on Europe's periphery in Russia and the Mediterranean littoral. The euro held up well through much of the financial crisis, "in particular, the euro's share in global foreign exchange reserves remained around 25 percent at end-2011." European Central Bank, "The International Role of the Euro," July 2012, 9–12 (Frankfurt am Main: Germany, 2012) available at http://www.ecb.europa.eu.

39. I argue that this is the main explanation for the evolution of EU security policy, though I review other explanations as well; see Barry R. Posen, "European Union Security and Defense Policy: Response to Unipolarity?" *Security Studies* 15, no. 2 (June 2006): 149–86.

40. The EU Common Security and Defence Policy web site lays out the various goals and accomplishments of ESDP; see http://www.consilium.europa.eu/showPage. aspx?id=261&lang=en. For current and planned operational capabilities, see European Union Common Security and Defence Policy, *Development of European Military Capabilities*," February 2010, available at http://www.consilium.europa.eu/uedocs/cmsUpload/100216-Factsheet_capacites_militaires-version4_EN.pdf.

41. Then British prime minister Tony Blair was reported to have considered the idea of cooperation with France on R&D and scheduling submarine patrols, though it does not appear that anything came of it; Andrew Gilligan, "Blair's Plans for a Eurobomb," *Spectator* (Britain), January 22, 2000, 10–11. More recently several French armament officials proposed cooperation with Britain in research and development on nuclear delivery systems; see Michael Taverna and Douglas Barrie, "Nuclear Fusion," *Aviation Week and Space Technology* 169, no. 15 (October 20, 2008): 32. Both articles note that the existing close cooperation between Britain and the United States in the nuclear field, indeed the dependence of Britain on the United States for missiles, would complicate such cooperation. Under the pressure of additional cuts in their respective defense budgets occasioned by efforts to recover from the global financial crisis, France and Britain are trying once again to deepen their military cooperation and signed a "Defence Co-operation Treaty" to this effect in November 2010. See "Q&A: UK-French Defence Treaty," November 2, 2010, available at http://www.bbc.co.uk/news/uk-politics-11672796; and UK Ministry of Defence, "UK-France Defence Co-operation Treaty Announced," November 2, 2010, available at http://www.mod.uk/DefenceInternet/DefenceNews/DefencePolicyAndBusiness/UkfranceDefenceCooperationTreatyAnnounced.htm.

A subordinate treaty addresses cooperation on a nuclear weapons research and development facility. Foreshadowing the agreement, and laying out the plausible rationale is Etienne de Durand, "Entente or Oblivion, Prospects and Pitfalls of

Franco-British Co-operation on Defence," *Future Defence Review*, Working Paper Number 8, Royal United Services Institute, September 2010, available at http://www.rusi.org/downloads/assets/FDR8.pdf.

42. Ursula Jasper and Clara Portela, "EU Defence Integration and Nuclear Weapons: A Common Deterrent for Europe?" *Security Dialogue* 41, no. 2 (April 2010): 145–68, reviews fifteen years of European debates about the organization of a joint Franco-British nuclear deterrent for the European Union, and why such proposals have not prospered. The two key reasons they offer are first that many European Union members wish to do nothing to weaken the U.S. nuclear deterrent commitment to Europe through NATO, and some non-NATO members of the EU are strongly committed to nuclear disarmament. Nevertheless they conclude that the notion is becoming "more practicable in the current stage of European construction."

43. Article IX of the treaty calls for the establishment of a "Council" and a "Defence Committee," but no command structure; NATO, "The North Atlantic Treaty," April 4, 1949, Article IX, available at http://www.nato.int/cps/en/natolive/official_texts_17120.htm.

44. Article V reads: "The Parties agree that an armed attack against one or more of them in Europe or North America shall be considered an attack against them all and consequently they agree that, if such an armed attack occurs, each of them, in exercise of the right of individual or collective self-defence recognised by Article 51 of the Charter of the United Nations, will assist the Party or Parties so attacked by taking forthwith, individually and in concert with the other Parties, such action as it deems necessary, including the use of armed force, to restore and maintain the security of the North Atlantic area.

"Any such armed attack and all measures taken as a result thereof shall immediately be reported to the Security Council. Such measures shall be terminated when the Security Council has taken the measures necessary to restore and maintain international peace and security"; see "North Atlantic Treaty," Article V.

45. National Intelligence Council, *Global Trends 2030: Alternative Worlds*, NIC 2012–001, Washington D.C. (December 2012), 16. See the two tables, "Traditional Four-Component Power Forecast" and "New Multi-Component Global Power Index Forecast." The "new" index adds some qualitative factors and shows somewhat slower change than the first, but the trends are the same, and the changes are significant.

46. John Hawksworth and Danny Chan, *The World in 2050, The BRICs and Beyond: Prospects, Challenges and Opportunities*, "Appendix B, Additional Projections for GDP at Market Exchange Rates," Price Waterhouse Coopers, January 2013, 11.

47. Barry R. Posen, "From Unipolarity to Multipolarity: Transition in Sight?" in *International Relations Theory and the Consequences of Unipolarity*, ed. G. John Ikenberry, Michael Mastanduno, and William C. Wohlforth (Cambridge: Cambridge University Press, 2011), 317–42.

48. For a grim depiction of China's ultimate ambitions to drive the United States from Asia and establish hegemony there, see Aaron L. Friedberg, *A Contest for Supremacy: China, America, and the Struggle for Mastery in Asia* (New York: W. W. Norton, 2011): 156–81.

49. Hugh White, "Power Shift: Rethinking Australia's Place in the Asian Century," *Australian Journal of International Affairs* 65, no. 1: 81–93, suggests that presuming China stays on its present growth trajectory there are only three choices for U.S.

policy in Asia: intense struggle for primacy waged mainly in the form of a military competition; abandonment of the Asian states to their own devices; and some form of accommodation, which he calls an "Asian Concert."

50. M. Taylor Fravel, *Strong Borders, Secure Nation: Cooperation and Conflict in China's Territorial Disputes* (Princeton, NJ: Princeton University Press, 2008).

51. Amitai Etzioni, "Who Authorized Preparations for War with China?" *Yale Journal of International Affairs* (summer 2013): 39–43.

52. White, "Power Shift," 85, 92.

53. Robert Ross, "The Problem with the Pivot, Obama's New Asia Policy Is Unnecessary and Counterproductive," *Foreign Affairs* 91, no. 6 (November/December 2012): 70–82.

54. Andrew Nathan and Andrew Scobell, "How China Sees America, Hint; as Hostile, Aggressive, and Determined to Block Beijing's Rise," *Foreign Affairs* 91, no. 5 (September/October 2012): 32–47.

55. George J. Gilboy and Eric Heginbotham, *Chinese and Indian Strategic Behavior: Growing Power and Alarm* (Cambridge: Cambridge University Press, 2012): xxi–xxii, 9–12, 69–71, 162–63.

56. Ibid., 94–132, develop their own military spending estimates, which add all relevant spending to the official defense budgets. In 2010, China spent just under three times what India spent at market exchange rates. Because the two economies are not presently at the same level, a Purchasing Power Parity method suggests India spends about two-thirds of what China does.

57. Economist Intelligence Unit (hereafter EIU), *Japan: Country Profile 2008* (London: Economist Intelligence Unit, 2008), 35–37. Japan did achieve robust growth from 2003–7, but this appears in retrospect to have relied too heavily on exports.

58. As the CIA reports, Japan is "among world's largest and technologically advanced producers of motor vehicles, electronic equipment, machine tools, steel and nonferrous metals, ships, chemicals, textiles, processed foods"; U.S. Central Intelligence Agency, "Japan" in *The World Factbook 2010*, available at https://www.cia.gov/library/publications/the-world-factbook/geos/ja.html. EIU similarly notes, "Japan is, for example, the world's largest maker of machine tools, with a growing lead in numerically controlled machine tools, and it is the world's second-largest vehicle manufacturer after the United States"; EIU, *Japan 2008*, 40–41.

59. For contemporary official U.S. military assessments of the requirements and possible costs of an initial amphibious assault on southern Kyushu planned for November 1945, see Joint War Plans Committee, "Details of the Campaign Against Japan," JWPC 369/1, June 15, 1945, in Douglas J. MacEachin, *The Final Months of the War With Japan: Signals Intelligence, U.S. Invasion Planning, and the A-Bomb Decision*, CSI 98–10001 (Washington, DC: Central Intelligence Agency: December 1998.) The United States planned on committing 766,700 troops and 2,794 aircraft to the assault (tab E). Roughly 1,000 warships and transports of every kind would have been committed to the operation. (I infer this figure from "tab G," which includes an estimate for the second phase of the operation, an assault on northwestern Kyushu.)

60. The CIA spells out Japan's vulnerability, observing, "[Japan has] negligible mineral resources," and "with virtually no energy natural resources, Japan is the world's largest importer of coal and liquefied natural gas as well as the second largest importer of oil"; CIA, "Japan." See also EIU, *Japan 2008*, 40–41.

[205]

61. Japan's National Defense Program Guidelines emphasize local defense, response to contingencies in and around Japanese territory and air space, and prevention of invasion. Reflecting these goals, maritime forces are divided into small units and scattered around the country—a force posture intended to provide coverage of the main sea lanes immediately around Japan. See Japan Ministry of Defense, *Defense of Japan 2009* (Tokyo: Erklaren, 2009), trans. Erklaren, Inc., 141–49.

62. EIU, *Japan 2008,* 27.

63. As of this writing, the new government of Prime Minister Shinzo Abe is considering prioritized improvements to certain military capabilities, including intelligence, the ability to respond to attacks in the remote islands, and ballistic missile defense capacity. See Japan, Ministry of Defense, "Defense Posture Review Interim Report," Provisional Translation, July 26, 2013, available at http://www.mod.go.jp/j/approach/agenda/guideline/2013_chukan/gaiyou_e.pdf. The United States and Japan agreed in October of 2013 to a series of measures designed to improve their joint strategic position. Unfortunately, the agreement alludes mainly to a series of changes in joint processes and planned studies and consultations. Only the United States commits to specific military improvements. See U.S. Department of State, "Joint Statement of the Security Consultative Committee: Toward a More Robust Alliance and Greater Shared Responsibilities," October 3, 2013 available at http://www.state.gov/r/pa/prs/ps/2013/10/215070.htm.

64. Yinan He, *The Search for Reconciliation: Sino-Japanese and German-Polish Relations since World War Two* (Cambridge: Cambridge University Press, 2009), 234–61, 287–88; Richard J. Samuels, *Securing Japan: Tokyo's Grand Strategy and the Future of East Asia* (Ithaca: Cornell University Press, 2007), 136–40, 148.

65. There are 6.7 metric tons of separated plutonium stored in Japan and 38 metric tons of Japanese-owned plutonium stored elsewhere in the world. These stocks are sufficient for more than a thousand nuclear weapons. See Emma Chanlett-Avery and Mary Beth Nikitin, *Japan's Nuclear Future: Policy Debate, Prospects, and U.S. Interests,* RL34487, Congressional Research Service, February 19, 2009), 3–5. Using this scale, the 6.7 metric tons in Japan would alone be sufficient for more than one hundred nuclear weapons.

66. Mitsubishi Heavy Industries has developed considerable expertise in the design and production of air-, land-, and sea-launched antiship cruise missiles. Japan builds high-quality submarines, which are armed with U.S. Harpoon antiship missiles. It is likely that Japan could develop the ability to place nuclear-tipped, land-attack cruise missiles on these diesel submarines quite quickly. The comparative proximity of China and Japan means that neither faces a difficult task building delivery systems that could reach the other. See International Institute for Strategic Studies, *The Military Balance 2010* (London: Routledge, 2010), 392–93; IISS, *Military Balance 2009,* 455–56.

67. Richard J. Samuels and James L. Schoff, "Japan's Nuclear Hedge: Beyond 'Allergy' and Breakout," in *Strategic Asia 2013–14, Asia in the Second Nuclear Age,* ed. Ashley J. Tellis, Abraham M. Denmark, and Travis Tanner (Seattle: National Bureau of Asian Research, 2013), 233–64, show that the Japanese national security elite has over time deliberately maintained the technological option to make nuclear weapons, views nuclear deterrence as central to Japanese national security, and is less confident in the extended deterrence commitment from the United States. Thus they see a future decision to acquire an independent nuclear deterrent as plausible.

68. Richard Samuels observes that even the twin Tsunami and nuclear reactor meltdown disasters of March 2011, and the associated demonstration of the utility of the U.S.-Japan military alliance for recovery work, had little effect on the more traditional security aspects of the alliance. Long-standing projects to improve the Japanese military, and to improve the ability of the allied militaries to cooperate in wartime, received no fillip from either the trials or the triumphs of the disaster. Richard J. Samuels, *3.11 Disaster and Change in Japan* (Ithaca: Cornell University Press, 2013), 80–109.

69. Narushige Michishita and Richard J. Samuels, "Hugging and Hedging: Japanese Grand Strategy in the 21st Century," in *Worldviews of Aspiring Powers: Domestic Foreign Policy Debates in China, India, Iran, Japan, and Russia*, ed. Henry R. Nau and Deepa M. Ollapally (New York: Oxford University Press, 2013), 146–80, 150, 162.

70. A recent study observes that "a review of recent articles and interviews with prominent Japanese opinion-makers and experts revealed a near-consensus of opposition to the development of nuclear weapons"; See Chanlett-Avery and Nikitin, *Japan's Nuclear Future*, 7.

71. Noting a strain of bandwagoning in the Japanese security policy debate, which calls for economic collaboration with China while simply discounting the implications for Japanese security, are Michishita and Samuels, "Hugging and Hedging," 169–70. They also cite a survey of Japanese analysts that suggests this is a minority view, 173.

72. Prior to the tsunami, one assessment argued that Japan was already on a path to a much more capable military and a more assertive foreign policy, and that this course was already deeply embedded in the Japanese foreign and security policy establishment, though the author hastened to offer the caveat that " 'remilitarisation' should not be read as an alarmist warning that Japan is necessarily intent on reverting to the kind of state it became between 1931 and 1945." Christopher Hughes, *Japan's Remilitarization*, Adelphi Papers 48, no. 403 (2008): 19.

73. "In a 2011 survey of the views of some fifty Japanese international affairs scholars and diplomats about the future of Japanese diplomacy, nearly half the respondents were, by our measures, 'balancers.' Seven could be characterized as " 'integrators.' While there were even fewer 'autonomists' and 'bandwagoners,' about one-quarter of these experts claimed that Japan should further promote its relationships multi-directionally rather than focusing on either the United States or China," Japanese Institute for International Affairs, ed., Kokusai Mondai (Tokyo: International Affairs, April 2011), cited in Michishita and Samuels, "Hugging and Hedging," 173.

74. Charles Glaser, "Will China's Rise Lead to War? Why Realism Does Not Mean Pessimism," *Foreign Affairs* 90, no. 2 (March/April 2011): 80–91.

75. M. Taylor Fravel and Evan S. Medeiros, "China's Search for Assured Retaliation: The Evolution of Chinese Nuclear Strategy and Force Structure," *International Security* 35, no. 2 (fall 2010): 48–87.

76. As noted at the web site of the U.S. Department of State, "In 1979, the United States changed its diplomatic recognition from Taipei to Beijing. In the U.S.-P.R.C. Joint Communiqué that announced the change, the United States recognized the Government of the People's Republic of China as the sole legal government of China and acknowledged the Chinese position that there is but one China and Taiwan is part of China. The Joint Communique also stated that within this context the people of the United States will maintain cultural, commercial, and other unofficial relations with the people on Taiwan.

"The United States does not support Taiwan independence. Maintaining strong, unofficial relations with Taiwan is a major U.S. goal, in line with the U.S. desire to further peace and stability in Asia. The 1979 Taiwan Relations Act provides the legal basis for the unofficial relationship between the U.S. and Taiwan, and enshrines the U.S. commitment to assisting Taiwan in maintaining its defensive capability. The United States insists on the peaceful resolution of cross-Strait differences and encourages dialogue to help advance such an outcome." U.S. State Department, Bureau of East Asian and Pacific Affairs, "U.S. Relations with Taiwan Fact Sheet," February 25, 2013, available at http://www.state.gov/r/pa/ei/bgn/35855.htm.

77. For an insightful review of the escalation potential of near-term U.S.-China crises, see Avery Goldstein, "First Things First: The Pressing Danger of Crisis Instability in U.S.-China Relations," *International Security* 37, no. 4 (spring 2013): 49–89.

78. Even strong advocates of a Grand Strategy of Restraint, Gholz, Press, and Sapolsky, "Come Home," 9, 14–15, 25–29, saw U.S. strategic interests in the Persian Gulf and recommended that the United States should ensure that no single regional power control a significant percentage of the energy resources in the Persian Gulf. In subsequent work Gholz and Press suggest that defending gulf states from conquest and protecting the sea lanes, should be easy, and recommend an "over the horizon" military presence in the region based mainly on carrier aviation. See also Eugene Gholz and Daryl Press, "Footprints in the Sand," *American Interest* 5, no. 4 (March–April 2010): 59–67.

79. See U.S. Department of Energy, Energy Information Agency, *Monthly Energy Review*, International Petroleum, Table 11.1b, World Crude Oil Production: Persian Gulf Nations, Non-OPEC, and World, September 2013, available at http://www.eia.gov/totalenergy/data/monthly/#international.

80. U.S. Dept. of Energy, Energy Information Agency, "World Oil Transit Chokepoints," (Last updated August 22, 2012), available at http://www.eia.gov/countries/regions-topics.cfm?fips=WOTC&trk=c.

81. U.S. Dept. of Energy, Energy Information Agency, *Monthly Energy Review*, Petroleum, Figure 3.3a, Petroleum Trade: Overview, June 2013, September 2013 available at http://www.eia.gov/totalenergy/data/monthly/#petroleum.

82. Anita Dancs with Mary Orisich and Suzanne Smith, *The Military Cost of Securing Energy* (Northampton, MA: National Priorities Project, 2008) suggest $100 billion of the 2009 defense budget, roughly 20 percent excluding war costs, could be attributed to ensuring the security of oil supplies, available at http://vcnv.org/files/NPP_energy_defense_spending_full_report.pdf ; Keith Crane, Andreas Goldthau, Michael Toman, Thomas Light, Stuart E. Johnson, Alireza Nader, Angel Rabasa, and Harun Dogo, *Imported Oil and U.S. National Security* (Santa Monica, CA: RAND Corporation, 2009), 25, suggest 12–15 percent of the FY 2009 defense budget, available at http://www.rand.org/pubs/monographs/MG838.

83. James T. Quinlivan, "Coup Proofing: Its Practice and Consequences in the Middle East," *International Security* 24, no. 2 (autumn 1999): 141–44.

84. Shahram Chubin, "Iran's Power in Context," *Survival: Global Politics and Strategy* 51, no. 1 (February/March 2009): 165–90.

85. Many doubt whether even a very hostile regime in Saudi Arabia could do a great deal of global economic damage. Other producers would take advantage of their absence from the market and consumers would find alternatives. Economies are more resilient than they once were, and what appears to have been oil-induced

shocks in the past now seem to have been caused as much by mistaken economic policies. See Philip E. Auerswald, "The Irrelevance of the Middle East," *American Interest* 2, no. 5 (May/June 2007): 19–37. So far as inflation is concerned, previous oil shocks seem to have wrought their damage and caused inflationary spirals in part due to the ability of organized labor to force up wages quickly; changes in the work force have eroded this propensity. Policy tools are also better than what they were. See *Energy, National Security and the Persian Gulf: Report of a Workshop,* MIT Security Studies Program Working Paper, May 2008, http://web.mit.edu/ssp/Publications/ confseries/Energy_national_security_and_Persian_Gulf.pdf, 11–15.

86. James Glanz and Robert F. Worth, "Attacks on Iraq Oil Industry Aid Vast Smuggling Scheme," *New York Times*, June 4, 2006. See also Friedrich Steinhäusler, P. Furthner, W. Heidegger, S. Rydell, and L. Zaitseva, "Security Risks to the Oil and Gas Industry: Terrorist Capabilities," *Strategic Insights* 7, no. 1 (February 2008), Center for Contemporary Conflict at the Naval Postgraduate School in Monterey, California, http:// hdl.handle.net/10945/11429.

87. Eugene Gholz, "The Strait Dope: Why Iran Can't Cut Off Your Oil," *Foreign Policy*, no. 174 (September/October 2009): 105. For a somewhat more alarmist treatment, see Simon Henderson, *Energy in Danger: Iran, Oil, and the West*, Policy Focus No. 83 (Washington DC: Washington Institute for Near East Policy, June 2008).

88. Gholz and Press, "Footprints in the Sand."

89. During the Iraq-Iran war the United States assumed the responsibility of protecting Kuwait's oil shipments in April 1987. After a U.S. warship was badly damaged by a mine, the tankers lead the way into the gulf, with U.S. warships following behind. The tankers could take the mine strike if it occurred.

90. United States military leaders typically offer guarded assessments. For example in 2005 Vice Admiral Lowell E. Jacopy of the Defense Intelligence Agency said that "Iran can briefly close the straits of Hormuz." Henderson, *Energy in Danger*, 4. A careful and conservative estimate that measures the plausible magnitude of Iran's present capabilities against recent military experience, suggests that the United States, using available assets and technologies, could take from one to four months to clear almost entirely a very determined Iranian mining effort supported by anti-ship cruise missiles. See Caitlin Talmadge, "Closing Time: Assessing the Iranian Threat to the Strait of Hormuz," *International Security* 33, no. 1 (summer 2008): 82–117, especially 97–98, 109–10, 115.

91. Henderson, *Energy in Danger*, 14–16.

92. Joshua R. Itzkowitz Shifrinson and Miranda Priebe, "A Crude Threat: The Limits of an Iranian Missile Campaign against Saudi Arabian Oil," *International Security* 36, no. 1 (summer 2011): 167–201.

93. For two arguments that the U.S. role in securing oil contributes to the global power position of the United States, see Steve A. Yetiv, *Crude Awakenings: Global Security and American Foreign Policy* (Ithaca: Cornell University Press, 2004), 76, 96; and Doug Stokes and Sam Raphael, *Global Energy Security and American Hegemony* (Baltimore, MD: Johns Hopkins University Press, 2010), 38–52.

94. The U.S. defense budget provides a significant security subsidy to every barrel of oil that leaves the gulf. Other states do what they wish with this subsidy. Some are happy to buy the oil without whatever risk premium would otherwise be included in the price. Other states, which slap the highest tax they can on oil consumption consistent with what their economies can tolerate, essentially pocket the difference.

This is another way that the U.S. taxpayer subsidizes European welfare states through the U.S. defense budget.

95. "Whether exaggerated or not, the specter of the United States coercing Persian Gulf oil producing states to reduce supplies to China, or even turning back super-tankers laden with petroleum en route to China, is taken very seriously by some Chinese strategic analysts." Bruce Blair, Chen Yali, and Eric Hagt, "The Oil Weapon: Myth of China's Vulnerability," *China Security* 2, no. 2 (summer 2006): 39, 47.

96. Against the backdrop of a functioning international market, the selective denial by Persian Gulf producers of exports to particular customers is essentially impossible. Blair et al., "Oil Weapon," 43–45.

97. See U.S. Central Intelligence Agency, "Israel" in *The World Factbook,* available at https://www.cia.gov/library/publications/the-world-factbook/geos/is.html; and U.S. Central Intelligence Agency, "European Union" in *The World Factbook,* available at https://www.cia.gov/library/publications/the-world-factbook/geos/ee.html.

98. "The IDF still retains its advantages over any probable combination of Arab states engaged in a regular war against Israel. Threats from the 'outer circle,' mostly by medium-range ballistic missiles, have preoccupied Israeli planners for almost two decades, and Israel has achieved significant capability to mitigate these threats (by acquiring long-range attack capabilities and by ballistic missile defense systems like the Arrow)." Yiftah S. Shapir and Shlomo Brom, "The Regional Military Balance," in *The Middle East Strategic Balance 2007–2008,* ed. Mark Heller (Tel Aviv: The Institute for National Security Studies, 2008), 48, available at http://www.inss.org.il/upload/%28FILE%291213863744.pdf.

99. Yiftah Shapir, "How Many Domes Does Beer Sheva Need? "INSS Insight No. 277, August 28, 2011, available at http://www.inss.org.il/publications.php?cat=21&incat=&read=5439.

100. For a good overview of the artillery and missile strikes on Israel during the Lebanon War and Israeli efforts to stop the attacks, see William Arkin, *Divining Victory: Airpower in the 2006 Israel-Hezbollah War* (Maxwell Air Force Base, AL: Air University Press, 2007), 55–74.

101. In the same period five Israeli civilians have been killed within the Green Line, Israel's pre-1967 border. See B'Tselem—The Israeli Information Center for Human Rights in the Occupied Territories, "Fatalities after Operation 'Cast Lead,' " available at http://www.btselem.org/statistics/fatalities/after-cast-lead/by-date-of-event.

102. IISS, *The Military Balance 2013,* 382–85; Agence France-Presse, "Ministry: Israel Tests Rocket System," July 12, 2013, available at http://www.defensenews.com/article/20130712/DEFREG04/307120015/Ministry-Israel-Tests-Rocket-System; Andrew Feickert, "Missile Survey: Ballistic and Cruise Missiles of Selected Foreign Countries," RL30427, Congressional Research Service, July 26, 2005, 36.

103. For a recent pessimistic assessment for the prospects for future negotiations, and an argument that in its own interests Israel should move forward unilaterally toward a two-state solution, see Shlomo Brom, "Israel and the Palestinians: Policy Options Given the Infeasibility of Reaching a Final Status Agreement," Institute for National Security Studies, *Strategic Assessment* 15, no. 2 (July 2012): 75–82.

104. The right of return is a central plank of the Palestinian national movement, and the inability of Palestinian leaders to compromise on this issue may be one of the major reasons why negotiations toward a two-state solution consistently fail. On the

other hand, there is evidence that Palestinian leaders in confidential negotiations have occasionally reduced their demands to figures in the tens of thousands. When revealed to the Palestinian public, however, such compromises have been widely condemned and then disavowed. See especially, Asher Susser, *Israel, Jordan, and Palestine: The Two-State Imperative* (Waltham, MA: Brandeis University Press, 2012), 61–68.

105. Brig. General Sedky Sobhy, "The U.S. Military Presence in the Middle East: Issues And Prospects," Strategy Research Project, U.S. Army War College, Carlisle Barracks, Pennsylvania, March 18, 2005: 20–22, available at http://www.dtic.mil/cgi-bin/GetTRDoc?AD=ADA432294. See also David D. Kirkpatrick and Kareem Fahim, "In Paper, Chief of Egypt Army Criticized U.S.," *New York Times* August 17, 2012, 1.

106. Akiva Eldar, "Israel's New Politics and the Fate of Palestine," *The National Interest*, July–Aug 2012, available at http://nationalinterest.org/article/israels-new-politics-the-fate-palestine-7069?page=show.

107. Tobias Buck, "Field of Dreams: Israel's Natural Gas," *Financial Times*, August 31, 2012.

108. Bruce Riedel, "American Diplomacy and the 1999 Kargil Summit at Blair House," Center for the Advanced Study of India, 2002, available at http://www.sas.upenn.edu/casi.

109. Barak Obama, "Address to the Nation on the Way Forward in Afghanistan and Pakistan," United States Military Academy at West Point, December 1, 2009, available at http://www.whitehouse.gov/the-press-office/remarks-president-address-nation-way-forward-afghanistan-and-pakistan.

110. For an only slightly more optimistic appraisal of Afghan security forces see Rod Nordland, Thom Shanker, and Matthew Rosenberg, "Afghans Fend Off Taliban Threat in Pivotal Year in Charge," *New York Times*, October 15, 2013, A6.

111. Arabinda Acharya, Syed Adnan Ali Shah Bukhari, and Sadia Sulaiman suggest that the Pakistani Taliban make money four different ways: they impose their own taxes, they collect donations from like-minded people across Pakistan, they receive payments from other militant organizations, and they engage in crime. See Arabinda Acharya, Syed Adnan Ali Shah Bukhari, and Sadia Sulaiman "Making Money in the Mayhem: Funding Taliban Insurrection in the Tribal Areas of Pakistan," *Studies in Conflict and Terrorism* 32, no. 2 (February 2009): 95–108.

112. Making this link between Pakistan and Afghanistan is C. Raja Mohan, "How Obama Can Get South Asia Right," *Washington Quarterly* 32, no. 2 (April 2009): 173–89, esp. 183–84.

113. Moreover, Ganguly and Howenstein show that India is moderately active in Afghanistan with aid, construction, and consular representation, which drives the Pakistanis to distraction. India would like to avoid a return of the Taliban regime, because they believe that it contributes to radicalization in the region, and thus rebellion in Kashmir. That said, there is no evidence that India runs any operations against Pakistan from Afghanistan. There is indeed a rivalry between the two powers over Afghanistan. See Sumit Ganguly and Nicholas Howenstein, "India-Pakistan Rivalry in Afghanistan," *Journal of International Affairs* 63, no. 1 (fall 2009): 127–40.

114. Sabrina Tavernise, Carlotta Gall, and Ismail Khan, "Pakistan, in Shift, Weights Attack on Militant Lair," *New York Times*, April 29, 2010. They note, "The Afghan

Taliban, under Mullah Muhammad Omar, remains Pakistan's main tool for leverage in Afghanistan. The arrest of the Taliban's top operational commander, Abdul Ghani Baradar, in January has not led to a broader crackdown against the Afghan insurgents. 'Does it indicate a shift in policy?' the Western diplomat said, referring to the arrest of Mr. Baradar. 'No. But it's still a good thing.' "

115. Formally, the FATA is governed directly from the Pakistani central state, which is itself a cause of resentment. Practically, however, the writ of the central state is weak.

116. Hilary Synnott, *Transforming Pakistan: Ways Out of Instability*, Adelphi Paper No. 406 (London: International Institute for Strategic Studies, 2009), 18–20. Cole suggests that Deobandis were "quietist" for much of the twentieth century but became radicalized by the Soviet invasion of Afghanistan in 1978. See Juan Cole, "Pakistan and Afghanistan: Beyond the Taliban," *Political Science Quarterly* 124, no. 2 (summer 2009): 233.

117. Riedel, "American Diplomacy."

118. C. Christine Fair, "Time for Sober Realism: Renegotiating U.S. Relations with Pakistan," *Washington Quarterly* 32, no. 2 (April 2009): 150–63, carefully assesses all the reasons why progress on external conflict resolution, internal reform, and abandonment of support for militants will be difficult to achieve in Pakistan.

119. Howard B. Schaffer, "U.S. Kashmir Policy in the Obama Administration and Beyond," *South Asia Journal* 3 (January 2012), available at http://southasiajournal. net/2012/01/u-s-kashmir-policy-in-the-obama-administration-and-beyond/.

120. Hilary Synnott, "How to Help Pakistan," *Survival* 52, no. 1 (February–March 2010): 17–23, explains these interconnections but then goes on to recommend that the West try to help Pakistan make major internal reforms that his own analysis suggests are improbable.

121. M. Ilyas Khan, "Pakistan Rules Out Offensive Against Punjab Militants," *BBC News*, June 3, 2010, available at http://www.bbc.co.uk/news/10228268. In late May, ninety people belonging to an obscure offshoot of Islam, the Ahmadi, were shot by Punjabi Islamic extremists, dubbed the "Punjabi Taliban." Some members of the civilian federal government called for a crackdown on these extremists, but the provincial government declined to do so, and the Pakistani Army discouraged them in any case. See Saeed Shah, "No Extremist Crackdown Likely in Pakistan's Punjab Province," *McClatchy Newspapers* (Washington, DC), June 6, 2010, available at http://www.mcclatchydc.com/2010/06/06/95406/no-extremist-crackdown-likely.html.

122. "Pakistan Helping Afghan Taliban-Nato," February 1, 2012, BBC News, Asia, available at http://www.bbc.co.uk/news/world-asia-16821218; Bruce Riedel, "Mumbai Massacre and Its Implications for America and South Asia," *Journal of International Affairs* 63, no. 1 (fall 2009): 111–26.

123. Riedel, "Mumbai Massacre," explains the deep connections between the Pakistan Army and Lashkar y Taiba. Riedel argues that despite Lashkar y Taiba's mischief, including the organization of the terrorist attack on Mumbai, more diffuse support for Al-Qaeda and international terrorism, and its meddling in Afghanistan, the Pakistani government has declined to crack down on the organization.

124. Anne Stenersen recounts how Al-Qaeda's connections to the Afghan Taliban have slightly weakened, while their connections to groups that ultimately came to form the Pakistan Taliban strengthened since 2001; see Anne Stenersen, "Al-Qaeda's

Allies: Explaining the Relationship between Al-Qaeda and Various Factions of the Taliban after 2001," Counterterrorism Strategy Initiative Paper (Washington, DC: New American Foundation, April 2010). See also Rohan Gunaratna and Anders Nielsen, "Al Qaeda in the Tribal Areas of Pakistan and Beyond," *Studies in Conflict and Terrorism* 31, no. 9 (2008): 775–807; Gunaratna and Nielsen track the various movements of Al-Qaeda and their relationships within Pakistan since 2001 in painstaking detail.

125. Pakistan has assisted in the apprehension of three key Al-Qaeda operatives in that country since 2002—Khalid Sheikh Mohammed, Ramzi bi al-Shibh, and Abu Zubaydah. See "Factbox: al Qaeda Leaders Killed or Captured in Pakistan," *Reuters*, May 2, 2011, available at http://www.reuters.com/article/2011/05/02/us-binladen-pakistan-alqaeda-idUSTRE74132J20110502.

126. Sabrina Tavernise, Carlotta Gall, and Ismail Khan, "Pakistan, in Shift, Weights Attack on Militant Lair," *New York Times*, April 29, 2010. South and North Waziristan have proven the most effective sanctuaries for militants of all kinds. As of this writing, the Pakistani armed forces have mounted significant operations in South Waziristan, but according to many observers North Waziristan quickly became the refuge for a range of militant groups, including Al-Qaeda, the Pakistani Taliban, the "Haqqani network" (which operates in Afghanistan and Pakistan), and perhaps also some Punjabi militants. The Pakistani armed forces were reported to understand the threat but to have not launched an operation. "Report says Pakistan's North Waziristan offensive likely in March," *Express Tribune*, January 25, 2014.

127. K. Alan Kronstadt, *Pakistan-U.S. Relations*, RL33498, Congressional Research Service, February 6, 2009, 66–68.

128. Steven Simon and Jonathan Stevenson have proposed a workable strategy. In particular, they offer a comprehensive legal and strategic rationale for targeted killing but at the same time recommend a series of reforms. Their main purpose is to argue that the Afghanistan development and counterinsurgency project is unnecessary and impractical, and to offer a more sustainable alternative; see Steven Simon and Jonathan Stevenson, "Afghanistan: How Much Is Enough?" *Survival* 51, no. 5 (October–November 2009): 47–67.

129. Polled in 2013, 72 percent of Pakistanis reported an unfavorable view of the United States, among the highest in the world. Only 11 percent reported a favorable view, the lowest in the world. Pew Research Global Attitudes Project, Global Indicators Database, available at http://www.pewglobal.org/database/indicator/1/survey/10/response/Unfavorable/ ; see also Juan Cole, "Pakistan and Afghanistan: Beyond the Taliban," *Political Science Quarterly* 124, no. 2 (summer 2009): 221–49, especially 226, 233–34, 240. In addition, consult C. Christine Fair, "Pakistan's Own War on Terror: What the Pakistani Public Thinks," *Journal of International Affairs* 63, no. 1 (fall/ winter 2009): 39–55, especially 46. Fair reports that in July 2009 almost 80 percent of Pakistanis polled disagreed with their government's cooperation with the United States in the "war on terror." See also Synnott, *Transforming Pakistan*, 90, 92, 180–81.

130. Cole, "Pakistan and Afghanistan," 246–47.

131. Jane Perlez, "U.S. Fears that Increased Aid to Pakistan Will Feed Graft," *New York Times*, September 21, 2009; Ken Dilanian, "State Dept. Rethinks How to Deliver Aid to Pakistan," *USA Today*, October 2, 2009; Alex Rodriguez, "Corruption Limits Aid to Pakistan," *Los Angeles Times*, March 28, 2010.

132. Robert J. Art, *A Grand Strategy for America* (Ithaca: Cornell University Press, 2003), 55–58, argues that the United States has a vital interest in great power "deep

peace" in Eurasia, in which the principal states not only do not fight, they do not compete. He advances many arguments for this position, but the one closest to this set of concerns is that a great power war on the continent has "a great risk of dragging the United States into it."

3. Command of the Commons

1. This chapter draws extensively on Barry R. Posen, "Command of the Commons: The Military Foundation of U.S. Hegemony," *International Security* 28, no. 1 (summer 2003): 5–46. Though I do still believe that without command of the commons, the United States could not even consider a hegemonic strategy, I have argued in the preceding chapters that the strategy has been tested and found wanting.

2. Defense spending does not dip below 3 percent of GDP until 2019, and falls to 2.8 percent of GDP by 2023. Congressional Budget Office, *The Budget and Economic Outlook: Fiscal Years 2013 to 2023*, "Figure 1–3, Projected Spending in Major Budget Categories," February 2013, 23, 25.

3. It was not "the taking of individual ships or convoys, be they few or many, that strikes down the money power of a nation; it is the possession of that overbearing power on the sea which drives the enemy's flag from it, or allows it to appear only as a fugitive; and which by controlling the *great common*, closes the highways by which commerce moves to and from the enemy's shores." Alfred Thayer Mahan, *The Influence of Sea Power upon History, 1660–1783* (Boston: Little, Brown, 1890): 138, quoted in Jon Tetsuro Sumida, *Inventing Grand Strategy and Teaching Command: The Classic Works of Alfred Thayer Mahan Reconsidered* (Baltimore, MD: The Johns Hopkins University Press, 1999): 46.

4. Kennedy distinguishes "naval mastery" from temporary, local naval superiority, or local command of the sea. "By . . . the term "naval mastery," however, there is meant here something stronger, more exclusive and wider-ranging; namely a situation in which a country has so developed its maritime strength that it is superior to any rival power, and that its predominance is or could be exerted far outside its home waters, with the result that it is extremely difficult for other, lesser states to undertake maritime operations or trade without at least its tacit consent. It does *not* necessarily imply a superiority over all other navies combined, nor does it mean that this country could not temporarily lose local command of the sea; but it does assume the possession of an overall maritime power such that small-scale defeats overseas would soon be reversed by the dispatch of naval forces sufficient to eradicate the enemy's challenge. Generally speaking, naval mastery is also taken to imply that the nation achieving it will usually be very favourably endowed with many fleet bases, a large merchant marine, considerable national wealth, etc., all of which indicates influence at a global rather than a purely regional level." Paul M. Kennedy, *The Rise and Fall of British Naval Mastery* (1976; repr. London: Macmillan, 1983), 9.

5. "By maritime strategy we mean the principles which govern a war in which the sea is a substantial factor. Naval strategy is but that part of it which determines the movements of the fleet when maritime strategy has determined what part the fleet must play in relation to the action of the land forces; for it scarcely needs saying that it is almost impossible that a war can be decided by naval action alone." Julian S. Corbett, *Principles of Maritime Strategy* (Mineola, NY: Dover, 2004): 15–16.

6. Maps of geographical chokepoints have become a favorite device of energy security analysts. See U.S. Energy Information Agency, "World Oil Transit Choke-

points," Last Updated: August 22, 2012, available at http://www.eia.gov/coun tries/regions-topics2.cfm?fips=WOTC.

7. Margaret and Harold Sprout, *Toward a New Order of Sea Power: American Naval Policy and the World Scene, 1918–1922* (Princeton, NJ: Princeton University Press, 1940), 10–16.

8. "But this eccentric movement, this advantage of interior position, had also a marked inherent disadvantage. However far the surge of Nipponese conquest might reach, always beyond its periphery were uncommanded seas over which Japan's enemies were bound ultimately to bring the full pressure of their superior strength. Because of the many islands of the East Indies, Japanese communications ran thru narrow seas permitting great opportunities to United Nations submarines, but our own lines ran across the broad Indian Ocean and the immense Pacific. Japan might push wide the *walls of her cage*, but she was isolated from her allies and surrounded by a hostile world." Bernard Brodie, *A Guide to Naval Strategy*, 3rd ed. (Princeton, NJ: Princeton University Press, 1944), 118.

9. The "first island chain" is the term used by Chinese strategists for "the line formed by the Aleutians, the Kuriles, Japan's archipelago, the Ryukus, Taiwan, the Philippines and Borneo." "Chinese Navy's New Strategy in Action," *IISS Strategic Comments*, vol. 16, comment 16, May 2010. See the map of new Chinese naval activity; for an alarmist treatment of China's possible military intent to seize one or more of the Ryukus in the event of war, in order to break out of the barrier formed by the chain, see Toshi Yoshihara and James R. Holmes, "The Japanese Archipelago through Chinese Eyes," *China Brief* 10, no. 16 (August 2010): 9–12; see also the map "The First and Second Island Chains," in Office of the Secretary of Defense, *Military and Security Developments Involving the People's Republic of China 2010*, Annual Report to Congress, U.S. Department of Defense, Washington, DC, 23, available at http://www. defense.gov/pubs/pdfs/2010_CMPR_Final.pdf.

10. "If time be, as is everywhere admitted, a supreme factor in war, it behooves countries whose genius is essentially not military, whose people, like all free people, object to pay for large military establishments, to see to it that they are at least strong enough to gain the time necessary to turn the spirit and capacity of their subjects in the new activities which war calls for. If the existing force by land or sea is strong enough so to hold out, even though at a disadvantage, the country may rely upon its natural resources and strength coming into play for whatever they are worth,—its numbers, its wealth, its capacities of every kind." Alfred Thayer Mahan, *Influence of Seapower*, 48. as quoted in Jon Tetsuro Sumida, *Inventing Grand Strategy*, 88.

11. "It [sea power] enables its possessors to exploit all their own resources, to draw upon the resources of the world for the raw materials and finished goods of their needs in war, to carry those goods whither they are needed, and to transport the fighting forces of the other arms to whatever points in the vast theatre of war where they can be most effectively used. Sea power did not win the war itself: it enabled the war to be won." Herbert Richmond, *Statesmen and Sea Power, Based on the Ford Lectures Delivered in the University of Oxford in the Michaelmas Term, 1943* (Oxford: Clarendon Press, 1946), 336.

12. Britain, France, Germany, and Italy together operate 84 destroyers and frigates. The U.S. Navy operates 103 cruisers, destroyers, and frigates. European surface combatants are smaller and less capable than those of the U.S. Navy, but they permit the surveillance and control of a great deal of additional sea space. Moreover, these navies either possess significant littoral combat experience such as Britain, or build some of the world's most lethal littoral weapons, such as France (antiship missiles)

and Italy (bottom mines.) IISS, *The Military Balance, 2011* (London: International Institute for Strategic Studies and Routledge, 2011), country entries.

13. Michael R. Gordon, "Threats and Responses: Allies; German and Spanish Navies Take on Major Role near Horn of Africa" *New York Times*, December 15, 2002, 36. Task Force 150 was initially an eight-ship flotilla conducting patrols in the Indian Ocean in search of al-Qaeda operatives. Its first commander was German, and its second commander was Spanish. It remains part of a larger multinational operation in the region, which presently "includes three dozen ships from Australia, France, Germany, Italy, Pakistan, Canada, Denmark, Turkey, the U.S. and U.K.," and other unnamed countries. U.S. Naval Forces Central Command, U.S. 5th Fleet Combined Maritime Forces, web site, available at http://www.cusnc.navy.mil/.

14. Corbett, *Principles of Maritime Strategy*, 16.

15. Kennedy, *Rise and Fall of British Naval Mastery*, 205–37.

16. Carlo Kopp, "Evolving Technological Strategy in Advanced Air Defense Systems," *Joint Forces Quarterly* 57, no. 2 (2010): 86–93, available at http://www.ndu.edu/press/lib/images/jfq-57/kopp.pdf.

17. The United States has organized a cooperative international effort of some ninety-seven countries to better enable the interdiction of cargos of illegal materials associated with weapons of mass destruction. This activity, whose effectiveness is difficult to judge, includes a general commitment to cooperation, a series of agreements to facilitate the boarding of suspicious ships, and a series of training activities to improve the ability of national naval forces to cooperate in interdiction efforts. Mary Beth Nikitin, *Proliferation Security Initiative (PSI)*, Congressional Research Service, 7–5700, RL34327, January 18, 2011:1–6, available at http://www.fas.org/sgp/crs/nuke/RL34327.pdf.

18. Clausewitz, *On War*, ed. and trans. Michael Howard and Peter Paret (Princeton, NJ: Princeton University Press, 1976, 1984), 180–82.

19. France spent the equivalent of $52 billion, Germany $45 billion, and the United Kingdom $60 billion (U.S.) in 2010. See NATO Public Diplomacy Division, "Financial and Economic Data Relating to NATO Defence," March 10, 2011, table 1.4, available at http://www.nato.int/cps/en/natolive/news_71296.htm?mode=pressrelease. The United States spent $79 billion on research, development, testing, and experimentation alone. See U.S. Department of Defense, Summary of the DOD Fiscal 2012 Budget Proposal, 8, available at http://www.defense.gov/Releases/Release.aspx?ReleaseID=14263. This has been the case for almost a decade. See International Institute for Strategic Studies, *The Military Balance 2002–2003* (London: IISS, 2002), 241, 252–53. My colleague, Harvey Sapolsky, called this to my attention.

20. Harvey M. Sapolsky, Eugene Gholz, and Allen Kaufman, "Security Lessons from the Cold War," *Foreign Affairs* 78, no. 4 (July/August 1999): 77–89.

21. John F. Newell III, *Airpower and the Battle of Khafji: Setting the Record Straight* (Air University Maxwell AFB, AL: School of Advanced Air Power Studies, June 1998), 54–61; See also Barry D. Watts and Thomas A. Keaney, "Effects and Effectiveness," vol. 2, pt. 2, *The Gulf War Air Power Survey* (Washington, DC: Government Printing Office, 1993): 234–42.

22. Estimating the personnel implications of force structure changes is as much art as science. It has roughly been the case since the Second World War that a U.S. division, including its own personnel, and those of supporting units, requires about 30,000–40,000 people to operate effectively—the so called "division slice." The lower

figure has been achieved recently when operating in developed theaters with either a great deal of host nation support and/or contractor support. And, not all of the supporting personnel are necessarily in the active forces; many are mobilized from the reserves. Today the army has a strength of about 553,000 to generate ten divisions (each with an average of four brigades.) Even if we assumed a 40,000-person division "slice," this leave 153,000 people in the so-called school-house army. I have assumed a 30,000 person slice for heuristic purposes.

23. U.S. Department of Defense, *Defense Budget Priorities and Choices* (Washington, DC: January 2012), 11–12, available at http://www.defense.gov/news/Defense_Budget_Priorities.pdf. In private briefings to Congress the Army hinted at much deeper cuts to come, to as few as 420,000 troops. Lance M. Bacon, "Chief, Congress and DOD hammer out Army's future manning levels," *Army Times* October 7, 2013, http://www.armytimes.com/article/20131007/NEWS/310070003/.

24. The Marine Corps is fully conscious of the growing risks to amphibious assaults. "While the global reach of U.S. naval forces provides an inherent means of overcoming geographic impediments to access . . . we must also recognize that military challenges to access are expanding. These include the continued use of mines and terrorist attacks against shipping, as well as the development of anti-access weapons with increased range, speed, and precision." See U.S. Marine Corps, *Marine Corps Operating Concepts, Assuring Littoral Access . . . Winning Small Wars*, 3rd ed. (Washington, DC: June 2010), 89–106, 95.

25. This is roughly what occurred at Guadalcanal, in the Solomon Islands, in August 1942. At the time of the U.S. landing, the Japanese had only had a small engineering contingent and limited forces on the island. The two sides then competed simultaneously to reinforce and deny the other reinforcement. See Richard B. Frank, *Guadalcanal: The Definitive Account of the Landmark Battle* (New York: Random House, 1990). One can imagine similar scenarios in the so-called "first island chain."

26. It is, however, reasonable to have more marines than ships; amphibious assaults against determined defenders are very costly; in the unlikely event that the United States ever has to do this kind of thing again, it is likely that the shipping can be readied for a second campaign before a Marine unit can repair itself, so it makes sense to have more marine units than shipping.

27. U.S. Department of Defense, *Defense Budget Priorities*, 11–12.

28. Since the late 1970s the marines have maintained Maritime Prepositioning Squadrons—small groups of ships anchored in harbors controlled by the United States, loaded with sufficient materiel to equip roughly one-third of a Marine division. This practice could continue, and depending on the scenario, would permit a Marine division landed from assault shipping to receive reinforcements through any austere port or airfield facilities they might seize.

29. The navy currently plans for a force of eight LHDs and two LHAs to provide the core assault shipping for the Marine Corps. All have large decks and can operate all types of Marine Corps helicopters and VSTOL aircraft such as the Harrier or F35B; the LHDs can also operate landing craft from well decks. They are roughly the size of WWII aircraft carriers. The marines assume that these ships, plus other more specialized vessels, can support an attack by two Marine Expeditionary Brigades (nearly a division.) Though I believe the United States needs some amphibious assault capability, I have found no compelling public rationale for any specific level and can offer no compelling alternative myself, so I leave the navy/marine shipbuilding program intact. See Eric Labs, *An Analysis of the Navy's Amphibious Warfare*

Ships for Deploying Marines Overseas (Washington DC: Congressional Budget Office, November 2011).

30. As in the case of the army, connecting force structure reductions to personnel reductions is an art form. The IISS counts 334,342 people in the active air force, and just over 150 squadrons of aircraft of all types, including training units. Crudely this implies an average of just over 2,000 persons in the organization as a whole is required to keep a squadron flying. Alternatively, IISS suggest that the Air Expeditionary Force, an assemblage of 135 aircraft that constitutes the typical deployment package for the Air Force requires 10,000–15,000 personnel. Hence one might say that in the field, at least 100 people per aircraft are required. This would imply also about 2000 per squadron, though this metric omits the training and support base in the United States. I thus add a few thousand to the total reduction. IISS, *The Military Balance 2010,* 38–40.

31. Alarmism about the fighters being developed by other powers is a staple of budget debates about fighter acquisition in the United States, in part because U.S. fighters are typically so expensive and thus require constant justification. See, for example, Rebecca Grant, *Losing Air Dominance,* Mitchell Institute Special Report, Air Force Association (September 2008):17–22, available at http://www.afa.org/AFA/PUBLICATIONS/MichellInstitutePapers.

32. For a primer on SEAD, and its cousin DEAD (destruction of enemy air defenses), see Christopher Bolkcom, "Military Suppression of Enemy Air Defenses (SEAD): Assessing Future Needs," RS21141, CRS Report for Congress, updated June 5, 2006, and Christopher Bolkcom, "Airborne Electronic Warfare: Issues for the 107th Congress," RL30841 Congressional Research Service, February 9, 2001. Both papers describe the history of the mission, current and future challenges, ongoing programs, and extant offensive systems at the time of publication. They are available at http://digital.library.unt.edu/explore/collections/CRSR/.

33. The SA-10, a NATO designation for the Russian S300, is said to be the most impressive of these systems. Discussing air defense suppression and the significant problems posed by the SA-10 is Owen R. Cote Jr., *The Future of the Trident Force,* Security Studies Program, Massachusetts Institute of Technology, May 2002, 25–29, available at http://web.mit.edu/ssp/publications/conference.html. http://web.mit.edu/ssp/Publications/confseries/Trident_ForceWEB.PDF. See also Cote, "'Buying . . . From the Sea': A Defense Budget for a Maritime Strategy," in Cindy Williams, ed., *Holding the Line: U.S. Defense Alternatives for the Early 21st Century* (Cambridge, MA: MIT Press, 2001), 146–50; and Cote, "Assessing the Undersea Balance between the U.S. and China," February 2011, SSP Working Paper WP11-1: 20–23, available at http://web.mit.edu/ssp/publications/working_papers/Undersea%20Balance%20WP11-1.pdf.

34. IISS, *The Military Balance, 2002–2003,* 148, credits China with 144 SA-10s. This implies perhaps a dozen batteries. See Federation of American Scientists, "SA-10 Grumble," available at http://www.fas.org/nuke/guide/russia/airdef/s-300pmu.htm.

35. "The PLA Air Force has continued expanding its inventory of long-range, advanced SAM systems and now possesses one of the largest such forces in the world. Over the past five years, China has acquired multiple S-300 battalions, the most advanced SAM system that Russia exports. It has also introduced the indigenously designed HQ-9." Office of the Secretary of Defense, "Annual Report to Congress Military and Security Developments Involving the People's Republic of China 2012," Washington, DC, May 2012, 24.

36. Cote, "Assessing," 20–23, discusses the great progress the United States has made in its ability to locate air defense radars precisely and quickly, but also the obstacles to exploiting this ability against modern air defense systems. He also suggests some innovative solutions.

37. Eric Labs, *Increasing the Mission Capability of the Attack Submarine Force* (Washington DC: Congressional Budget Office: March 2002), 31, hints at regular SSN support of battle groups: "If the submarines transferred to Guam under this option were removed from San Diego, the SSN presence there would end, making it difficult for attack submarines *to train with carrier battle groups and thus to support them during their deployments*" (my emphasis). In subsequent work he notes plans to attach an SSN to amphibious groups. "Under a plan announced in 2003, the navy has begun reorganizing its fleet so that three surface combatants (a cruiser, a destroyer, and a frigate) and *one attack submarine operate with each amphibious ready group* [my emphasis]. The resulting task force was called an expeditionary strike group, or ESG." See also Eric Labs, *The Future of the Navy's Amphibious and Maritime Prepositioning Forces* (Washington, DC: Congressional Budget Office, November 2004), 4.

38. Labs, *Mission Capability*, ix, 1, 5, 31.

39. Once adversary submarines become very quiet, some form of active sonar will be required to find them. Submarines themselves do not regularly employ active sonars because this gives their position away. Thus, against very quiet submarines, in adversary waters, a forward-deployed SSN will ultimately become less useful for offensive action.

40. Les Aspin, Secretary of Defense, *Report on the Bottom-Up Review*, October 1993, U.S. Dept. of Defense, 19, 49–53.

41. Benjamin S. Lambeth, *American Carrier Air Power at the Dawn of a New Century* (Prepared for the United States Navy) (Santa Monica, CA: RAND Corporation, 2005), iii.

42. Thomas A. Keaney and Eliot A. Cohen, *Gulf War Air Power Survey, Summary Report* (Washington, DC: Government Printing Office, 1993): 13, 56–57, 60–61. By the end of the first day of combat, "air superiority—the ability of one side's aircraft to operate in selected airspace at a given time without prohibitive interference from the other side" was achieved. By the end of the fifth day, Iraqi radar-guided surface-to-air missiles became largely ineffective in engaging U.S. aircraft.

43. A. Jewell et al., *USS Nimitz and Carrier Airwing Nine Surge Demonstration*, CRM 97-111.10 (Alexandria, VA: Center for Naval Analysis, April 1998), 4. See also Lambeth, *Carrier Air Power*, 64, suggesting that as many as 250 sorties of all types is achievable.

44. Aircraft carrier wings are constrained by the "deck cycle." A carrier can put roughly 30 aircraft into the air at a time, in a complex launch process that involves steaming into the wind. It has a similar aircraft recovery process. Thus, four carriers operating together would probably mount attacks in a series of waves, each one with perhaps 120 aircraft.

45. The present navy inventory of Tomahawk missiles is probably between three and four thousand weapons, though I have been unable to find an exact figure. The newest "Block IV" version costs between a half a million and a million dollars each, and some two thousand have been delivered to the fleet since 2004. See http://www.raytheon.com/newsroom/feature/tomahawk_02-10/. This is an accurate and flexible weapon. Cruise missiles are costly, but the most modern fighter aircraft now cost nearly 100 million dollars each. The employment of large numbers of

cruise missiles simultaneously to suppress lethally and saturate air defenses is beginning to seem like a bargain.

46. Fifty-six Arleigh Burke Destroyers have 96 vertical cells each capable of launching cruise missiles or surface-to-air missiles. Twenty-two Ticonderoga class cruisers have 122 cells each. A four-carrier assault force would have perhaps sixteen escorts. The antiship missile threat necessitates loading these ships mainly with air-defense missiles, but some land attack cruise missiles could be accommodated. The four Ohio class nuclear submarines could each carry 154 land attack cruise missiles.

47. Against targets that are buried, and or protected by layers of concrete and steel, heavier precision-guided bombs are preferred. A B2 can carry sixteen two-thousand-pound precision-guided bombs, or a smaller number of even larger precision-guided bombs specially designed to penetrate hard targets. Though some navy fighters can carry one-ton weapons, the navy appears to prefer flying with weapons not heavier than a thousand pounds. As the United States only possesses twenty B2s, and its other long-range aircraft such as the B52 or B1B probably ought not to be sent even against a degraded air defense, it will ultimately become necessary to find another way to attack very hard structures, if the target set is large.

48. For an exhaustive treatment of the life cycle of a nuclear powered aircraft carrier, see Roland J. Yardley, James G. Kallimani, John F. Schank, and Clifford A. Grammich, *Increasing Aircraft Carrier Forward Presence: Changing the Length of the Maintenance Cycle* (Santa Monica, CA: RAND Corporation, 2008): ix–xx, available at http://www.rand.org/pubs/monographs/MG706/. Under a variety of alternatives a CVN can either be deployed or ready for combat in thirty days, roughly 65 percent of the time. Thus a nine-carrier force would yield six ready to fight within a month.

49. Six of the seven fought in the Pacific; the seventh, the Ranger was not considered sufficiently capable for combat against the Japanese Navy. "A Brief History of U.S. Navy Aircraft Carriers Part IIa—The War Years (1941–1942)," available at http://www.navy.mil/navydata/nav_legacy.asp?id=2.

50. This is driven by the importance of the E2C airborne warning and control aircraft to fleet air defense. Each carrier normally has four or five such aircraft, which permit at least one to be aloft at any one time. Damage to one carrier, however, could prevent the launch and recovery of such aircraft. The grounding of the E2s could significantly increase the vulnerability of the carrier to complete destruction, and of the rest of the task force. Thus it would be prudent to maintain two carriers together to provide mutual support.

51. I estimate that this could imply a reduction of twenty thousand to thirty thousand active uniformed naval personnel. But I can find no reliable way of matching people to warships. A carrier and its air wing typically have five thousand to six thousand people aboard. Four surface escorts for each carrier would add perhaps three hundred people each, for a total of twelve hundred. A supply ship/oiler is usually associated with the battle group. Additional personnel ashore are required at a ratio of perhaps 1:1.

52. Because this plan calls for the early retirement of two nuclear powered aircraft carriers, another possibility suggests itself. The USN could cancel the acquisition of two large amphibious assault ships, convert the nuclear carriers to Marine Corps use instead, and postpone the acquisition of two major amphibious assault ships for many years.

53. Robert Rubel, "The Future of Aircraft Carriers," *Naval War College Review* 64, no. 4 (autumn 2011): 13–27, succinctly reviews the range of missions that carriers have

fulfilled historically and offers a careful analysis of their future. He doubts that they will remain sufficiently survivable to mount sustained air operations close to the shores of a peer competitor. Though conditions will vary, in the most difficult cases it will be necessary to attack with cruise missiles, or conventional ballistic missiles, from stealthy platforms. In these same conditions, amphibious attack will also be ruled out.

54. Wayne P. Hughes, *Fleet Tactics and Coastal Combat*, 2nd ed. (Annapolis: Naval Institute Press, 2000), 26–27, 36–39, notes that Nelson won many of his greatest victories "inshore" against enemy fleets that ought to have been covered by shore batteries. He was, however, diligent in finding ways to neutralize or circumvent those batteries. Hughes then develops a series of general principles for doing so, though notes that it is not always possible. The fleet has one main disadvantage: combat power is concentrated in a handful of sinkable platforms whereas littoral defenses are dispersed, and are difficult to damage catastrophically. The fleet has certain advantages—mobility and the ability to concentrate forces are the main ones. Some defenses can be avoided; some can be crushed by concentrated firepower; some can be isolated and weakened prior to attack, some can be attacked from an unexpected quarter—the land if a beach can be found to land marines. Occasionally, none of these nostrums will work, but the objective will still need to be attacked, in which case a costly slugfest will prove necessary.

55. General Bruce Carlson, USAF (Ret), "National Reconnaissance Office Update," speech, Annual Air & Space Conference and Technology Exposition, September 13, 2010, available at http://www.nro.gov/news/speeches/2010/2010-02.pdf.

56. Union of Concerned Scientists, UCS Satellite Database (includes launches through 1/31/11), available at http://www.ucsusa.org/nuclear_weapons_and_ global_security/space_weapons/technical_issues/ucs-satellite-database.html. They identified 957 total satellites, so the United States has almost half the satellites in space.

57. According to the *Quadrennial Defense Review Report*, released on September 30, 2001, "The ability of the United States to access and utilize space is a vital national security interest." According to the report, "Ensuring freedom of access to space and protecting U.S. national security interests are key priorities that must be reflected in future investment decisions," 45.

58. "National Security Space Strategy," U.S. Dept. of Defense and U.S. Director of National Intelligence, Washington, DC, 2010 (unclassified summary), 5.

59. The United States has laws on the books that permit the NOAA to prohibit U.S. companies from providing imagery to other countries and presumably groups, if it is determined that U.S. national security requires it. It also appears that these commercial actors must maintain sufficient legal and physical control over their satellites to permit compliance with U.S. government wishes. See *The Federal Register*, April 25, 2006, part 3, Department of Commerce National Oceanic and Atmospheric Administration, 15 CFR Part 960, Licensing of Private Land Remote-Sensing Space Systems; Final Rule: 24474–24491, available at http://www.gpo.gov/fdsys/pkg/ FR-2006-04-25/html/06-3841.htm.

60. GPS cost $4.2 billion (1979 prices) to bring to completion, significantly more money than was originally projected. This is the cost of the development and deployment of the system, and the acquisition of sufficient satellites (118), to achieve and sustain a 24-satellite array. By 1997, $3 billion (1979 dollars) had been spent on "user equipment," the military terminals that calculate location on the basis of the

satellites' signals. See U.S. Department of Defense, "Systems Acquisition Review Program Acquisition Cost Summary as of June 30, 1997." See also U.S. General Accounting Office, *Navstar Should Improve the Effectiveness of Military Missions—Cost Has Increased*, PSAD-80-91, February 15, 1980, 14.

61. The United States formerly corrupted the GPS satellite signals to reduce the accuracy that a nonmilitary user terminal could achieve. On May 1, 2000, President Clinton ended this policy due to the vast commercial possibilities of highly accurate positional information. At that time, the United States believed that it could employ new techniques to jam the GPS signals regionally in a way that would prevent an adversary from exploiting them, but not dilute the accuracy elsewhere. See President Bill Clinton: "Improving the Civilian Global Positioning System (GPS)," May 1, 2000, available at http://clinton4.nara.gov/WH/New/html/20000501_2.html.

62. Advocates of Galileo explicitly argue that Europe must have its own satellite navigation systems or lose its "autonomy in defense." See Dee Ann Divis, "Military Role for Galileo Emerges," *GPS World* 13, no. 5 (May 2002): 10, available at http://www.globalsecurity.org/org/news/2002/020514-gps.htm. Four satellites in the Galileo system were in orbit by the end of 2012. See also "China Launches Two More Beidou Navigation Satellites," *BBC News-Technology*, April 30, 2012, available at http://www.bbc.com/news/technology-17896353.

63. "Threats to United States Space Capabilities," by Tom Wilson, Space Commission staff member, prepared for the *Report of the Commission to Assess United States National Security Space Management and Organization* (Washington D.C.: Government Printing Office, January 11, 2001), available at http://www.fas.org/spp/eprint/article05.html. Secretary of Defense Donald Rumsfeld chaired this commission.

64. A technically competent country with limited resources may be able to develop a capability to damage or destroy U.S. reconnaissance satellites in low earth orbit. See Allen Thomson, "Satellite Vulnerability: A Post-Cold War Issue," *Space Policy* 11, no. 1 (February 1995): 19–30, available at http://www.fas.org/spp/eprint/at_sp.htm.

65. Tim Ross and Holly Watt, "WikiLeaks: US vs. China in Battle of the Anti-Satellite Space Weapons," *Telegraph*, February 2, 2011, available at http://www.telegraph.co.uk/news/worldnews/wikileaks/8299491/WikiLeaks-US-vs-China-in-battle-of-the-anti-satellite-space-weapons.html.

66. Wilson, "Threats to United States Space Capabilities," offers the most accessible discussion of satellite vulnerability and modes of attack.

67. This is based on my simple addition of the maximum estimated cost increases associated with hardening satellites, providing them the capability for autonomous operations, giving them some onboard attack reporting capability, making them maneuverable, providing them with decoys, and providing them with some self-defense capability. See Wilson, "Threats to United States Space Capabilities," pt. 6, "Countermeasures—Strategies for Enhancing Survivability."

68. Ross and Watt, "WikiLeaks: US vs. China in Battle of the Anti-Satellite Space Weapons."

69. Federation of American Scientists, Space Policy Project, Military Space Programs, "Anti-Satellite Weapons, Overview," (last updated March 1997), available at http://www.fas.org/spp/military/program/asat/overview.htm. Dwayne Day, "Smashing RORSATs: the origin of the F-15 ASAT program," *Space Review*, January 11, 2010, available at http://www.thespacereview.com/article/1540/1.

70. Jim Wolf, "U.S. Deploys Satellite Jamming Systems," *Reuters*, October 29, 2004, reports the deployment of the Counter Communications System. This system is

operated by the U.S. Air Force 4th Space Control Squadron, which "provides combat space superiority effect" and "deploys globally to conduct mobile and transportable space superiority operations." See also Department of the Air Force, "U.S. Air Force Fact Sheet, 4th Space Control Squadron," available at http://www.peterson.af.mil/library/factsheets/factsheet_print.asp?fsID=4707&page=1.

71. See for example, Theresa Hitchens, "Weapons in Space: Silver Bullet or Russian Roulette," in *Space Weapons, Are They Needed?*, ed. John M. Logsdon and Gordon Adams (Washington, DC: Space Policy Institute, George Washington University, 2003), 115–56. available at http://www.gwu.edu/~spi/assets/docs/Security_Space_Volume.Final.pdf ; Charles V. Pena and Edward L. Hudgins, *Should the United States "Weaponize" Space?* Policy Analysis No. 427 (Washington, DC: Cato Institute, March 18, 2002), 5–10.

72. U.S. Department of Defense, "Total Military Personnel and Dependent End Strength by Service, Regional Area, and Country, as of December 31, 2012," available at the Department of Defense, Defense Management Data Center, https://www.dmdc.osd.mil/appj/dwp/reports.do?category=reports&subCat=milActD utReg. The total deployed includes active duty, reservist, and National Guard personnel. Congressional Research Service, *National Guard Personnel and Deployments: Fact Sheet*, January 17, 2008, is the most recent public assessment. Roughly 28 percent of troops deployed to Iraq and Afghanistan from 2001–7 were either from the guard or the reserves.

73. The Pentagon uses two terms for the commonsense term *base*. Worldwide, the Pentagon has some 5,000 "sites" distributed across some 523 "installations." Some installations have several sites, which are themselves quite large. I use the term *base* for any "site" large enough for the Pentagon to list. Office of the Deputy Under Secretary of Defense (Installation and Environment), "DOD Base Structure Report FY 2013 Baseline," 2–7. available at http://www.acq.osd.mil/ie/. A review of the sites controlled by the U.S. Air Force in Japan gives an idea of the variability of the term "site." The Air Force has 16 sites in Japan, ranging in size from 64 to 6,077 acres, and ranging in replacement cost from 18 million to 5.8 billion dollars. See Deputy Under Secretary of Defense (Installation and Environment), "Air Force," 18. Three of these sites are actual air force bases—Kadena, Misawa, and Yokota. It should also be noted that bases in U.S. Trust Territories such as Guam and Puerto Rico, are not counted as "Foreign." Despite the ambiguities, the quoted document, which appears annually, is the most authoritative public statement of the size and dollar value of the U.S. base structure.

74. U.S. Dept. of Defense, "Strengthening U.S. Global Defense Posture—Report to Congress," Washington, DC, 2004; Ryan Henry, "Transforming the U.S. Global Defense Posture," *Naval War College Review* 59, no. 2 (spring 2006): 19–28.

75. Henry, "Transforming," 23–24.

76. U.S. Dept. of Defense, "Strengthening U.S. Global Defense Posture," 13.

77. For both a political and economic cost-benefit assessment of overseas bases to the implementation of current U.S. grand strategy, see Michael J. Lostumbo et al., *Overseas Basing of U.S. Military Forces: An Assessment of Relative Costs and Strategic Benefits* (Santa Monica, CA: RAND Corporation, 2013), 287–304, esp. 289.

78. Ibid. "Appendix D-U.S. Military Overseas Prepositioned Equipment," 383–88.

79. U.S. Joint Forces Command, *Partnership Opportunities Catalogue, FY 2011–2012*, Norfolk, VA, 140–43. The index lists eighteen "multi-national" exercises of varying size that the United States planned for Fiscal Years 2011 and 2012, which were

considered appropriate for U.S. interagency participation. As this is a forward-looking interagency planning tool, it includes no details as to which nations would actually participate in the planned exercises: 40, 41. This is only a partial list of multinational exercises but it is not obvious why some exercises are included in this publication and some are not. As of July 1, 2013, this publication is no longer accessible on the worldwide web, perhaps because Joint Forces Command was disestablished.

80. "EUCOM and its components are actively engaged in more than 100 exercises and operations that enhance their ability to play an active role in transatlantic security and defend the United States forward." U.S. European Command, "Key Activities, Exercises and Operations," available at http://www.eucom.mil/key-activities/exercises-and-operations. With the withdrawal of U.S. forces from Europe, these exercises would diminish significantly.

81. *Foreign Military Training, Fiscal Years 2009 and 2010, Joint Report to Congress,* vol. 1, U.S. Dept. of Defense and U.S. Dept. of State, 1–924, offers much detail on the direct training programs of individual service members from other countries. This program does not cost much, and represents only a fraction of U.S. activities. There are additionally two unpublished volumes, which are classified, suggesting that much of this training is politically sensitive.

82. Robert M. Gates, "Helping Others Defend Themselves," *Foreign Affairs* 89, no. 3 (May/June 2010): 2–6, argues that the United States can limit the necessity to intervene militarily in other countries through more intense engagement, including the training of local security forces. There are cases where this will make sense, but it is equally plausible that close training relationships implicate the United States in internal political fights that risk deeper involvement and the alienation of some domestic factions.

83. Lostumbo et al., *Overseas Basing,* "Appendix C Security Cooperation Cost Differential between Forward-Based and U.S.-Based Forces," 379.

84. During the tragic attack on the U.S. diplomatic mission in Benghazi, on September 11, 2012, the European Command's quick reaction force of Special Forces soldiers, normally based in Stuttgart, was on a training mission in Croatia. Media accounts have not reported what exactly they were doing there, but a good guess is training Croatian forces. While an alert unit surely must train to stay sharp, sending them off to Croatia would seem to defeat the purpose of having a "quick reaction force." Michael P. Gordon and Eric Schmitt, "Libya Attack Shows Pentagon's Limits in Region," *New York Times,* November 4, 2012, A4.

85. In the last major defense drawdown, 1989–99, active military personnel and DOD civilians fell by 35 percent, and active force structure fell by roughly 33 percent across all the services, while the defense budget fell by roughly 26 percent. I have drawn (or estimated) these figures from CBO, "Budgeting for Defense: Maintaining Today's Forces," Congress of the United States, Congressional Budget Office, September 2000: ix–x, available at http://www.cbo.gov/sites/default/files/cbofiles/ftpdocs/23xx/doc2398/intro.pdf.

Index

Afghanistan
  Al-Qaeda presence, 10, 38–39, 85,
    120–21, 126
  corruption, 122
  India, relations with, 123
  military program, 122
  NATO, relations with, 37–40, 122
  opium production, 122
  Pakistan, relations with, 122–28
  Pashtuns, 122, 127
  political environment, 121–22, 127
  population patterns, 122
  Soviet Union, relations with, 83
  state-building efforts, 11, 25, 66
  Taliban regime, 38–39, 51, 120–23,
    126–28, 141
  United States, relations with, 11, 15,
    24–26, 35–40, 51, 66–67, 121–22,
    127–28, 147, 158–59
  war costs, 25–26, 39
Ahmadinejad, Mahmoud, 77
air defense systems, 59, 114, 136, 143,
  149, 155
aircraft carriers, 12, 138, 151–56,
  161–62
Al-Assad, Bashar, 115
Albania, 50, 57
Albright, Madeleine K., 7, 9, 14, 164
Allawi, Ayad, 49
Al-Maliki, Nouri, 35, 48, 66
Al-Qaeda
  affiliated organizations, 85, 127
  Afghanistan presence, 10, 38–39, 85,
    120–21, 126
  Barack Obama intervention, 121–22
  George Bush intervention, 86, 120–21
  Iraq presence, 58, 85
  ISAF role, 39
  Muslim roots, 11, 45, 83–85
  nuclear ambitions, 81, 84
  Pakistan presence, 85, 121–22, 126–28
  September 11 attacks, 7, 45, 83, 120
  United States response, 10, 38–39, 45,
    66, 83–87, 120–21, 127–28, 133, 143,
    159, 165
  See also terrorism
Al-Zawahiri, Ayman, 83–84
American Enterprise Institute, 16
amphibious operations, 12, 103, 143,
  147–48, 151–52, 156, 171
Arab Spring, 25, 119
Armitage, Richard, 43
Aum Shinrikyo, 81
Australia, 92, 102, 161
Azores, 161

B2 aircraft, 154
Baker, James, 47
balance of power, 11, 20, 28–31, 69, 72,
  96–98, 129, 140, 145
Balkan wars, 9
ballistic missiles, 74–76, 99, 116, 151, 157
Bangladesh, 124
Barelvism, 124

Beidou system, 157
Benghazi, 57
Biden, Joe, 47
Bin Laden, Osama, 83–84, 121, 165
Bosnia, 9, 25, 50, 55–57, 67, 91, 164
Brazil, 29, 94
Britain
  balancing efforts, 71, 172
  China, relations with, 18
  economic environment, 87–89
  geographic position, 138
  Germany, relations with, 78, 129,
    172–73
  gross domestic product (GDP), 88
  hegemony capabilities, 88–89
  India, relations with, 123, 125
  Japan, relations with, 138
  military program, 27, 64, 87–88, 138,
    142, 146
  nuclear program, 73, 90
  political environment, 87
  population patterns, 88
  trade practices, 63–64
  United States, relations with, 97, 146
  World War II strategy, 5, 33–34, 97,
    104, 129
Brussels, 89
Brzezinski, Zbigniew, 9
Bush, George H. W., 7–8, 164
Bush, George W.
  Al-Qaeda, efforts against, 86, 120–21
  anti-American sentiment, 54
  election strategy, 11, 164–65
  Global Force Posture Review, 15, 159
  India policy, 31, 97
  Iran policy, 14
  Iraq policy, 14, 48
  Japan policy, 43
  military force structure, 14–15, 48
  North Korea policy, 14
  Operation Enduring Freedom,
    120–21
  Primacy agenda, 9, 14
  space strategy, 156
  strategic rhetoric, 11
  troop deployment, 14–15, 48, 159

Canada, 18–19, 63
capitalism, 53, 93, 95, 168–69
Carlson, Bruce, 156
Caucasus, 116
chemical weapons, 10, 113

Chen Shui Bian, 104
Cheney, Richard, 9
China
  balancing efforts, 29–32, 65, 171
  Beidou system, 157
  Britain, relations with, 18
  economic environment, 92–96, 165
  geographic position, 138–39, 150,
    171–72
  gross domestic product (GDP), 17–18,
    92–94
  hegemony capabilities, 6, 8, 20, 29, 34,
    65, 71, 91–96, 105, 171–72
  India, relations with, 80, 91, 96–98,
    120, 165, 171
  Iran, relations with, 29
  Japan, relations with, 34, 41, 44, 66,
    79, 91, 99–102
  military program, 17, 31–32, 65, 79,
    92–96, 100, 103, 149–52, 157
  nuclear program, 44, 71, 73, 76, 95–96,
    102–3, 171
  oil interests, 29, 112
  Pakistan, relations with, 97
  political environment, 82, 93–96
  population patterns, 17, 92, 94
  Russia, relations with, 30–32, 65, 71,
    74, 80, 91, 96, 98, 150, 171
  South Korea, relations with, 94
  Taiwan, relations with, 102–4
  trade practices, 63, 93–94, 99–100
  United Nations, influence on, 29
  United States, relations with, 14,
    17–18, 30–32, 63, 76, 91–96, 132,
    171–72
  Vietnam War role, 25, 52, 59
Clapper, James, 85
Clausewitz, Carl von, 22–23, 144
Clinton, Bill, 9–10, 12, 14–15, 24, 43, 72,
  153, 165
Clinton, Hillary, 5
Cold War
  alliance structure, 33–34, 36, 71
  balancing efforts, 30, 34, 36, 93
  combat personnel, 10, 15
  communism, role of, 95
  German strategy, 78–79
  Israel/Arab conflict, 45
  Japanese strategy, 41, 78
  rogue state survivors, 7
  roll-back strategies, 5
  Soviet Union strategy, 18, 30

submarines, 151
United States strategy, 10, 18, 33–34, 74, 93, 146, 159, 164
command and control centers, 79, 130, 149–51, 154
communism, 52, 55, 59, 95
Cooperative Security, 6–9, 11
Corbett, Julian, 141–42
Croatia, 50, 55
cruise missiles, 74, 111, 116, 151, 154–57
Czechoslovakia, 172

Dayton Agreement, 55
Democratic Party, 5, 7, 10, 15, 118, 173
Democratic People's Republic of Korea. *See* North Korea
Deobandism, 124
Department of Defense (DOD), 10, 12, 36, 48, 63, 145, 163. *See also* United States military
Diego Garcia, 161
diffusion of power, 29, 115, 167–68, 174
drones, 86, 158
Durand Line, 123

Egypt, 45, 51, 83–84, 113–14, 118
European Union (EU)
alliance structure, 35–36, 88
Bosnia Herzegovina reconstruction, 55–56
Common Security and Defense Policy, 89
euro strength, 18, 88
gross domestic product (GDP), 17, 88
member states, 78, 87–90
military programs, 17, 31, 35–36, 89–90
Political and Security Council, 89–90
population patterns, 17, 88
status quo power, 89
wealth, 35, 88
See also individual countries

F22 aircraft, 149
F35 aircraft, 149
FBI (Federal Bureau of Investigation), 85
Finland, 172
First World War. *See* World War I
Foreign Affairs, 5
France
balancing efforts, 71, 172
economic environment, 88–89

French Revolution, 22, 28, 51
Germany, relations with, 78, 172–73
gross domestic product (GDP), 88, 94
hegemony capabilities, 88–89
Louis XIV reign, 28
military program, 27, 41, 88, 129, 145
nuclear program, 73, 90
political environment, 87
population patterns, 88
United States, relations with, 29
Vietnam, relations with, 52
free/cheap riding, 21, 33, 35–44, 61, 65–66, 71, 143, 145, 166
French Revolution, 22, 28, 51
Friedman, Tom, 47

Gaddafi, Muammar, 24, 38, 57
Gates, Robert, 40, 46
Gaza, 114–15, 117, 119
genocide, 56–57
geography, 18–21, 41, 61, 67, 94–94, 102, 105–6, 110, 123–25, 129, 138–40, 150, 171
Georgia, 30, 35
Germany
alliance structure, 78
balancing efforts, 71, 78–79, 172
Britain, relations with, 78, 129, 172–73
Cold War strategy, 78–79
economic environment, 87–88
European Union, role in, 78
France, relations with, 78, 172–73
gross domestic product (GDP), 88, 94
hegemony capabilities, 20, 88–89
military program, 4, 79, 87–88, 129, 145
Nazis, 34, 104, 129, 170
nuclear program, 72, 78–80, 88, 167, 171
political environment, 87–88
population patterns, 88–89
Russia, relations with, 31
submarines, 129
trade practices, 63
United States, relations with, 78–79, 167
World War II role, 4, 28, 34, 71, 78, 129, 170
Gilpin, Robert, 62
Global Force Posture Review, 15, 159
Global Trends 2025: A Transformed World, 165

Global Trends 2030: Alternative Worlds, 91–92, 165
GLONASS system, 157
Gorbachev, Mikhail, 31
Grotto, Andrew, 77
Guam, 148, 161

Haiti, 9, 25, 56
Hamas, 114, 117
Hazeras, 122
helicopters, 35, 40, 59, 146, 152
Herzegovina, 55–56, 67
Hitler, Adolf, 28
Hizbollah, 32, 114–15
humanitarian activities, 2, 10–11, 25, 37, 56–60, 86, 128
Hussein, Saddam, 11, 14, 49–51, 108

identity politics, 22, 50–54, 59, 67, 86, 131, 163
Ikenberry, G. John, 5, 62
improvised explosive devices (IEDs), 59
India
    Afghanistan, relations with, 123
    Britain, relations with, 123, 125
    China, relations with, 80, 91, 96–98, 120, 165, 171
    economic environment, 94, 97–98, 125
    geographic position, 139
    George W. Bush policy, 31, 97
    gross domestic product (GDP), 17, 92, 94
    hegemony capabilities, 20, 29, 71, 91–92
    Japan, relations with, 78
    military program, 17, 92, 97–98, 125
    nuclear program, 31, 71, 94, 97, 120, 171
    Pakistan, relations with, 74, 120, 123–28
    political environment, 125
    population patterns, 17, 92, 97, 125
    United States, relations with, 31, 97–98, 120, 126, 128
Indonesia, 92, 99
International Atomic Energy Agency (IAEA), 82
International Criminal Court, 56
International Peace Cooperation Law (Japan), 43
International Security and Assistance Force (ISAF), 38–40, 121

Iran
    China, relations with, 29
    economic environment, 108, 141
    George W. Bush policy, 14
    hegemony capabilities, 108–9
    Iraq, relations with, 110–11
    Israel, relations with, 72–73, 77, 114–16
    military program, 32, 108
    nuclear program, 5, 14, 29, 31, 72–73, 76–77, 116, 141
    oil interests, 107–9
    Pakistan, relations with, 120
    political environment, 77, 109
    population patterns, 108
    Strait of Hormuz, 107, 110–11
    trade practices, 141
    United States, relations with, 14, 66, 76–77, 109
Iraq
    Al-Qaeda presence, 58, 85
    George W. Bush policy, 14, 48
    hegemony capabilities, 108
    internal insurgencies, 48–50, 58–59, 67
    Iran, relations with, 110–11
    Justice and Accountability Commission, 49
    Kuwait, relations with, 107, 111, 141, 146
    military program, 48–50, 141, 146, 154
    nuclear program, 14, 72
    oil interests, 49–50, 107, 141
    political environment, 48–50, 58, 67
    Saudi Arabia, relations with, 146
    state-building efforts, 25, 57–58, 66
    United States, relations with, 10–11, 14–15, 24–26, 32, 35, 48–50, 57–59, 140–41, 146–47
    war casualties, 26, 50, 58–59
    war costs, 25–26, 58–59, 67
Isolationism, 6
Israel
    economic environment, 113, 118
    gross domestic product (GDP), 113
    Hamas conflict, 114, 117
    Hizbollah conflict, 32, 114–15
    Iran, relations with, 72–73, 77, 114–16
    Iron Dome defense system, 114
    military program, 47–48, 113–16, 118–19, 149
    nuclear program, 73, 113, 116–17, 170

Palestine conflict, 45–47, 115, 117–20, 132
   political environment, 117–20
   population patterns, 113
   terrorism threats, 32, 114–16
   trade practices, 113
   United Nations involvement, 46
   United States, relations with, 44–48, 54, 66, 106, 116–20, 132, 166
   West Bank settlements, 46–47, 106, 115, 117, 119
Italy, 130

Jackson, Andrew, 16
Japan
   alliance structure, 40–44, 78
   balancing efforts, 71, 78–79
   Britain, relations with, 138
   China, relations with, 34, 41, 44, 66, 79, 91, 99–102
   Cold War strategy, 41, 78
   economic environment, 8, 78, 98–102, 139
   geographic position, 138–39
   George W. Bush policy, 43
   gross domestic product (GDP), 17, 36, 42–43, 92, 94, 98
   hegemony capabilities, 20
   India, relations with, 78
   International Peace Cooperation Law, 43
   military program, 17, 34, 36, 40–44, 66, 78–79, 92, 98–102, 130, 138
   North Korea, relations with, 44
   nuclear program, 72, 78–80, 94, 98, 101, 167
   oil interests, 100, 112
   political environment, 40–44, 78, 98
   population patterns, 17, 92, 98
   Russia, relations with, 78
   Taiwan, relations with, 41
   trade practices, 98–100
   United States, relations with, 4, 16, 29–30, 40–44, 63, 66, 71, 78–79, 98–102, 159–61, 167
   World War II role, 78, 138, 170
Jordan, 117
Justice and Accountability Commission (Iraq), 49

Kadena Air Force Base, 161
Kaiser Wilhelm, 28

Karzai, Hamid, 35, 66, 121
Kashmir, 125–27
KC130 aircraft, 149
Kennan, George, 87
Kennedy, Paul, 70, 136
Keohane, Robert, 62
Kerry, John, 119
Khomeini, Ayatollah, 77
Kindleberger, Charles, 62
Kissinger, Henry, 9
Koizumi, Junichiro, 43
Kosovo, 10, 24–25, 35, 37, 50, 56–57, 91, 164
Krauthammer, Charles, 9
Kurds, 49–51
Kuwait, 107, 111, 141, 159
Kyushu, 99

Lebanon, 111, 114–15
Liberman, Peter, 63–64
Libya, 24–25, 38, 56–57, 91
Louis XIV, 28
Luzon Straits, 152

Maghreb, 85
McCain, John, 5
Meade, Walter Russell, 16
Mecca, 110
Medina, 110
Mexico, 18–19, 63
Miller, Aaron David, 45
mines, 102, 110–11, 142, 157
Morsi, Mohamed, 114
Mubarak, Hosni, 113–14
Muslims, 11, 50–51, 55, 83–85, 110, 123–25

Napoleon Bonaparte, 28, 129–30
National Intelligence Council, 17, 91, 165
National Reconnaissance Office, 156
National Security Space Strategy, 156
nationalism, 22, 51–54, 60, 67, 96, 123, 140, 165
NATO (North Atlantic Treaty Organization)
   Afghanistan, relations with, 37–40, 122
   alliance structure, 16, 36–38
   Bosnia Herzegovina intervention, 55–56
   command structure, 16, 30, 90–91

NATO (North Atlantic Treaty
  Organization) *(continued)*
  enlargement, 31, 164
  gross domestic product (GDP), 35–36
  Libya, relations with, 38
  military program, 30, 36, 89
  NATO Response Force (NRF), 37–38
  origins, 74, 78
  political role, 16, 160
  Prague Summit, 37
  Riga Summit, 37
  Serbia, relations with, 37
  Soviet Union, relations with, 9, 87
  troop deployment, 36–40
  United States, relations with, 5, 16,
    34, 37–38, 72, 90–91
Nazis, 34, 104, 129, 170. *See also*
  Germany
Nelson, Horatio, 155
Netanyahu, Benjamin, 47
Nixon, Richard, 30
North Korea (Democratic People's
  Republic of Korea)
  economic environment, 73, 105
  George W. Bush policy, 14
  Japan, relations with, 44
  malnourishment, 105
  military program, 105
  nuclear program, 14, 31, 44, 72–73,
    82, 105
  Pakistan, relations with, 120
  political environment, 82
  population patterns, 104–5
  South Korea, relations with, 72, 102,
    104–5
  United States, relations with, 31,
    43–44, 72
Nuclear Non-Proliferation Treaty
  (NPT), 31, 73, 78, 82
nuclear proliferation, 5–9, 14, 30–31,
    60–62, 69, 72–73, 78, 82, 106, 120,
    132–33, 151, 167–68
nuclear weapons
  aircraft carriers, 153–56, 161
  Al-Qaeda ambitions, 81, 84
  Britain, 73, 90
  China, 44, 71, 73, 76, 95–96, 102–3, 171
  costs, 21, 73
  deterrence role, 4, 7, 14, 21–23, 61–62,
    70–78, 101, 116, 133
  France, 73, 90
  Germany, 72, 78–80, 88, 167, 171

India, 31, 71, 94, 97, 120, 171
International Atomic Energy Agency
  (IAEA), 82
Iran, 5, 14, 29, 31, 72–73, 76–77,
    116, 141
Iraq, 14, 72
Israel, 73, 113, 116–17, 170
Japan, 72, 78–80, 94, 98, 101, 167
North Korea, 14, 31, 44, 72–73,
    82, 105
Pakistan, 73–74, 82, 120, 125, 170
plutonium, use of, 82–83
rogue states, 6–7, 22
Russia, 71, 73, 94, 170–71
security measures, 81–83, 133, 162
South Africa, 82
South Korea, 72, 94, 167
Soviet Union deterrence, 28, 74–76,
    134
strategic role, 19–21, 31, 133, 139
submarines, 74, 76, 151–52, 162
terrorism, role in, 72, 76, 80–81, 116,
    162, 167
United States arsenal, 19, 23, 29,
    43–44, 61–62, 72–73, 82, 116, 140,
    151, 167
United States, threats against, 7,
    14, 19–20, 69–78, 82, 102–3, 116,
    133–34, 167
uranium, use of, 83
See also weaponry
Nye, Joseph, 43

Obama, Barack
  Afghanistan policy, 39, 159
  Al-Qaeda, efforts against, 121–22
  Asia pivot, 6, 95
  China policy, 95
  Iraq policy, 48, 86
  Japan policy, 43
  nuclear weapons stance, 73, 82
  Quadrennial Defense Review
    (QDR), 14
  space strategy, 156
  Taliban, efforts against, 121–22
  troop deployment, 12, 14, 39, 48, 159
oil industry, 18, 29, 49–50, 97, 100,
    106–13, 141, 169
Okinawa, 148, 159, 161
Operation Desert Shield, 146
Operation Desert Storm, 25, 43, 107,
    141, 146, 153–54

Operation Enduring Freedom, 26, 38–39, 120–21
Operation Iraqi Freedom, 25, 29, 107, 146, 153
opium, 122

Pakistan
  Afghanistan, relations with, 122–28
  Al-Qaeda presence, 85, 121–22, 126–28
  China, relations with, 97
  corruption, 124
  economic environment, 122–23, 125
  Federally Administered Tribal Areas (FATA), 124, 126
  India, relations with, 74, 120, 123–28
  Iran, relations with, 120
  military program, 123–28
  North Korea, relations with, 120
  nuclear program, 73–74, 82, 120, 125, 170
  Osama bin Laden, death of, 83
  Pashtuns, 51, 122–24, 126
  political environment, 82, 122–24, 128
  population patterns, 124
  Taliban presence, 121–24, 126–27
  United States, relations with, 56, 86, 120–22, 127–28
Palestine, 45–47, 115, 117–20, 132
Palestine Liberation Organization (PLO), 117–18
Panama Canal, 139
Pashtuns, 51, 122–23, 126–27
Pearl Harbor, 138
Pentagon, 10, 26, 36, 49, 108, 147–50, 158–62. *See also* United States military
Persian Gulf War, 107, 140–41
Philippines, 35
Pletka, Danielle, 16
plutonium, 82–83
polarity, 16, 29, 63, 93–94, 98, 129, 164–65, 168
post-traumatic stress disorder, 26
Powell, Colin, 12
Prague Summit, 37
Primacy, 6, 8–11, 14, 17
Princeton Project on National Security, 10
Punjabis, 123–24, 126

Qatar, 107, 115
Quadrennial Defense Review (QDR), 14

radar, 41, 149, 154
RAND Corporation, 160–61
Reagan, Ronald, 116
Realists, 9–11, 29, 33, 63, 67, 168–72
reckless driving, 33–35, 44–50, 61, 65–66, 143, 166
Red Sea, 111
Refugee Convention, 56–57
refugees, 6–7, 47, 56–57, 117–18
Republic of Korea. *See* South Korea
Republican Party, 5, 8–11, 15–16, 118, 173
Rice, Condoleezza, 11, 47
Riga Summit, 37
rogue states, 6–8, 22, 27, 65
Rumsfeld, Donald, 16, 37–38, 156
Russia
  balancing efforts, 30–31, 65, 71, 98
  China, relations with, 30–32, 65, 71, 74, 80, 91, 96, 98, 150, 171
  economic environment, 87–88, 98
  geographic position, 139
  Germany, relations with, 31
  GLONASS system, 157
  gross domestic product (GDP), 17, 71, 92, 94
  hegemony capabilities, 20, 71, 79, 87–89
  Japan, relations with, 78
  military program, 17, 87–88, 92, 98, 113–14, 149–50, 152, 157
  nuclear program, 71, 73, 94, 170–71
  population patterns, 17, 71, 88–89, 92
  resurgence, 8
  United States, relations with, 29–31, 76
Rwanda, 57
Ryukyu Islands, 99, 152

Sarotte, Mary, 31
satellites, 86, 156–58
Saudi Arabia, 51, 83–84, 107–15, 118, 146
Scandinavia, 79
Second World War. *See* World War II
Selective Engagement, 6–7, 129, 170
September 11 attacks, 6–7, 11, 14, 24–27, 38, 43, 50–51, 81, 83, 118, 120, 165
Serbia, 10, 24, 37, 50, 55, 57
Shanghai Cooperation Organization, 30
Shias/Shiites, 48–49, 51, 58, 115, 120, 122, 124
Sindhis, 124
Singapore, 161

Sobhy, Sedky, 118
Somalia, 9, 25, 50, 56
South Africa, 82
South Korea (Republic of Korea)
  China, relations with, 94
  economic environment, 104–5
  gross domestic product (GDP), 92, 105
  military program, 92, 104–5
  North Korea, relations with, 72, 102,
    104–5
  nuclear program, 72, 94, 167
  population patterns, 92, 104–5
  trade practices, 105
  United States, relations with, 72,
    104–5, 159, 167
Soviet Union
  Afghanistan, relations with, 83
  Cold War strategy, 18, 30
  collapse, 5–8, 22, 67, 76, 83, 87
  economic environment, 18, 93
  hegemony capabilities, 20, 34, 52,
    74, 94
  NATO, relations with, 9, 87
  nuclear deterrence, 28, 74–76, 134
  political environment, 82, 95
  United States, relations with, 4–6, 20,
    71, 74–76, 134, 153
  Vietnam War role, 25, 59
  World War II strategy, 5, 33–34, 52
Steinberg, James, 14
Strait of Hormuz, 107, 110–11, 137
Strait of Malacca, 97
Strategic Defense Initiative, 116
submarines, 12, 75–76, 102–3, 116, 129,
  138, 150–52, 162
Sudan, 10
Sunnis, 48–51, 58–59, 115, 120, 122, 124
Suppression of Enemy Air Defenses
  (SEAD), 149–50, 154. *See also* air
  defense systems
Supreme Allied Commander Europe
  (SACEUR), 90
Sweden, 172
Syria, 30, 85, 111, 114–15

Taiwan
  China, relations with, 102–4
  economic environment, 104
  geographic size, 102–3
  gross domestic product (GDP), 102
  Japan, relations with, 41
  military program, 102

political environment, 35, 103–4
population patterns, 102
trade practices, 104
United States, relations with, 35, 41,
  102–4
Tajiks, 51, 122–23
Taliban, 38–39, 51, 120–24, 126–28, 141,
  159
tanks, 114, 149, 154
Tea Party, 16
terrorism
  Hamas, 114, 117
  Hizbollah, 32, 114–15
  Israel, threats to, 32, 114–16
  non-state actors, 80
  nuclear weapons, role of, 72, 76,
    80–81, 116, 162, 167
  political goals, 80
  private organizations, role of, 1
  rogue states, role of, 6
  United States, threats against, 5, 45,
    72, 133, 143–44
  war costs, 25
  See also Al-Qaeda
Theater Security Cooperation Management Information System, 162
Tito, Josip Broz, 55
torpedoes, 142, 152, 155
Turkey, 111

Union of Concerned Scientists, 156
United Arab Emirates (UAE), 107, 112
United Kingdom. *See* Britain
United Nations, 16, 29–30, 43, 46, 82
United States
  Afghanistan, relations with, 11, 15,
    24–26, 35–40, 51, 66–67, 121–22,
    127–28, 147, 158–59
  alliance structure, 2, 8–9, 16–18, 29,
    33–38, 67, 140–44, 160–61, 171–73
  Britain, relations with, 97, 146
  China, relations with, 14, 17–18,
    30–32, 63, 76, 91–96, 132, 171–72
  currency strength, 18–19, 64–65, 88
  economic environment, 10, 16–19,
    63, 70, 92–94, 107, 135–36, 140,
    165–66, 174
  France, relations with, 29
  geography, 18–19, 69–71
  Germany, relations with, 78–79, 167
  gross domestic product (GDP), 16–17,
    27, 35–36, 63, 92, 94, 135, 163, 166

immigration, 18
India, relations with, 31, 97–98, 120, 126, 128
Iran, relations with, 14, 66, 76–77, 109
Iraq, relations with, 10–11, 14–15, 24–26, 32, 35, 48–50, 57–59, 140–41, 146–47
Israel, relations with, 44–48, 54, 66, 106, 116–20, 132, 166
Japan, relations with, 4, 16, 29–30, 40–44, 63, 66, 71, 78–79, 98–102, 159–61, 167
national assets, 18
national debt, 18–19
NATO, relations with, 5, 16, 34, 37–38, 72, 90–91
neighbor relationships, 18–19
North Korea, relations with, 31, 43–44, 72
nuclear threat against, 7, 14, 19–20, 69–78, 82, 102–3, 116, 133–34, 167
oil interests, 45, 106–13
Pakistan, relations with, 56, 86, 120–22, 127–28
Palestine, relations with, 45–47, 118–20, 132
political environment, 5–16, 33, 95, 101, 118–19, 131, 163–66, 173
population patterns, 17–18, 92
Russia, relations with, 29–31, 76
Saudi Arabia, relations with, 109–10
South Korea, relations with, 72, 104–5, 159, 167
Soviet Union, relations with, 4–6, 20, 71, 74–76, 134, 153
Taiwan, relations with, 35, 41, 102–4
terrorism threats, 5, 45, 72, 133, 143–44
trade practices, 63–65, 107, 110, 140–42, 150
United States military
    Air Force, 12, 105, 143, 145, 148–50, 154, 159–62, 166
    aircraft carriers, 151–56
    Al-Qaeda, response to, 10, 38–39, 45, 66, 83–87, 120–21, 127–28, 133, 143, 159, 165
    Army, 12, 118, 145–47, 149, 159–61
    Army War College, 118
    base structure, 15, 30, 41, 53, 99, 155–56, 158–61

casualties, 24–26, 58–59, 141
Coast Guard, 144
Cold War strategy, 10, 18, 30, 33–34, 74, 93, 146, 159, 164
Department of Defense (DOD), 10, 12, 36, 48, 63, 145, 163
geographic position, 138–40
ground forces, 8, 90, 105, 143–46, 162
humanitarian role, 10, 25, 50, 56–60, 86, 128
ideology, 24–25, 50–51
Marine Expeditionary Units (MEUs), 148
Marines, 12, 145–49, 154, 159–61, 166
maritime strategy, 138–44, 161–63, 166
Navy, 12, 99, 139, 141, 150–56, 159–62, 166
nuclear arsenal, 19, 23, 29, 43–44, 61–62, 72–73, 82, 116, 140, 151, 167
Operation Desert Shield, 146
Operation Desert Storm, 25, 43, 107, 141, 146, 153–54
Operation Enduring Freedom, 26, 38–39, 120–21
Operation Iraqi Freedom, 25, 29, 107, 146, 153
Pentagon, 10, 26, 36, 49, 108, 147–50, 158–62
Persian Gulf War, 107, 140–41
political influences, 9–12, 14
space strategy, 156–58
spending, 12, 14, 24–27, 34–36, 40, 58–59, 92, 104, 107–8, 145, 149, 152, 163–65, 174
Suppression of Enemy Air Defenses (SEAD), 149–50, 154
Taliban, efforts against, 121–22, 159
technological superiority, 7–8, 18, 23, 26–27, 59, 145
troop deployment, 12–15, 36, 39, 48, 92, 107, 121, 127, 146–49, 158–63
U.S. Central Command (CENTCOM), 107
World War II strategy, 5, 25, 33–34, 97, 104, 147, 170
    See also weaponry
uranium, 83
Uzbeks, 51, 122

Vietnam War, 25, 52, 58–59, 149

Warsaw Pact, 30, 37, 67
weaponry
  air defense systems, 59, 114, 136, 143,
    149, 155
  aircraft carriers, 12, 138, 151–56, 161–62
  B2 aircraft, 154
  ballistic missiles, 74–76, 99, 116, 151,
    157
  chemical weapons, 10, 113
  command and control centers, 79,
    130, 149–51, 154
  cruise missiles, 74, 111, 116, 151, 154–57
  drones, 86, 158
  F22 aircraft, 149
  F35 aircraft, 149
  helicopters, 35, 40, 59, 146, 152
  improvised explosive devices (IEDs),
    59

mines, 102, 110–11, 142, 157
radar, 41, 149, 154
satellites, 86, 156–58
submarines, 12, 75–76, 102–3, 116,
  129, 138, 150–52, 162
tanks, 114, 149, 154
torpedoes, 142, 152, 155
weapons of mass destruction, 9, 51,
  115–16, 167
See also nuclear weapons
Wilson, Woodrow, 6, 9
World War I, 71, 130, 139, 170, 173
World War II, 4–5, 33–34, 52, 71,
  78, 97, 104, 129–30, 139, 147,
  170

Yanbu, 111
Yemen, 85